NB

The Tempest

SHAKESPEARE IN PERFORMANCE

Advisory Editors: **David Bevington and Peter Holland**

Text Editor: **Richard Preiss**

Youth
Zone

methuen | drama

First UK edition published 2008

A & C Black Publishers Limited
38 Soho Square
London W1D 3HB
www.acblack.com

© 2008 Sourcebooks Inc.
First printed in the U.S. by Sourcebooks MediaFusion

ISBN 978-0-7136-8407-0

A CIP catalogue record for this book is available from the British Library.

This book is produced using paper that is made from wood grown in managed, sustainable forests. It is natural, renewable and recyclable. The logging and manufacturing processes conform to the environmental regulations of the country of origin.

Cover Design by Jocelyn Lucas

Cover Illustration © Ann Elson 2008

CD manufactured by Lemon Media

Printed and bound by Antony Rowe Ltd, Chippenham, Wiltshire

Contents

ABOUT SOURCEBOOKS MEDIAFUSION

Launched with the 1998 *New York Times* bestseller
We Interrupt This Broadcast and formally founded in 2000,
Sourcebooks MediaFusion is the nation's leading publisher
of mixed-media books. This revolutionary imprint is dedicated
to creating original content—be it audio, video, CD-ROM,
or Web—that is fully integrated with the books we create.
The result, we hope, is a new, richer, eye-opening,
thrilling experience with books for our readers.
Our experiential books have become both bestsellers
and classics in their subjects, including poetry (*Poetry Speaks*),
children's books (*Poetry Speaks to Children*),
history (*We Shall Overcome*), sports (*And The Crowd Goes Wild*),
the plays of William Shakespeare, and more.
See what's new from us at www.sourcebooks.com.

The Tempest, written about 1611, never appeared in print during Shakespeare's lifetime. Like many of his plays, its only early text is contained in the 1623 First Folio ("F") collection of *Mr. William Shakespeare's Comedies, Histories, & Tragedies,* which thus provides the copy for all modern editions, including this one. Such a singularity makes the editor's task relatively straightforward—there are no competing, inevitably different textual states to collate, as there are with *Hamlet* and *King Lear*—but by no means an easy one. The relatively clean, uniform quality of F's text, for instance, has at times sponsored deceptively simple theories of its provenance and lent its readings an authority that can be difficult to overrule. Coupled with its privileged place in the Folio, scholars formerly assumed that the play derived entirely from an authorial manuscript. The unusual fullness of its stage directions, however, suggests a theatrical provenance as well; at the same time, these directions are too gnomic and oblique (e.g. the banquet disappearing in 4.1 with what F calls merely *"a quient deuice"*) to have served the production needs of an acting company. The current scholarly consensus is that the King's Men's scribe, Ralph Crane, transferred Shakespeare's "foul papers," or original draft, into a "fair copy" suitable for publication, taking liberty along the way to enlarge the stage directions with the benefit of a "spectator's hindsight," from someone who had seen the play in performance but who did not or could not report on its precise mechanical details.

Crane's unspecified interventions, along with his idiosyncratic punctuation and lineation, may also be partly responsible for F's ambivalent attitudes to prose and verse. Most famously, this creates a problem for the rendering of Caliban. F has him speak in verse with Prospero in 1.2, and likewise enter 2.2 with a verse soliloquy, but immediately after the arrival of Trinculo revert to prose; thereafter, in 3.2, both Stephano and Trinculo sometimes receive verse as well. Despite their irregular representation, though, Caliban's speech rhythms are recognizably more structured, giving rise to the editorial tradition of juxtaposing a Caliban who consistently speaks in iambic pentameter against his prosaic interlocutors. Beyond the force of the metrics themselves, the warrant for this tradition is, admittedly, entirely interpretive; it pushes us toward a poignant, almost tragic insight into his character. Caliban, the deformed savage, displays a mastery of the language he curses Prospero for teaching him, attaining a poetic sensibility his debauched, supposed cultural superiors lack. And yet, as with all the political relations in this play, the flip side of such mastery is bondage. Even in his lust for rebellion and sovereignty he betrays himself a slave to rules, and to rule itself, to hierarchical orders of thought and power. Internalizing the values of the very world he wants to reject, he tells Stephano and Trinculo of how, when he dreams, it is not of freedom, but of "riches / Ready to drop on me." (3.2.129-130)

F's punctuation has been standardized to produce, where possible, a text oriented toward performance. For instance, since actors do not speak in parentheses, inset speech digressions are typically marked by em dashes, offering a wider potential range of vocal modulation. Orthography has been silently modernized and stage directions added, with the aim of elucidating sense and action while not foreclosing meaning; more significant variations and interpolations are treated in notes. Staging commentary is restricted only to the practical issues left open by the text. Where commentary refers to a past production, it uses the director's name as shorthand, giving the year.

Richard Preiss

On the CD

ACT 3, SCENE 1, LINES 60–97

11. Narration: Sir Derek Jacobi
12. Jamie Glover as Ferdinand, Jennifer Ehle as Miranda, and
    Bob Peck as Prospero
    The Complete Arkangel Shakespeare • *2003*
13. Benedict Cumberbatch as Ferdinand, Emilia Fox as Miranda, and
    Ian McKellen as Prospero
    Naxos AudioBooks • *2004*

ACT 3, SCENE 2, LINES 76–105

14. Narration: Sir Derek Jacobi
15. Ben Onwukwe as Caliban, John Hodgkinson as Stephano,
    Ian Talbot as Trinculo, and Scott Handy as Ariel
    Naxos AudioBooks • *2004*
16. Wayne Best as Caliban, Peter Donaldson as Stephano,
    Stephen Quimette as Trinculo, and Michael Therriault as Ariel
    The CBC Stratford Festival Reading Series • *1998*

ACT 3, SCENE 3, LINES 53–82

17. Narration: Sir Derek Jacobi
18. Adrian Lester as Ariel
    The Complete Arkangel Shakespeare • *2003*
19. Scott Handy as Ariel
    Naxos AudioBooks • *2004*

ACT 4, SCENE 1, LINES 1–32

20. Narration: Sir Derek Jacobi
21. William Hutt as Prospero and Paul Miller as Ferdinand
    The CBC Stratford Festival Reading Series • *1998*
22. Ian McKellen as Prospero and Benedict Cumberbatch as Ferdinand
    Naxos AudioBooks • *2004*

ACT 4, SCENE 1, LINES 146–163

23. Narration: Sir Derek Jacobi
24. Donald Wolfit as Prospero
    Living Shakespeare • 1962
25. William Hutt as Prospero
    The CBC Stratford Festival Reading Series • 1998
26. Ian McKellen as Prospero
    Naxos AudioBooks • 2004

ACT 5, SCENE 1 LINES 106–134

27. Narration: Sir Derek Jacobi
28. William Hutt as Prospero, Eric Donkin as Alonso,
    Brian Tree as Gonzalo
    The CBC Stratford Festival Reading Series • 1998
29. Donald Wolfit as Prospero, Richard Warner as Alonso,
    George Merritt as Gonzalo
    Living Shakespeare • 1962
30. Ian McKellen as Prospero, Roger Hammond as Alonso,
    David Burke as Gonzalo
    Naxos AudioBooks • 2004

EPILOGUE, LINES 1–20

31. Narration: Sir Derek Jacobi
32. Donald Wolfit as Prospero
    Living Shakespeare • 1962
33. William Hutt as Prospero
    The CBC Stratford Festival Reading Series • 1998
34. Ian McKellen as Prospero
    Naxos AudioBooks • 2004

Featured Audio Productions

NAXOS AUDIOBOOKS (2004)

Alonso, King of Naples,	Roger Hammond
Sebastian, his brother	John McAndrew
Prospero, Duke of Milan	Ian McKellen
Antonio, his brother	Neville Jackson
Miranda, Prosperos' daughter	Emilia Fox
Ferdinand, Alonso's son	Benedict Cumberbatch
Gonzalo	David Burke
Adrian, a lord	Simon Treves
Francisco, a lord	Tim Bentinck
Caliban, a savage	Ben Onwukwe
Trinculo, a jester	Ian Talbot
Stephano, a drunken butler	John Hodgkinson
Master	Simon Treves
Boatswain	Tim Bentinck
Ariel, an airy spirit	Scott Handy
Juno	Elaine Claxton
Ceres	Laura Paton

Directed by John McAndrew

THE COMPLETE ARKANGEL SHAKESPEARE (2003)

Prospero	Bob Peck
Miranda	Jennifer Ehle
Ariel	Adrian Lester
Antonio	Simon Russell Beale
Ferdinand	Jamie Glover
Caliban	Richard McCabe
Trinculo	Desmond Barrit
Alonso	Jack Klaff
Gonzalo	Christian Rodska
Sebastian	Chook Sibtain
Stephano	Arthur Cox
Boatswain	Nicholas Murchie
Ceres	Sian Radinger
Iris	Adjoa Andoh
Juno	Abigail Docherty
Francisco	Robert Whitelock

Other parts played by members of the cast
Directed by Clive Brill

LIVING SHAKESPEARE (1962)

Master of Ship	John Arnatt
Boatswain	Tenniel Evans
Gonzalo	George Merritt
Miranda	Rosalind Iden
Prospero	Sir Donald Wolfit
Ariel	Mai Zetterling
Caliban	Denis Shaw
Ferdinand	Michael Gwynn
Sebastian	Tenniel Evans

Antonio	Simon Lack
Alonso	Richard Warner
Stephano	George Arnatt
Trinculo	John Humphry

Directed by Dennis Vance

THE CBC STRATFORD FESTIVAL READING SERIES(1998)

Prospero	William Hutt
Caliban	Wayne Best
Stephano	Peter Donaldson
Alonso	Eric Donkin
Antonio	Colin Fox
Miranda	Jennifer Gould
Ferdinand	Paul Miller
Trinculo/Boatswain	Stephen Quimette
Ariel	Michael Therriault
Gonzalo	Brian Tree
Sebastian	Richard Zeppieri
Ceres	Barbara Dunn-Prosser
Iris	Barbara Fulton
Juno	Pamela Gerrand

Directed by Richard Monette

Note from the Series Editors

For many of us, our first and only encounter with Shakespeare was in school. We may recall that experience as a struggle, working through dense texts filled with unfamiliar words. However, those of us who were fortunate enough to have seen a play performed have altogether different memories. It may be of an interesting scene or an unusual character, but it is most likely a speech. Often, just hearing part of one instantly transports us to that time and place. "Friends, Romans, countrymen, lend me your ears," "But, soft! What light through yonder window breaks?," "To sleep, perchance to dream," "Tomorrow, and tomorrow, and tomorrow."

The Sourcebooks Shakespeare series is our attempt to use the power of performance to help you experience the play. In it, you will see photographs from various productions, on film and on stage, historical and contemporary, known worldwide or in your community. You may even recognize some actors you don't think of as Shakespearean performers. You will see set drawings, costume designs, and scene edits, all reproduced from original notes. Finally, on the enclosed audio CD, you will hear scenes from the play as performed by some of the most accomplished Shakespeareans of our times. Often, we include multiple interpretations of the same scene, showing you the remarkable richness of the text. Hear Sir Ian McKellen as Prospero and Emilia Fox as Miranda dramatize Shakespeare's words. Compare McKellen's Prospero to Sir Donald Wolfit's 1962 performance for the Living Shakespeare. The actors create different worlds, different characters, different meanings.

As you read the text of the play, you can consult explanatory notes for definitions of unfamiliar words and phrases or words whose meanings have changed. These notes appear on the left pages, next to the text of the play. The audio, photographs, and other production artifacts augment the notes and they too are indexed to the appropriate lines. You can use the pictures to see how others have staged a particular scene and get ideas on costumes, scenery, blocking, etc. As for the audio, each track represents a particular interpretation of a scene. Sometimes, a passage that's difficult to comprehend opens up when you hear it out loud. Furthermore, when you hear more than one version, you gain a keener understanding of the characters. Is Prospero a cunning villain out for revenge or an overprotective father? Does his control over Ariel and Caliban force us to loathe him or sympathize with him? Do our feelings for him change as the play progresses? The actors made their choices and so can you. You may even come up with your own interpretation.

The text of the play, the definitions, the production notes, the audio–all of these work together, and they are included for your enjoyment. Because the audio consists of performance excerpts, it is meant to entertain. When you see a passage with an associated clip, you can read along as you hear the actors perform the scenes for you. Or, you can sit back, close your eyes, and listen, and then go back and reread the text with a new perspective. Finally, since the text is actually a script, you may find yourself reciting the lines out loud and doing your own performance!

You will undoubtedly notice that some of the audio does not exactly match the text. Also, there are photographs and facsimiles of scenes that aren't in your edition. There are many reasons for this, but foremost among them is the fact that Shakespeare scholarship continues to move forward and the prescribed ways of dealing with and interpreting text are always changing. Thus a play that was edited and published in the 1900s will be different from one published in 2008. Finally, artists have their own interpretation of the play, and they too cut and change lines and scenes according to their vision.

The ways in which *The Tempest* has been presented have varied considerably through the years. We've included essays in the book to give you glimpses into the range of the productions, showing you how other artists have approached the play and providing examples of just what changes were made and how. Our text editor, Richard Preiss, in his essay, "In Production: Rough Magic: *The Tempest* of Theater History," explains how each historical era has reinvented the play to suit its own tastes and needs, and makes the intriguing claim that at its basic level, *"The Tempest* is an early modern analog of films like *Pirates of the Caribbean* or *Harry Potter"*. In "As Performed by Shakespeare Behind Bars at the Luther Luckett Correctional Complex in LaGrange, Kentucky, 2003", director Curt L. Tofteland gives an account of his experience in directing the inmates of the

Luther Luckett Correctional Complex as part of the program, Shakespeare Behind Bars. Comparing the prison and the inmates to Shakespeare's island and its inhabitants, he notes striking parallels between the inmates and the characters they have chosen to portray. Douglas Lanier's essay on *The Tempest* in popular culture provides examples of the play's influence in various genres such as music (it is the Shakespearean play most frequently adapted to operatic form), poetry (W. H. Auden, Robert Browning, and Sylvia Plath have all composed poems on aspects of the play), and even film and television, such as the 1956 science fiction film *Forbidden Planet* as well as the TV series *Gilligan's Island, Fantasy Island,* and *Lost*—all loosely based on Shakespeare's play. Finally, for the actor in you, (and for those who want to peek behind the curtain), we have an essay that you may find especially intriguing. Andrew Wade, voice coach of the Royal Shakespeare Company for sixteen years, shares his point of view on how to understand the text and speak it.

One last note: we are frequently asked why we didn't include the whole play, either in audio or video. While we enjoy the plays and are avid theatergoers, we are trying to do something more with the audio (and the production notes and the essays) than just presenting them to you. In fact, our goal is to provide you tools that will enable you to explore the play on your own, from many different directions. Our hope is that the different pieces of audio, the voices of the actors, and the old production photos and notes will all engage you and illuminate the play on many levels, so that you can construct your own understanding and create your own "production"— a fresh interpretation unique to you.

Though the productions we referenced and the audio clips we have included are but a miniscule sample of the play's history, we hope they encourage you to delve further into the works of Shakespeare. New editions of the play come out yearly; movie adaptations are regularly being produced; there are hundreds of theater groups in the U.S. alone; and performances could be going on right in your backyard. We echo the words of noted writer and poet Robert Graves, who said, "The remarkable thing about Shakespeare is that he is really very good—in spite of all the people who say he is very good."

We welcome you now to The Sourcebooks Shakespeare edition of *The Tempest*.

Dominique Raccah

Marie Macaisa

Dominique Raccah and Marie Macaisa
Series Editors

Introduction to the Sourcebooks Shakespeare **The Tempest**
Sir Derek Jacobi

Rough Magic: The Tempest of Theater History

THE TEMPEST IN PRODUCTION

Richard Preiss

The Tempest is about old worlds imagining new ones: it is a play that prefigures the very problem of its theatrical adaptation. To ask how this play ought to be staged has been, for the past four centuries, a way of asking how *any* Shakespeare play ought to be staged, and it has been a litmus test of each generation's attitude toward the poet's authority. Each historical moment has re-invented it to suit its own tastes and needs, no matter how much (or little) deference has been paid to the playwright's "intention." The very nature of the play, indeed, makes such a calculation difficult. At a basic level, *The Tempest* is an early modern analog of films like *Pirates of the Caribbean* or *Harry Potter*: even when it premiered in 1611 it was a special effects extravaganza, with staging requirements—a sea storm, shipwrecks, spells, flying spirits, monsters, disappearing banquets—that would have pushed the technologies of Renaissance theater to their limit. How, then, are we to realize the play "faithfully" in later eras? For dramatist George Bernard Shaw, the play's poetry was "so magical that it would make the scenery of modern theatre ridiculous"; for critic Michael Billington, "it cries out for directorial embellishment." Do we use only the devices Shakespeare had at his disposal, or do we incorporate more advanced techniques, reasoning that he too would have used them had they been available? Such choices bear crucially on our interpretation of the play. How much of its meaning resides in its spectacle, its capacity to induce in us what Prospero calls Miranda's "amazement"? Few plays are so conscious of the relation between theater and power, subtly reminding us of our *own* susceptibility to surfaces, and of the charmed circle in which we ourselves stand (or sit) to watch it. *The Tempest* builds into its themes the work it actively performs upon its audience, and thus its "original" form can never be recovered simply because its original audience, to whose horizon of "amazement" those effects were calibrated, can never be recovered. The primal, "Shakespearean" version of the play is a utopia, forever out of reach; like its characters—imprisoned by the past—*The Tempest* can only beckon toward uncertain futures, demanding that we remake it in our own changing image.

ORIGINS AND PROBLEMS

Tempest criticism has historically tried to combat this idea of evanescence. Much has been made of the fact that the play appears first in the 1623 Folio of Shakespeare's *Comedies, Histories and Tragedies*, even though it was one of his very last plays before retiring in 1613. Since the nineteenth century, it

"Sir George Somers discovers the Bermudas" illustration by R. Caton Woodville in the Illustrated London News, 13 June 1903, page 903
Photo Courtesy of Mary Evans Picture Library

has been lifted from this textual setting to form a separate class—with other late plays like *The Winter's Tale*, *Pericles* and *Cymbeline*—called "Romances": the term attempts to taxonomize our feeling that these plays inhabit a hybrid genre between comedy and tragedy, sharing a sentimental concern for the fate of families, a painful awareness of time and loss, and a commitment to non-realistic (i.e., supernatural) modes of dramatic resolution. But the Folio's privileging of *The Tempest* has always lent it a special aura, sponsoring the belief that Shakespeare intended it as his valediction to the stage, a crystallization of his views on the nature of theater and of the playwright's craft. Prospero certainly thinks like a dramatist, orchestrating his revenge from afar by moving people into position like chess pieces; indeed, Ferdinand and Miranda are discovered "playing at chess" in the climax. Yet the play would be very thin were Prospero merely a glorified projection of the author. Though he renounces his "art" at the end, vowing to break his staff and "drown [his] book," both he and it—and by extension the theatrical art it resembles—come in for as much judgment as those he judges; it is not even clear that he fulfills his promise of renunciation, let alone forgiveness.

Ultimately, however, the play's claim to personal retrospective rests on proving that *The Tempest* really was Shakespeare's last play, a hypothesis that is likewise false. The earliest reference to it is a record of a performance at Court, on November 1, 1611. This was not necessarily the first production, but other sources Shakespeare used suggest it was an early one. As the only play with no direct source in contemporary literature, Shakespeare instead borrowed material from a letter written in July, 1610 by William Strachey, detailing the 1609 voyage of Sir George Somers to the Jamestown colony in Virginia, for his account of the opening storm, the features of the island, and perhaps even a sketch of the plot. Somers and his crew were wrecked in a "most dreadful tempest" and marooned on the island of Bermuda for nearly a year, during which time some of them found the island so alluring they mutinied and conspired to remain there indefinitely.

Strachey's letter reached England by September, 1610, and though it was not printed until 1625, it would have circulated in manuscript. The play is indebted to several pamphlets about Bermuda, in fact, as well as to the many travel reports that had flooded England in the preceding decades with fabulous stories of enchanted New World islands and innocent, ignorant natives; and aspects of both Caliban and Gonzalo's "commonwealth" speech derive almost *verbatim* from Michel de Montaigne's (1533-1592) essay "Of the Cannibals," translated in 1603. But if Strachey's letter dates *The Tempest* to late 1610 or early 1611, then it surely was not Shakespeare's last play. We know that *Henry VIII* was new in 1613, when, at its premiere, cannon fire set the roof of the Globe Theatre ablaze and burned the playhouse to the ground. Shakespeare collaborated with his fellow playwright John Fletcher on two other plays, *Two Noble Kinsmen* and *Cardenio* (since lost), which likewise postdate *The Tempest*. *Henry VIII* may also have been a joint work with Fletcher, and scholars often use this to qualify *The Tempest* as Shakespeare's last *solo* composition, yet we cannot even determine the chronology between *The Tempest* and *The Winter's Tale*. Arguments for it as a "farewell" are either inconsistent with the evidence, or use the themes of the play circularly, as self-referential proof. Thus, *The Tempest* remains an island, cut off from the psychological origins we would invoke to make the task of interpreting it easier.

We know that *The Tempest* was performed at court for King James, first in 1611 and again in 1613, when it appeared in a list of fourteen plays comprising a celebration of the marriage of James's daughter Elizabeth to a German prince. Because *The Tempest* has a wedding masque in it—masques were elaborate, highly stylized allegorical pageants of power and ceremony—critics in search of biographical keys to the play have argued that it was revised for this occasion, and that Prospero is a figure for James himself. But here again, both the play and its circumstances discourage this equation.

James I of England from the period 1603–1613
Paul Van Somer I (1576–1621)

The Tempest actually deals with the *danger* of arranged royal marriages: Prospero's masque forbids Ferdinand and Miranda's sexual desire, while Sebastian reminds Alonso that "loosing" his daughter to a foreign husband was his first mistake. Not only were plays deemed suitable fare for court festivities, they were never expressly commissioned for them.

The King's Men performed for James when his pleasure commanded it; the rest of the year their livelihood relied on a paying public, and plays were written primarily to make money. *Lack* of evidence, then, that *The Tempest* was ever staged at one of the King's Men's two commercial playhouses, the Blackfriars or the Globe, cannot be taken as evidence against it. Shakespeare's rival Ben Jonson, at least, expected the audience of his *Bartholomew Fair* (1614) to know the play. Jonson mocked the fantastic elements in Shakespeare's late work by calling one of his own characters "Mooncalf," a nickname Stephano gives Caliban, and his induction further announced that "the author is loath to make Nature afraid in his plays, like those that beget Tales, Tempests, and suchlike drolleries."

Yet compared with Shakespeare's other plays, *The Tempest*'s hold on the public's imagination was not especially deep or lasting. We do not know how often (if at all) it was revived by the King's Men before the closing of the theaters in 1642, but the number of contemporary allusions to it is small. In contrast to bestsellers like *Richard III*, *Henry V,* and *Hamlet*, which went through multiple individual printings, *The Tempest* was never printed outside the Folio. Ironically, it was only a radical adaptation—what a purist today might call travesty—that ensured the play's future. During the English Civil War (1642-1660), playhouses were closed by order of Parliament, whose Puritan majority opposed theater on religious grounds and who also wanted to censor public debate in a nation fiercely divided by the execution of its King, Charles I. When the playhouses reopened after the Restoration of the monarchy in 1660, professional theater in England had been dormant for a generation, and, without new scripts, the reconstituted playing companies had only old, pre-War material to revive. Returning to this repertory was part of a larger cultural project of mass amnesia—as if to pretend that the intervening years of revolution had never happened—but the actors were also ordered by Charles II to update the plays, to tailor them to current fashion. This meant the fashion of France, where Charles had lived in exile, and where neoclassical drama, along with a tolerance of actresses, were the norm. Aesthetics and politics are always intimately related, but for the sensitive era of the Restoration they were inseparable; in a play like *The Tempest*, both needed cleaning up.

RESTORATION REVISIONS: DAVENANT'S ADAPTATION AND SHADWELL'S OPERA

The Tempest was revived in November 1667, in a version by John Davenant, with additions by John Dryden. *The Enchanted Island*, as it was called, used less than a third of Shakespeare's text. Most notably, Prospero's role was greatly diminished: in contrast to a modern tradition that can find no way around him, Prospero was now no longer the star of the show—nor could he be. Too much of his story involved the troublesome idea of deposing a monarch, and so the revenge plot shriveled. Antonio was relegated to minor character status, Sebastian was eliminated altogether, and Prospero was reduced from an omnipotent scourge to a chorus-like master of ceremonies. Even his betrothal masque for Ferdinand and Miranda, along with the famous line "Our revels now are ended," was excised. In place of dramatic gravity, Davenant introduced more love plots, banishing the play's darkness with neoclassical symmetry and light. Miranda received a sister, Dorinda, who falls in love with Hippolito, another castaway who happens to be Prospero's cousin, "heir of the dukedom of Mantua." Hippolito and Dorinda's romance forms a counterpart to Ferdinand and Miranda's, since just as Miranda has never seen a man, Hippolito has never seen a woman; Prospero has raised him in total isolation because his stars predicted that the sight of a woman would kill him. The prediction happily proves false, and with this bizarre revision Davenant also managed both to expose and to defuse a theme implicit in Shakespeare's original: Prospero's phobic attitude to sex and the inexorable movement from sex toward death. The parallel courtship further solved another post-Restoration problem of the play: its lack of parts for actresses, not only Dorinda but Hippolito, too, were played by women. Davenant appears to have relished the opportunity to reverse the transvestite conventions of Shakespeare's theater—and the gender crossing also pleased the audience, since Hippolito remained a "breeches part" until the early nineteenth century. Charles II showed his own approval by starting an affair with the actress who played Hippolito, Moll Davis.

But Davenant did not stop the doubling there. Ariel received a female counterpart and love-interest, the she-spirit Milcha. Caliban's sexuality, conversely, had to be toned down, and so he too was given a sister—oddly named after his mother—called Sycorax, for whose affections Stephano and Trinculo compete. Not only did this negate his threat to "people...this isle with Calibans" by trying to rape Miranda, since he is no longer the last of his line, but it also shrewdly removed the charge of tyranny implicit in Caliban's accusation that Prospero usurped him, since he was never "mine own king."

Davenant evacuated the political stakes, and emotional claims, of Caliban's primacy on the island, reducing him from malign rebel to goofy servant. He further dissipated the severity of the conspiracy against Prospero by yet again multiplying it and distributing it, inventing two more equally hapless goons in the characters Mustacho and Ventoso—whose arguments for control of the island are made to sound like the republican rhetoric of the Civil War, so that their ambitions can easily be spotted as illegitimate and ridiculous. To an already musical play, finally, Davenant added more songs and dances. Ferdinand and Ariel share a duet called "the Echo Song," and the psychological terrorism of Prospero's banquet is mitigated by the presence of "eight fat spirits with Corn-o-Copia." Davenant's idiom is generally bawdier, sacrificing the play's poignancy and its undertone of menace in favor of gaiety and romp. This is a play where at the end Prospero does not have to renounce his magic, because magic is without consequences to begin with. The avid playgoer Samuel Pepys saw the first performance, and called it "the most innocent play that ever I saw"; he judged it to have "no wit, but yet good, above ordinary plays." Less than a week later he saw it again, finding it "very pleasant, and full of so good variety that I cannot be more pleased almost in a comedy." He saw it three more times over the next four months.

Davenant's *Enchanted Island* is not *The Tempest*, but it was not trying to be, and like any adaptation it deserves to be taken seriously on its own terms, as both a reading of the play and a refinement of it for its affirmational historical moment: the Restoration was "restoring" a whole social order, not "Shakespeare." (The original play is, ironically, about how *tenuous* the foundations of such an order are; perhaps this was the reason to rewrite it.) Davenant's version cannot be dismissed if only for the simple reason that audiences would see its text for the next 170 years. Paradoxical as it may sound, until the early nineteenth century, a vast gulf separated the textual and theatrical traditions that mediated Shakespeare to the public. Though the eighteenth century would see the first sustained effort to fix Shakespeare's texts as he had intended them—itself a process that involved a great deal of "fixing," emendations based on each editor's sense of what "sounded right" or "worked better," procedures we would today consider grossly subjective and invasive—this was deemed scholarship for the library. Theatrical professionals did not necessarily believe that this "authentic" text made the best material for the repertory. Plays needed to be "improved" for the stage as well as on the page, and *The Tempest* was no exception.

Davenant had established a structural template with immediate appeal, but the Restoration *Tempest* would find its most enduring form in Thomas

Shadwell's version, which in 1674 mounted the Davenant/Dryden script as an opera. Most of the songs were retained, and new ones—along with more dances and a new instrumental score—were composed, pushing the orchestra to twenty-four musicians. But the opera was truly innovative as a visual experience. The Duke's Men, the play's owners, had moved to a new theater in Dorset Garden, where a larger playing area made more complex special effects possible, which Shadwell exploited to create the most marvelous spectacle of the age. His opening directions, no less cryptic than Shakespeare's, give us a sense of the vast machinery involved: "a thick, Cloudy Sky, a very Rocky Coast, and a Tempestuous Sea in perpetual Agitation. This Tempest (supposed to be raised by Magic) has many dreadful objects in it, as several spirits in horrid shapes flying down among the Sailors... and when the ship is sinking, the whole house is darkened, and a shower of fire falls upon them." A gorgeous tableau of a rising sun was followed by many embellishments, such as a chorus of devils and a ballet of Winds and Tritons. John Downes, the prompter, remembered "particularly one Scene Painted with *Myriads* of *Ariel* Spirits; and another flying away, with a Table Furnisht out with Fruits, Sweet meats, and all sorts of Viands," and "all things was perform'd in it so Admirably well," he went on, "that not any succeeding Opera got more Money."

Shadwell's opera, based on Davenant's text, would reign supreme as the form of Shakespeare's play for the next seventy years, and was largely responsible for the victory of the Duke's Men over the rival King's Men. The King's had passed over *The Tempest* when monopolies over the pre-War dramatic stock were dispensed in 1660, but by 1675 they were reduced to parodying it, in a mock-opera called *The Mock-Tempest*. Shadwell's opera was revived in 1690, for which the composer Henry Purcell provided Dorinda with a new song; the score underwent extensive revisions and additions. At the newer, bigger theater in Drury Lane, the play was offered in six of the first nine theatrical seasons of the 1700s (by then the companies had amalgamated), with a 1707 advertisement assuring it would be performed with "all the Original Flyings and Musick." From 1710 to 1732, with Drury Lane being managed by the first of the great actor-directors, Colley Cibber, it was revived twenty times in twenty-three seasons. Cibber noted in his diary that "the greatest profit in so little time had yet been known in my memory." No one especially cared that it was not "Shakespeare," because it was great theater, consonant with the tastes and values of the age. But its extraordinary success was a prompt to begin reconsidering just what "Shakespeare" meant, and what rights he had in the realization of his texts. The Licensing Act of

1737, which subjected all new drama to such harsh censorship that Shakespeare suddenly became a staple of the national repertory, made a collision course between these textual and theatrical traditions inevitable. *The Tempest* was one of the first intersections.

THE RETURN OF THE PLAY

The reinstatement of Shakespeare's play was a fitful, piecemeal process. In 1746 James Lacy offered a production that claimed to be "as written by Shakespeare, never acted there before"; it was actually a blend of Shadwell's, retaining his fifth act masque of Neptune and Amphitrite, and ran for just six performances. It would take the charisma and showmanship of the eighteenth century's premier actor-manager, David Garrick, to make Shakespeare's play competitive with its operatic adaptation—but not before he first tried to do it merely as a different opera. In 1756 he presented a new *Tempest* which replaced Shadwell's score, and abandoned Davenant's text in favor of a new libretto written only around the outlines of Shakespeare's original plot. This too failed—Garrick later denied responsibility for it—and a year later, in 1757, he presented Shakespeare's play, the first time the Folio text had been performed on stage in over a hundred years. Garrick still cut about 400 lines, but the purely dramatic version remained commercially viable—thanks, no doubt, to the fact that it was Garrick playing Prospero—until his retirement in 1776.

The very next year, when Richard Sheridan took over Drury Lane, the opera began to creep back. Sheridan kept Shakespeare's text, but reinserted Shadwell's masque of Neptune and a "Grand Dance of Fantastic Spirits." Like Lacy's 1746 blend, Sheridan's struck a nerve—it was one thing to *rewrite* Shakespeare as opera, but another to stage his actual *words* as such—and critics scorned it for all the pantomime and melodrama they had formerly praised in Shadwell. Yet audiences still loved its gaudy stage machinery, so much so that habitual latecomers demanded the opening storm scene be moved to Act 2. Ironically, a competing version of Shadwell's opera got only six performances between 1776 and 1779. Its days were numbered, but the opera's dip in fortune was temporary. In 1787 John Philip Kemble revived it yet again at Drury Lane, restoring Hippolito, Dorinda, and their friends to thunderous applause. Producing Shadwell annually for fifteen years, Kemble moved to Covent Garden in 1803, where he began to offer a streamlined version that drastically cut the visual effects, but still retained Davenant's text. Gradually the play was shedding Shadwell's frills, and moving back toward its first Restoration incarnation: through *The Tempest*, theater history was rewinding. By 1815, the critic William Hazlitt could declare even the Restoration text defective compared to Shakespeare. For him, Kemble's version was "vulgar and ridiculous...a travestie, a carica-ture," full of "all the heavy tinsel and affected formality which Dryden had borrowed from the French."

Hazlitt's concern for the "Englishness" of a play about a group of Italians on an island resembling a Frenchman's description of America may be mis-placed, but the rise of European nationalism it signals was the final histori-cal contingency that completed the turn toward "authentic" realizations of Shakespeare. In 1838 William Charles Macready staged the most narrowly Shakespearean production to date. It was still a machine-play, and it retained a few Shadwell songs for Ariel—and critics still faulted it for too much pantomime—but it firmly re-established Shakespeare's text. Whereas *The Tempest* had naturally indulged the eighteenth century appetite for spec-tacle, however, the Romantics were chiefly interested in character—by now the centerpieces of the Shakespeare canon had become *Hamlet* and *King Lear*—and it was the interior of the play, not its exterior, that needed to be charted. What was required of it now was depth, soul, emotional profundity. Though nearly two centuries of commercial success had accorded it pride of place in the repertory, its stage history had not prepared *The Tempest* for such a cultural renovation. The play was as much comedy as tragedy; it had few soliloquies; its "hero" never seemed to suffer a crisis of conscience or self-doubt; it had all these trappings of the supernatural to detract from its inner focus. Where was its dramatic conflict, its spiritual struggle, its timeless bat-tle between individual and cosmos? What, in short, was its "human angle"?

CALIBAN AND MODERNITY: BENSON'S APE AND TREE'S ABORIGINE

It was Caliban who allowed the play to reinvent itself for the modern era, precisely because the category of "the human" itself was undergoing a fresh renegotiation, through a myriad of discourses—biological, racial, imperial—with which he suddenly resonated. Shakespeare's Restoration heirs had found nothing redeeming in him (Dryden wrote him off as a "witch," a "devil" and a "slave"), and throughout the eighteenth century, he was played as comic and burlesque, a foil to offset the more conventional clowning of Stephano and Trinculo. By the early 1800s, however, as the Shakespearean text reasserted itself, critics began to see his as the plum role and the ripest for creative interpretation. The new literary interest in the gothic already colors Leigh Hunt's praise for John Emery's Caliban in 1806 wherein

Caliban "approaches to terrific tragedy, when he describes the various tortures inflicted on him by the magician...the monster hugs and shrinks into himself, grows louder and more shuddering as he proceeds, and when he pictures the torment that almost turns his brain, glares with his eyes and gnashes his teeth with an impatient impotence of revenge." As the play's malevolence gradually became re-invested in Caliban, the diabolical quality of Prospero's art—which two centuries of opera had already diluted—further softened, to the point where Charles Kean's 1857 Princess's Theater production could replace his misshapen Spirits with "naiads, wood nymphs and satyrs...bearing fruit and flowers."

But the Victorians were not, like Trinculo, merely trying to turn Caliban into a one-man freak show. Scientific inquiry into the nature of language, thought and human origins put increasing pressure on the distinction between man and beast; the acceleration of the British colonial project, furthermore, brought the empire into contact with native peoples in Africa and Australia who, because they were labeled primitive and inferior, tested the validity of the imperialist claim to be able to civilize. The French Revolution of 1789 had ignited a wave of republicanism across Europe, and a philosophical interest in individual rights; anti-slavery sentiment in Britain had by 1807 succeeded in abolishing the practice across the Commonwealth. Works like Mary Shelley's *Frankenstein* (1818) asked if monsters could be made by men as well as nature, and what responsibility science had for its creations. Caliban's twisted body became a metaphor for his soul, and what captivity—or education—had done to it. In Macready's 1838 version, George Bennett played him as a victim of Prospero's oppression, improvising a moment during their first meeting (still often used today) where Caliban lunges at him, only to be repelled by a charm. As this "salvage and deformed slave" attracted deeper cultural significance, a new narrative—the tension between his innate dignity and his outward barbarity—was gradually scripted for him. For Romantic critics, who had shifted the seat of the quintessentially human faculty from reason to the imagination, he became a noble savage, worthy of sympathy the more his privation and wretchedness were understood. Coleridge famously argued that Caliban had the poetic temperament to elevate himself above his brutality, and so that brutality became increasingly necessary to counterpoint with his poetry. Audiences *wanted* to see him as an animal so they could see him as human. In 1854 William Burton played him as a snarling, taloned fiend, which *The New York Times* called "immense...not the great god Pan himself was more the link between the man and beast than this thing." Such language reminds us that Darwin's *Origin of Species* was only five years away; in 1873, in fact, a scholar named Daniel Wilson published *Caliban: The Missing Link*, in which he tried to prove that Shakespeare's character furnished evidence of evolution. In American *Tempest* parodies, meanwhile, Caliban often spoke the line "ain't I a man and a brother?"—an anti-slavery slogan, and a phrase that often cropped up in evolutionary debates as well.

As Darwin's theory gained credence, coupled with the aftermath of the American Civil War and growing anxiety over the fate of British Imperialism, by the turn of the twentieth century Calibans experimented ever more boldly with the biological, anthropological and colonial. Frank Benson, influenced by Wilson's book, conducted "fieldwork" for the role in his 1891 Stratford production by studying apes at the zoo. He gave an athletic, zany performance that included hanging upside down from a tree branch and appearing with a fish in his mouth; Benson's caricature was so good, in fact, that audiences laughed at him, and a stagehand reportedly mistook him for a real monkey. (The parallels with Andy Serkis's recent film portrayal of Gollum in Peter Jackson's *Lord of the Rings* trilogy are striking, and Tolkien's conception of the creature may itself be indebted to late-Victorian stage Calibans.) The character's costume also reflected this quasi-scientific interest in his morphology. Augustin Daly directed an American *Tempest* in 1897 that covered Caliban in

Sir Herbert Beerbohm Tree ca. 1900

fur, with scales on his legs; Sir Herbert Beerbohm Tree's 1904 *Tempest* draped him in seaweed, similarly literalizing his description as half-man, half-fish.

Tree cemented the Victorian refashioning of Caliban into an object of pathos. Taking on the role himself—a further sign of the play's new dramatic core—Tree greatly enhanced Caliban's sensitivity to music, choreographing for him extended dances reminiscent of tribal ritual, complete with a necklace of shells. Tree's aborigine was still an extension of Benson's ape, but the image of a Caliban who shared the same capacity for beauty, order and wonder as his European counterparts—only to be destroyed by it—painfully evoked a fragile, innocent humanity. To punctuate this point, and recognizing that the play seems to forget about him upon Prospero's departure, Tree ended with an emotionally devastating tableau:

> Caliban creeps from his cave, and watches the departing ship bearing away the freight of humanity which for a brief spell has gladdened and saddened his island home, and taught him to "seek for grace." For the last time, Ariel appears, singing the song of the bee…Caliban listens for the last time to the sweet air, then turns sadly in the direction of the parting ship. The play is ended. As the curtain rises again, the ship is seen on the horizon, Caliban stretching his arms towards it in mute despair. The night falls, and Caliban is left on the lonely rock. He is a King once more.

John Ryder's 1871 production at the Queen's Theatre had introduced a similar coda, but devoid of irony: his Caliban had lain basking in the rays of the setting sun, glad to be rid of his foreign occupiers. Thirty years later, Tree's Caliban was now a fully tragic figure.

THE RECONSTRUCTIONIST MOMENT

Tree's 1904 *Tempest* was also the last in the line of great Victorian spectaculars. The new emphasis on character study, especially Caliban's, had thus far not disrupted the stage tradition of scenic excess inherited from Shadwell, even if they were increasingly incompatible. Charles Kean's 1857 production set the benchmark for visual fantasy with a full-scale shipwreck and lavish dances; the show was criticized for not leaving room for acting—indeed, despite cutting hundreds of lines of dialogue, the play still ran five hours—but in style it was widely imitated. A Chicago production at McVickers Theater in 1889 also built a life-size sailing vessel onstage for scene 1, with actual people scurrying about its simulated decks. By 1904 Tree would abandon much of the play's machinery, but he was excited by the possibilities of electricity, and used subtle lighting effects to suggest moods and accents. He also contributed his share of pantomimes, including an acrobatic ballet of nymphs suspended from wires, who sang "Come unto these yellow sands" after Ariel's exit at the end of Act 1. Writing in his program, Tree defended the production values of the past two centuries by maintaining that "of all Shakespeare's works, *The Tempest* is probably the one which most demands the aids of modern stagecraft."

Yet by the start of the twentieth century—complementing "The New Bibliography," a scholarly rejection of the editorial "improvements" habitually imposed on Shakespeare's texts—modern stagecraft was also giving way to historically stricter casting and staging. Until now simplicity had been an aesthetic, not a principled, choice. For the shipwreck, for example, a 1900 revival of Benson's production had used the economic device of a swinging lantern on a darkened stage, amid the cries of the sailors. In 1897, however, William Poel directed a *Tempest* for the Elizabethan Stage Society without any scenery, and with the musical accompaniment of only a tabor and pipe. In 1919, William Bridges-Adams took Poel's academic nostalgia even further, attempting to recreate not only the play's original performing *conditions*, but what he believed was its original *performance*. A curtain displayed the coats-of-arms of Princess Elizabeth and her new husband, and the rest of Bridges-Adams's staging tried to simulate the experience of actually *watching* a court entertainment, like the one *The Tempest* served for King James in 1613. Historical "authenticity" was not a new criterion in the theater, of course, for by the early nineteenth century, actors were uniformly adopting historically consistent dress. However, such dress was always that of the period being *represented* in the play, not that of the period in which it was first *performed*. This trend of "reconstructing" Shakespeare, of making theater itself a subject of history rather than a medium for the histories it imagines, was short-lived. Yet this movement did occasion the reappraisal of at least one character: Ariel. Ever since the demise of Shadwell's opera (in which he had a girlfriend), Ariel had always been played by a woman, as a Tinkerbell; after the 1920s, with the return to a boy actor's part, the issue of Ariel's gender—if still unresolved as *either* male or female—would now always become a choice, and often a provocative, unsettling one. Ariel's humanity, like Caliban's inhumanity, could no longer be taken for granted.

DROWNING THE BOOK

Between Ariel and Caliban stands Prospero, and their excavation now forced the issue of his relationship both to them and to the rest of the play. Prospero had in the past been portrayed as a benign old wizard: serene, majestic, compassionate to his wards and fatherly in his protection of Miranda. Since the mid-twentieth century he has become the play's star turn once again, however, and theater directors have strived to destabilize his control over himself and others, as well as our ethical response to him. John Gielgud, the greatest modern interpreter of the role, began this process by the simple choice of playing him as his own age: when he took the part in a 1930 Old Vic production (for the first of many times), Gielgud was twenty-six. We think of Prospero as old, but the facts of the story do not require him to be more than thirty; Gielgud's performance hinted at the link between Prospero's self-image and his power, and the role of magic as an extension of his fantasy life. In Peter Brook's landmark production at Stratford in 1957, Gielgud was playing him for the third time, and made him a melancholic introvert, indifferent to affection, torn by the competing desires to forgive his enemies and to avenge his wrongs. To underscore this ambivalence, Brook (in the manner of a post-Freudian *Hamlet*) made his stage a projection of Prospero's psyche, its shadowy caverns and dense vegetation symbolic of a dreamscape. Brook wanted to dislocate the audience from Prospero's sense of reality, so he adopted a spare, skeptical attitude to the play's visuals. Borrowing from Benson's 1891 production, he depicted the opening storm with only a suspended, wildly swinging lantern. Critics found the play too dark, but its minimalism opened up new interpretive avenues, cheapening the magic by which Prospero coerces our support, and making the audience's disorientation an intellectual as well as sensory experience. Brook would fully submit the play to this "theater of cruelty" in his smaller, more experimental 1968 *Tempest*, which ended with Caliban seizing the island, raping Miranda and sodomizing Prospero.

This may have been extreme, but other productions of the later twentieth century have similarly been "revisionist" insofar as they identify the play's vision with Prospero's, and attempt to alienate and reject it. Peter Hall's 1974 National Theatre version used Gielgud again—reluctantly, since Hall felt Gielgud was still too "gentle and nice," and he wanted "the play to happen *to* Prospero." Hall also returned to reconstructionist stage principles, this time for ironic effect. He produced the play with all the elaborate technology of a Jacobean court entertainment, such as painted slats of ocean waves, wires for ascents and descents, and wing-and-shutter scenery for scene shifts. Whereas these contraptions were conventional for a seventeenth century audience, however, the intent was to make a twentieth century one find their artifice self-conscious and gimmicky, their obviousness jarring and comic. Gielgud's Prospero, a man obsessed with his power but whose power itself now appeared flimsy, even silly, thus came off as something of a schizophrenic; Ariel flitted about the stage continuously on a makeshift trapeze to suggest that he existed only in Prospero's mind. Hall said the protagonist on which he modeled his Prospero was Macbeth, and the fact that *The Tempest* could even be thought of in these nightmarishly intense terms tells us how much its stage history was now being resisted, or in this case used against itself.

Other directors, meanwhile, have resorted to more legible systems of reference to interrogate Prospero's agency. Liviu Ciulei's 1981 Minneapolis production gave him in a labcoat for a robe and a ruler for a staff, with an Einstein-like wig to suggest a Cold-War critique of nuclear-era science; Robert Falls at Chicago's Goodman Theater in 1987 made his staff an umbrella composed of shiny, space-age fabric, a satellite dish with which he commanded extraterrestrial spirits. Declan Donnellan's 1988 Cheek By Jowl production showed Prospero watching the entire action from a stage-left dressing room, periodically applying make-up to himself in front of a mirror: his face gradually reflected the spiritual toll of his preoccupation with vengeance, until by the end he had deformed into a gaunt, hollow-eyed ghoul. For the Melbourne Theatre Company in 1990, Gale Edwards adopted an architectural approach, constructing a set dominated by a massive, revolving bust of Prospero's head, with a gaping hole at the back (ostensibly, his brain) which then doubled as Caliban's cave—heavy-handedly implying Prospero as the source of both the play and the "thing of darkness" he refuses to acknowledge. Silviu Purcarete's 1995 Nottingham production further highlighted, and questioned, Prospero's superiority by depicting him in eighteenth century dress, an amalgam of philosopher-prince, amateur scientist and decadent aesthete, attended by multiple Ariels whose lines Prospero spoke in a dubbed voice-over.

A more mainstream way of complicating the play's politics—and of making them speak to our own—has been to interracialize its cast. With the possible exception of only *Othello*, *The Tempest* more than any Shakespeare play became a site for the culture wars triggered in America by the end of the Jim Crow period, and worldwide by the decay of imperialism. As late as the 1930s Caliban was still being played as a Neanderthal, but the first portrayal of him as an African enthralled to a white master—a forced but inevitable reading today—occurred in 1934, in Roger Livesay's performance at London's Old Vic. Livesay was merely a white actor in blackface, however, accompanied by exaggerated Negro stereotypes: only in Margaret Webster's 1945 Broadway *Tempest* did Canada Lee become the first African-American to break Caliban's color line, and as the Civil Rights movement opened doors for black actors, the character quickly became a showcase for more trenchant political statements. Earle Hyman performed him in 1960 as a fat, sing-songy parody of Uncle Remus; James Earl Jones in 1962 as a green reptile; Henry Baker at the 1970 Washington D.C. Shakespeare Festival was described as "a black militant... angry and recalcitrant" in his defiance of Prospero. Just as quickly, though, casting black actors for the role also became seen as endorsing its racism, and post-1960s productions responded by multiplying the number of minorities onstage. Perhaps the most stridently postcolonial *Tempest* was Jonathan Miller's 1970 Mermaid production, which depicted *both* Caliban and Ariel as black, thus juxtaposing their respective subjections to Prospero: while Caliban was a ragged field slave, Ariel was a dapper house servant, lending Uncle Tom connotations to his being Prospero's chief "minister" for tormenting his counterpart. Tina Packer's 1980 Shakespeare and Co. production made Stephano a black man, further satirizing Caliban's enslavement to him. George C. Wolfe's 1995 New York Shakespeare Festival *Tempest* used a black Ariel to different effect, allying him and Caliban in mutual hatred of Prospero. Sam Mendes' 1993 Royal Shakespeare Company production stunned audiences by having a hitherto dutiful Ariel, upon being set free, spit in Prospero's face.

Other, more "multicultural" *Tempest*s have expanded the range of permutations. Since the 1980s, Caliban has been played as a Native American, a Rastafarian, a Maori, a punk, an adolescent and even as a female banshee; Peter Brook's most recent production in 1990 reversed the race of the entire cast. Yet directors have also tired of reducing the play to ethnic binaries, and have begun returning to more plastic, theoretical engagements with its categories of identity. Hall's 1974 Caliban had worn makeup bisecting his face into half-human and half-animal, prompting us to ask which we see; Hall's 1988 version offered a hyper-monstrous Caliban dripping with blood and slime, his genitals encased in a wooden box. Mendes's 1993 RSC production took this one-dimensionality to a literalist extreme by painting the single word "MONSTER" across Caliban's bare chest.

BRAVE NEW WORLDS: "DIRECTOR'S SHAKESPEARE" AND GLOBAL TEMPESTS

Productions like Mendes's exemplified a new wave of interest in the play as part of the phenomenon of "director's Shakespeare," a term that has less to do with a play's having a director than with the idea that every play, on some level, is *about* the presence of a director within it, insofar as it must teach us how to watch it. *The Tempest*, with its meta-theatrical themes of illusion and control, neatly fits this bill, and recent avant-garde treatments have tried to foreground that theatricality by making the audience's experience part of the play's analysis of power. Mendes reduced the conventional logic of the stage to surrealistic absurdities. Prospero's cell looked like the prop room for the very play he was in, replete with books, clothing, a chessboard, and a toy playhouse; actors came and went in a basket through a trapdoor, as if the stage were a makeshift metaphor for the audience's mind. At the opening, Ariel climbed out of the basket, stood on it, and pushed a suspended lantern, at which point the thunder and lightning began. If this gesture invites us to think of the creation of the storm and of the theater itself as interrelated acts, it also—if we may by now recognize it as a variation on Benson and Brook— reminds us that theater is inevitably cyclical and citational. Mendes, like Hall, exposes the play's art as art, but points it at the dynamics of *all* fiction-making, not just Prospero's; Peter Greenaway's 1991 *Prospero's Books* applied to film the same imagistic and narrative fragmentation.

This interpretive mode has flourished internationally, probably because it lays out an abstract, conceptual framework for the play that transcends language barriers. Giorgio Strehler's 1978 *Tempest* for the Piccolo Teatro di Milano infused Shakespeare's fantasy with a self-reflexive awareness of its own media, taking place entirely on the deck of the ship supposedly wrecked in the opening storm—as if the island were itself an imaginary nautical construct, adrift at sea; Prospero shattered his staff at the end, at which point the set crumbled into ruins. A 1983 Madrid version directed by the Argentine Jorge Lavelli, with a female Prospero, piped in Ariel's lines via the house stereo, expanding on the idea that he is a figment of Prospero's mind. For the opening scene, Leo de Berardinis's 1986 Bologna production reverted to the same non-realistic pantomime that had been standard in the nineteenth century, but without explanatory help from realistic scenery or action. Instead of panicked sailors, white-haired zombies slowly emerged from the dark background; to the prelude from Wagner's *Parsifal*, they expressed their torment in low moans, framing the play as a memory being relived after the fact. Other productions have invoked the play's spectacular stage tradition in order to parody it, presenting the island as a three-ring circus peopled with actual clowns and acrobats. Robert LePage's 1992 *La Tempête* in Montreal was set in a rehearsal room—complete with wall-to-wall mirrors and a study table—in which the actors reviewed, prepared and improvised upon the script they were supposed to be performing. Prospero gave a speech comparing the play to the writings of Jorge Luis Borges, and the storm consisted of a toy ship sailing across the table. Over the course of the play, the rehearsal gradually grew indistinguishable from the play itself, and by Act 5 all the actors had "become" their characters. A 1992 Japanese *Tempest* directed by Yukio Ninagawa wove the story into two native art forms, Noh and Kabuki, Japan's classical opera and its comic theater respectively. Caliban wore Kabuki dress, while the ceremonial elements, such as the masque, were done in traditional Noh chant; each scene, whether he was in it or not, was initiated by a clap from Prospero. Another 1992 Japanese production, a life-size puppet show directed by Minoru Fujita, rewrote the happy ending in favor of the revenge plot, portraying Prospero and Alonso as feuding warlords.

Far from exhausted, the play's colonial themes have found new relevance in settings where the local experience of empire has enabled a homegrown perspective. Krystyna Skuszanka's 1959 production in Krakow developed an ambiguous political allegory to evade state censorship under Poland's Soviet-style government. Prospero was characterized as both a progressive, enlightened social scientist and, at the same time, a totalitarian dictator whose cold rationality cannot contain the unpredictable energy of the human spirit; Gonzalo's "commonwealth" speech must have come dangerously alive in a Communist context, as a subversive meditation on the perils of idealism. In 1971, Cuban poet Roberto Fernandez Retamar sparked a Latin American renaissance for *The Tempest* when, in his essay "Caliban," he asked "what is our history, what is our culture, if not the history of Caliban?" In response, the decade witnessed a new eagerness to stage the play in the modern-day countries whose colonization it foreshadowed. Derek Jarman's 1979 film turned Prospero's emotional isolation into a metaphor for closeted homosexuality, making Shakespeare's play a risky, exuberant anthem of gay liberation on the cusp of the first outbreak of the AIDS epidemic. Michael Bogdanov's 1997 BBC film set the play in the economically depressed docklands of Cardiff, Wales, using real residents in his cast, and marking Prospero and the courtiers as London property developers whose private quarrels are killing an indigenous way of life. And while by 1989 casting a black Caliban would have been a common sight in the West, in South Africa, at the peak of its struggle with apartheid, a Pretoria production—translated into the colonial language Afrikaans—did just that, his stark nakedness daring audiences to see him as inhuman. The dizzying array of adaptations attests to how versatile, and irreducibly visual, the play can still be.

Over the past 400 years *The Tempest* has, like the battered vessel with which it begins, endured all the upheavals history has thrown at it—regicide, Restoration, science, empire, slavery, democracy, technology—as well as every sea-change in Shakespeare reception that accompanied them. Constantly torn apart and rebuilt, revised and restored and revised again, the play has emerged a prism through which we can view that history itself, the events that shaped our world rendered visible in what successive generations did to the play and asked the play to do to them in turn. Shakespeare may not have been able to foresee how a drama once used to pay a king a political compliment could have become so scathing a political weapon; but he would not have been surprised at how—whether indulged, resisted or deconstructed—the play's "magic" has continued to haunt, fascinate, frustrate and elude us, and allowed us to think about the nature of the art that holds us captive every time we see it performed. *The Tempest* embodies theater as much as theater has embodied it, and it is still sailing.

As Performed

BY SHAKESPEARE BEHIND BARS AT THE LUTHER LUCKETT CORRECTIONAL COMPLEX IN LaGRANGE, KENTUCKY, 2003

Curt L. Tofteland

[*The essay that follows is a first-hand account by Curt L. Tofteland on directing the inmates of the Luther Luckett Correctional Complex in Shakespeare's* The Tempest *for the program,* Shakespeare Behind Bars *(SBB). Tofteland describes the experience through his eyes as director and recounts his inmates' challenges as they prepared for their individual roles. Comparing the prison and the inmates to Shakespeare's island and its inhabitants, he draws intimate parallels between the inmates' experiences and those of the characters', providing a unique insight into the play. The rehearsal process was documented in the film,* Shakespeare Behind Bars, *by Philomath Films and released in 2005. - Editor*]

It is 8:45 AM, September 9, 2002. The oppressive heat and humidity of a late Kentucky summer have yet to grip the countryside. On a hill, erupting from the earth, like mushrooms following a rainstorm, are the sand colored buildings of the Kentucky State Reformatory (KSR). A curtain of heat, radiating skyward from the pasture, makes KSR appear as a distant desert mirage. The double razor wire fence surrounding the massive correctional complex reflects the intense sunshine. The glistening razor wire cuts through the dreamlike quality of the picture, solidly grounding me in reality.

The metaphor of my journey to a world within a world is not lost on me. I am on the road to meet my Shakespeare Behind Bars brothers at the nearby Luther Luckett Correctional Complex, a medium security adult male prison. I drive past the barbed wire fence that keeps the cattle within the pasture and me on the outside. Within the pasture, is yet another world enclosed by double razor wire fences, an even more restricted world where the criminal offenders are kept in and the cattle—and I—are kept out.

The prison floats in isolation. An island within an island. Like the island that Prospero, Miranda, Ariel, and Caliban inhabit.

I keep driving. Just past KSR, the natural world reestablishes itself in the form of white barns, a grain silo, and other familiar farm outbuildings. Beyond the farmstead, the Roderer Correctional Complex sternly stands guard at the far end of the pasture.

In the foreground, an inmate wearing a bright orange jump suit with the word **JAIL** stenciled in black letters on his back drives a green John Deere tractor, pulling a trailer laden with large round bales of dried hay. The inmate exists between the barbed wire world and the razor wire world. He has been allowed this privilege of restricted freedom by the warden (Prospero). The inmate is a trustee. He exists between the world of freedom and the world of imprisonment. He is Ariel, doing the tasks the warden has commanded him to do, with the promise that if he obeys and perfectly completes the tasks, he will gain his release. He will have served his time in the world in-between and finally reenter the world of freedom.

Behind the razor wire fences, reside the criminal offenders (Calibans) who have been convicted of committing heinous crimes against their fellow human beings. Some people will say they are past redemption. Others, that they are incapable of reformation, echoing Prospero's view of Caliban:

> A devil, a born devil, on whose nature
> Nurture can never stick; on whom my pains,
> Humanely taken all, all lost, quite lost.
> And as with age his body uglier grows,
> So his mind cankers. I will plague them all,
> Even to roaring.

> (4.1.189-194)

As I round the bend in the road, the Luther Luckett Correctional Complex comes into view. It is an assemblage of one story, dull white buildings squatting in rural Kentucky between Buckner and LaGrange. I turn left and cross the asphalt gulf that will carry me to the island known as Luckett.

As I approach Box One, the officer recognizes my car and waves me past.

At the stop sign, I face a T-shaped intersection. Ahead of me is the double razor wire barrier. On my right, a sign reads "STOP! Authorized Vehicles Only Past this Point." Here, a perimeter blacktop road encircles two stands of razor wire fence; this asphalt perimeter is patrolled by an armed officer twenty-four hours a day, seven days a week, fifty-two weeks a year.

I look to my left, to the guard tower looming over the scene, its opaque windows reflecting the late summer sunshine. Behind the one-way glass sit highly skilled marksmen who have been trained to shoot to kill.

I park my car and enter Building One. I am on the island. I encounter the personal security checkpoint. I pass through a metal detector and pick up my personal belongings on the other side. My route takes me past the administrative offices for the prison and through two sets of sliding security doors. For a few moments, I am trapped between them. I feel like Ariel, confined to the in-between world.

When freed, I stand before the elevated control room of double-paned, bulletproof security glass through which I am scrutinized by the officer who controls all the sliding security doors in Building One.

Still more security measures follow. When I step through the final sliding door, I am now securely within the inner sanctum of Building One on Luckett island.

I begin to stack the chairs and tables to create an open area for our rehearsal at the end of the long rectangular room opposite the humming vending machines. When I am finished, I stand facing the door from whence will enter the inmate participants of Shakespeare Behind Bars.

I await the Calibans.

Through the double paned, bulletproof glass on my right, a group of inmates trudge up the walkway from the yard. Dressed from head to ankle in khaki clothing, the color of the faded pasture grass that surrounds the prison, walk the band of brothers who make up the all male acting ensemble of Shakespeare Behind Bars (SBB).

I founded this company with the assistance of Dr. Julie Barto, Kentucky Department of Corrections psychologist, in 1985. Our vision was and is to prepare offenders who have served their time for their crime to return to the streets as productive and contributing members of our society. Our mission is to discover the heart of human behavior through the exploration of the works of William Shakespeare. Our journey is deeply personal, leading the inmates to insight, understanding, acceptance, responsibility, transformation, redemption, and the hope of forgiveness.

For the inmates, Shakespeare Behind Bars is a journey into the authentic self; it is the courage to abandon the mask and turn a genuine face to the world. It is a quest into their most vulnerable selves.

Shakespeare Behind Bars is a voluntary program with the number of participants capped at 30. The inmates receive no institutional credit for their participation, and any Luther Luckett Correctional Complex inmate is welcome to join the SBB circle. New recruits have two requirements: they must have a twelve-month institutional record clear of infractions, and they must secure sponsorship from an SBB core member.

Although inmates who join the ensemble have little or no theatrical experience, they are treated with the same expectations of dedication and discipline as professional actors who are in the process of rehearsing a play.

Even so, the Shakespeare Behind Bars rehearsal process follows the guidelines of a professional company with two notable exceptions. One of the few rules I enacted when I created the SBB program was the elimination of actors' auditioning for roles. The SBB ensemble members are empowered to cast themselves. Over the years, there have been instances in which several members of the ensemble desired the same role. The group always resolved these disputes amongst themselves using nonviolent communication and conflict resolution to decide who most needed the role.

The second notable exception in our rehearsal process is the casting of the female roles. A male playing a female role, although the law in Shakespeare's day, is rare in our modern professional theater. A male inmate playing a female role in a prison production of a play by William Shakespeare was nonexistent until our 1996 Shakespeare Behind Bars production of *The Two Gentlemen of Verona*.

In the early days of the SBB program, it took enormous courage for an inmate to step forth and assume the role of a female character. Prior to our

Curt Tofteland directs cast members in the 2005 documentary film *Shakespeare Behind Bars* by Philomath Films
Courtesy of Philomath Films; Photo: Hank Rogerson

first performance, I told the cast that if they broke character when the audience's response became personal, the audience, not the actors, would be in control of the production.

In our first performance for the prison yard, when the first actor appeared on stage costumed in female apparel, there was pandemonium. The inmate audience exploded with howls of laughter, jeers, and heckling. Our actors absorbed the audience reaction and endured with patience and nobility. In what seemed like a pregnant eternity, the audience's reaction decreased and finally ceased when they realized their noisy intrusion was having no effect on our actors.

Each time a new actor playing a female entered the stage, the audience howled. And each time, the actors went on, refusing to break character despite the ridicule.

As the performance proceeded, fewer and fewer audience members participated in the disturbance. We could feel the audience's respect growing. In the talk-back we held at the conclusion of the performance, many of the audience members expressed their admiration for the actors, particularly those playing the female roles. A bond grew between the inmates, both on and off the stage. All recognized the courage it took to risk doing something so divergent from the testosterone-driven male behavior which is the norm on the prison yard. This early experience was one of the many life lessons we SBB members hold dear to our hearts—the courage to risk.

Today, playing a female role in a Shakespeare Behind Bars production has become a rite of passage. SBB members step up to play these roles needing minimal encouragement from the ensemble.

In the *Shakespeare Behind Bars* documentary, we have the opportunity to view the journey of an SBB ensemble member taking on the role of Prospero's daughter. When we meet Red in the documentary, we see him attempt a mock escape when I ask who is playing the only female role in *The Tempest*. After Red's mock escape, we cut away to hear him say, "They put the role on me. I rebelled and said, 'Let me choose the role. Don't you choose the role for me.'"

It appears that the SBB code of casting has been broken by not allowing Red to choose to play the role of Miranda. Red seems to say he was coerced by his fellow SBB members. In reality, Red was actively being encouraged to play Miranda. However, he always held the power to refuse. And in the spirit of generosity, Red chose to support the production once he realized Miranda did not fit any of his SBB brothers.

Red looks over his costume as Miranda in the 2005 documentary film *Shakespeare Behind Bars* by Philomath Films
Courtesy of Philomath Films; Photo: Hank Rogerson

What made Red's decision to play Miranda even more remarkable is that he has a developmental reading disorder. To keep the disorder hidden, Red always arrived at each rehearsal with his lines memorized for the scenes we were working that day. I often held him up to the rest of the ensemble as a professional-level actor whom they should all emulate.

Eventually Red's secret was revealed when we decided to jump to a scene he hadn't memorized. Red protested that he hadn't begun work on that scene. We told him we understood and that he could read Miranda's lines from the script. When it came time for Red to read, he struggled. In that moment, I recognized his reading disorder and stopped the rehearsal. Red was visibly embarrassed. The years of ridicule he had endured while navigating his schooling were fully resting upon his slumped shoulders. I told him that it didn't matter to us that he couldn't read well. We recognized the nobility of his heroic attempt.

When asked how he memorized, Red revealed that his roommate read Miranda's lines out loud. Red repeated the lines until they were written on his brain.

Throughout the *Shakespeare Behind Bars* documentary, we view Red's miraculous transformation as he explores the depths of Miranda's character.

Such transformations are at the heart of *The Tempest*. Just as Red and his fellow actors took risks to go beyond the limits set for them, characters in this play must choose to take risks if they are to change. The play challenges them to let go of the past and move into the future. This is the transformation that the Shakespeare Behind Bars actors are seeking in their own lives. We chose to explore *The Tempest* for nine months because the play speaks deeply to the redemptive power of change, which is forgiveness.

Through the process of the play, Prospero transforms from a revengeful human being to one who discovers empathy, mercy, and the power of forgiveness.

From among multiple interpretations of *The Tempest,* we chose to examine the play as an allegory. We see Ariel and Caliban as the opposite extremes of Prospero. Caliban is represented on the earth-bound plane (the shadow). Ariel is represented in the ethereal plane (the light). Prospero represents the rational part of the human being that contains free will—the will and ability to choose. Prospero is the fulcrum between the world of shadow (Caliban) and the world of light (Ariel).

We explore the idea that when each offender committed his crime he acted out of his Caliban self, for whom moral principles, a sense of right and wrong, are beyond understanding.

Caliban, the criminal, attempts to rape Miranda.

Prospero accuses him: "thou didst seek to violate / The honor of my child" (1.2.349-350). Caliban defiantly shows no remorse, replying,

> Oh ho, oh ho! Would't had been done!
> Thou didst prevent me; I had peopled else
> This isle with Calibans.
>
> (1.2.351-353)

Caliban also seeks revenge for his imprisonment by plotting the murder of Prospero: "Yea, yea, my lord. I'll yield him thee asleep, / Where thou mayst knock a nail into his head" (3.2.51-52). He even tells his coconspirators, Stephano and Trinculo, when it might be done:

> Why, as I told thee, 'tis a custom with him
> I' th' afternoon to sleep. There thou mayst brain him,
> Having first seized his books: or with a log
> Batter his skull, or paunch him with a stake,
> Or cut his wesand with thy knife.
>
> (3.2.76-80)

THE TEMPEST [28

As the other dimension of Prospero, Ariel feels empathy for those whom Prospero seeks to revenge and urges him to forgiveness:

> Your charm so strongly works 'em
> That if you now beheld them, your affections
> Would become tender.
>
> PROSPERO
> Dost thou think so, spirit?
>
> ARIEL
> Mine would, sir, were I human.

(5.1.17-20)

Ariel's empathic words give Prospero pause. As he reflects upon them, the authentic meaning is revealed. His transformation begins. In an instant, he discovers empathy. Twelve years of revengeful plotting evaporates. He embraces mercy and the power of forgiveness.

Prospero moves from the shadow into the light with these words:

> And mine shall.
> Hast thou—which art but air—a touch, a feeling
> Of their afflictions, and shall not myself,
> One of their kind, that relish all as sharply
> Passion as they, be kindlier moved then thou art?

(5.1.20-24)

Prospero's view of justice evolves. True, he was a victim of deceit and treachery by his brother. And as in the Old Testament biblical passage of "an eye for an eye and a tooth for a tooth," Prospero feels justified in his revenge upon his perpetrator. He has waited a long time and gone to great length to develop his art and set the stage for his revenge. He now holds the power to wreak revengeful havoc. But in his epiphany, Prospero discovers his noble self. And it is in nobility that he is able to abate his anger. As his anger dissipates, Prospero realizes that revenge is the common action and that the rarer action lies in his higher self where virtue abides.

Prospero's transformation continues:

Though with their high wrongs I am struck to th'quick,
Yet with my nobler reason, 'gainst my fury
Do I take part. The rarer action is
In virtue than in vengeance. They being penitent,
The sole drift of my purpose doth extend
Not a frown further. Go, release them, Ariel;
My charms I'll break, their senses I'll restore,
And they shall be themselves.

(5.1.25-32)

It is in his virtue that Prospero finds the power of forgiveness, extending it even to Antonio:

Flesh and blood,
You, brother mine, that entertained ambition,
Expelled remorse and nature; whom, with Sebastian—
Whose inward pinches therefore are most strong—
Would here have killed your king: I do forgive thee,
Unnatural though thou art.

(5.1.74-79)

For you, most wicked sir, whom to call brother
Would even infect my mouth, I do forgive
Thy rankest fault—all of them.

(5.1.130-132)

In this moment, Prospero represents the victims of the Shakespeare Behind Bars inmates. The inmates hope their victims too will find within their nobility the virtue that will allow them to forgive their perpetrators. It is a worthy hope, but one that is denied because the offenders are locked away on an impenetrable island, isolated from society.

In forgiving the conspirators, Prospero has come to terms with the part of him that desired and sought revenge. He must embrace Caliban, his shadow self: "this thing of darkness I / Acknowledge mine" (5.1.273-274). And with Prospero's acknowledged forgiveness, Caliban too is transformed, elevated from the savage beast to a higher being. It is Caliban's choice to rise above his former self: "and I'll be wise hereafter, / And seek for grace" (5.1.291-292).

Caliban's journey of transformation through the play—from "a savage and deformed slave" to a civilized and free creature who will "be wise hereafter, and seek for grace"—mirrors the Shakespeare Behind Bars inmate's journey of transformation, from a convict, who doesn't have the capacity for empathy or remorse for his crime, to a human being who, in seeking for "grace," discovers empathy, remorse, grief, and the desire to give something positive back to society.

In the final couplet of the play, Prospero makes it clear that forgiveness frees us. In this, his voice merges with those of the Shakespeare Behind Bars inmates: "As you from crimes would pardoned be, / Let your indulgence set me free" (Epilogue.19-20).

Note:

Hank Rogerson of Philomath Films contacted me in January 2002 regarding making a documentary about Shakespeare Behind Bars. After viewing a previous documentary by Philomath Films, I invited Hank to visit Luther Luckett to view our performance of *Hamlet* in May 2002. We received permission from the Kentucky Department of Corrections to film the documentary. Larry Chandler, Warden LLCC, and Karen Heath, Director Department of Recreation LLCC, were instrumental in the making of the film.

In September 2002, Philomath Films began filming our nine-month preparation of *The Tempest*. Filming was completed following *The Tempest* Tour in September of 2003. The final cut of the film was completed in December 2004.

Shakespeare Behind Bars was selected as one of 16 documentaries (out of 624 submissions) to present its world premiere at the 2005 Sundance Film Festival. The documentary has gone on to 40+ film festivals around the world, garnering 11 awards. It has had a commercial release, been screened in Europe on the British Broadcasting Corporation, in Canada on the Canadian Broadcasting Corporation, in the United States on the Public Broadcasting Service, and on cable on the Sundance Channel. The documentary is now available on DVD, and more information can be found on http://www.shakespearebehindbars.com/.

Shakespeare Behind Bars
Written and directed by Hank Rogerson
Produced by Jilann Spitzmiller
Philomath Films (2005)

HANK ROGERSON is a producer, director, writer, and actor who works in both fiction and non-fiction film. He wrote and directed *Shakespeare Behind Bars*, which had its world premiere at the Sundance Film Festival and has won 11 awards, including Best of Show, Best Documentary, and a Special Jury Prize. Hank co-produced, directed, and edited *Homeland*, a documentary about four families on the Pine Ridge Indian Reservation that aired nationally on PBS in 2000. Hank also co-directed and produced *Circle of Stories*, a multi-media web project that brings to life the vibrant art of Native American storytelling at pbs.org.

JILANN SPITZMILLER is an award-winning producer, director, and writer who produced *Shakespeare Behind Bars*; she was also a producer and director on other Philomath Films projects including *Homeland* and *Circle of Stories*. Philomath Films is a three-time recipient of ITVS funding and twice has received funding from the Sundance Institute. Jilann is also a cinematographer and has freelanced extensively on documentaries, with her work appearing on NBC, PBS, A&E, Bravo, and Discovery Health. She co-directed and co-produced *Critical Condition* for National PBS about the nation's health insurance crisis. Jilann is also a documentary consultant and teaches documentary workshops around the country.

"A Sea-Change / Into Something Rich and Strange"

THE TEMPEST IN POPULAR CULTURE

Douglas Lanier

Claiming pride of place among the plays in the First Folio, *The Tempest* has had a long and robust afterlife in performance and popular adaptation, despite shifts in cultural and critical fashion. One reason for its resilience may be that it has many of the qualities of myth. Compared to many other Shakespeare plays, the plot of *The Tempest* is relatively uncomplicated. Its characters have been reduced to uncomplicated archetypes, and its narrative is located in a seabound never-never land, despite a few real-world details. Despite its simplicity *The Tempest* interweaves a remarkable number of thematic strands that adaptors have teased out and developed for their own ends. *The Tempest* is the family saga of a father and daughter, a tale of political intrigue, a castaway adventure, a fantasy story of magicians, monsters and fairies, the chronicle of an old man's last days, a religious allegory, a musical and special-effects extravaganza, a colonialist screed, and Shakespeare's fictionalized leave-taking of the stage. What's more, *The Tempest* has prompted very strong and radically opposing responses from audiences and critics over time. For some, the play offers the portrait of a benevolent, omnipotent magus who, like the playwright himself, marshals magical forces to craft a fairy-tale ending for himself and his daughter. For others, Prospero is a manipulative colonial tyrant obsessed with control who engages in the very usurpation that he himself has suffered. The play offers ample materials for both responses. As adaptors have fastened upon various strands in the play, adaptations have tended towards two broad interpretive directions, one that emphasizes *The Tempest*'s charming qualities, its fantasy and romantic elements and benevolent tone, or one that focuses on its connections with the troubling legacies of colonial and patriarchal politics.

"MARVELOUS SWEET MUSIC":
The Tempest AND MUSICAL ADAPTATION

Prompted by Ariel's many songs and Caliban's talk of "sounds, and sweet airs, that give delight" (3.2.124), composers have long found the mellifluous isle a rich source of inspiration. Indeed, *The Tempest* is the Shakespearean play most frequently adapted to operatic form. John Dryden and William Davenant's 1667 stage adaptation–later revised by Thomas Shadwell in 1674–added not only Sycorax, a sister of Caliban, and Dorinda, a second daughter of Prospero (with her corresponding consort, Hippolito), but also extensive musical passages by Matthew Locke appropriate to this version's expanded courtship themes. Henry Purcell and John Weldon's musical setting of Shadwell's text in 1695 expanded the musical elements even more, creating one of the very first Shakespearean operas, one which remained popular on the stage for more than fifty years. Many operatic versions were to follow. In the last years of the eighteenth century, several composers tried their hands at setting Friedrich Wilhelm Gotter's play *Die Geisterinsel* (1795), a tale of magical storms and retribution based upon *The Tempest* in which Prospero and company were menaced by Sycorax. Yet despite the evident craftsmanship of Gotter's story, these operas were not crowd-pleasers. Jacques Halévy's *La Tempesta* (1850) was the high-water mark of nineteenth-century operatic versions, and it rang fascinating changes on Shakespeare's tale. In Halévy's version (clearly influenced by Gotter's play), Sycorax, Caliban's mother, plays an expanded role, encouraging her son to imprison Miranda and Ariel and tricking Miranda into nearly killing Ferdinand to save her father. The emphasis on magic and fairies, the melodramatic plot and amplified pathos, and the stark contrast between savage and civilized are in accord with Victorian stage treatments of the play.

Twentieth-century composers have continued to find the play an attractive source, with versions ranging from the conventional (for example, Heinrich Sutermeister's 1942 *Die Zauberinsel* [*The Magic Island*] and Frank Martin's 1956 *Der Sturm* [*The Storm*]) to the avant-garde (for example, Luciano Berio's 1984 *Un Re in Ascolto* [*A King Listens*], with a libretto by the novelist Italo Calvino). Again, despite the popularity of *The Tempest* as a subject for opera, none of these adaptations have made their way into the standard repertory. The play has also inspired song cycles and instrumental music. The analogy between the sounds of the sea-swept island and tempestuous emotions proved irresistible to many composers writing in the Romantic tradition, among them Hector Berlioz, Peter Tchaikovsky, Jean Sibelius, and William Alwyn, all of whom have written orchestral suites based upon the play. And given Ariel's penchant for singing in Shakespeare's original text, it is unsurprising that many composers–Frank Martin, Ralph Vaughan Williams, Alexander Goehr, Judith Weir, Harrison Birtwhistle and Michael Nyman among them–have produced musical settings and song cycles based upon Ariel's songs. One of the most intriguing is George Benjamin's *Sometimes Voices* (1998), which brilliantly depicts Caliban's wonder and terror at the island's quasi-musical noises.

Popular composers have also tried their hands at making a musical of *The Tempest*, though like their classical counterparts, few of their efforts have found wide audiences. Of them Bob Carlton's *Return to the Forbidden Planet* (1989) has had the greatest popular success. *Return* is a retro-musical, a look back at the culture of baby-boomers' youth with a nostalgic yet ironic smile. A textbook example of postmodern pastiche, Carlton's musical is a campy mash-up of three cultural "classics"–Shakespeare's *The Tempest*, the science fiction film *Forbidden Planet*, and rock-and-roll hits like "Great Balls of Fire" and "All Shook Up." In this version, Dr. Prospero, a mad scientist, and his daughter Miranda are marooned on the planet Albatross with Ariel the robot, only later to be discovered by Captain Tempest and his crew of space explorers. The pleasure of this musical lies in its arch citation of Shakespearean and space opera commonplaces. Though the characters use dialogue from *The Tempest* and lines cribbed from other Shakespearean plays, they behave in accordance with B-movie clichés and fall into singing wittily-chosen pop standards (at her first sight of Captain Tempest, for example, Miranda bursts into "Good Vibrations"). Much of this musical's appeal springs from the audience's knowing recognition of its citations, the participatory qualities of its staging (audiences are encouraged to sing along), and its affectionate send-up of high cultural Shakespeare. The show's strong element of nostalgia has interesting though perhaps unintentional resonances with Prospero's penchant for remembering his past.

Judging simply from song titles, it is clear that *The Tempest*'s association with music remains powerful for popular songwriters. Songs entitled "Ariel" and "Caliban" reveal well-established connotations of these names, "Ariel" often the sign of jazz, salsa, dream pop or New Age instrumental tunes, "Caliban" the sign of more raucous styles like rock, punk, and metal. "Full Fathom Five" is also a popular though far less specific reference point, with versions by artists as diverse as Cowboy Nation, Marianne Faithful, Ian Carr, Méav, Miranda Sex Garden, Pearls Before Swine, and Victory at Sea. Laurie Anderson sardonically references the speech in her song "Blue Lagoon" (on *Mister Heartbreak*, 1984) and again in "The Ugly One with the Jewels" (on *The Ugly*

One with the Jewels, 1995); in the Decemberists' song triptych "The Island" (on *The Crane's Wife*, 2006), the third section, entitled "You'll Not Feel the Drowning," freely paraphrases Ariel's song, recasting it as a song of revenge, not transformation. A number of *Tempest*-themed songs bear New Age or Latin musical associations, both appropriate respectively to the play's magical atmosphere and Caribbean setting. Loreena McKennitt's mystical "Prospero's Speech" (on *The Mask and Mirror*, 1994) and Locust's ambient "Prospero" (on *Weathered Well*, 1994) are instances of the former; Ruben Blades' "Blackamán" (on *Agua de Luna*, 1986), a song of Caliban's liberation, exemplifies the latter. More ambitious have been the group Mynde's song cycle based upon *The Tempest*, developed into a complete alternative rock opera in 1996, and *The Caribbean Tempest*, Kit Hesketh-Harvey's 1999 production of the play with extensive added reggae and calypso music (its first production in Barbados starred pop diva Kylie Minogue as Miranda).

Musical Adaptations of The Tempest

Marcha Malamet, Dennis Green, and Howard Ashman, Dreamstuff (1976)	part of the Shakespeare rock musical craze of the period
Dennis Watkins and Chris Harriott, *Beach Blanket Tempest*, (1984, revised 1990)	a campy Australian musical which melds Shakespeare's narrative with clichés of 60s beach movies; its Prospero is an Elvis-like magus
Zden?k Barták, *The Tempest: Millennium Musical* (1999)	a Korean pop musical in celebration of the new century, written by a Czech composer
Neil K. Newell and C. Michael Perry, *Such Stuff as Dreams, or The Tempest: The Musical* (2001)	a prequel, focusing on Prospero and Miranda's arrival on the island and their battle with Sycorax
Maggie MacDonald and Bob Wiseman, *The Rat King* (2006)	a post-apocalyptic free adaptation in which Ed Cannon, a tyrannical mad scientist, seeks a suitor for his daughter Carlyn while manipulating the Rat King, a mute servant boy who was raised with rats

"THIS INSUBSTANTIAL PAGEANT":
The Tempest ON STAGE AND IN VERSE

Prospero's speech on the fleeting nature of stage performance, a speech that culminates in the line "We are such stuff / As dreams are made on" (4.1.156-157), is only one of many famous references to theater within the play. Those references, as well as the spectacular nature of many of its scenes, have sparked the imaginations of many playwrights, for *The Tempest* is one of the most frequently adapted of Shakespeare's plays. (The line "We are such stuff / As dreams are made on" has had its own distinct afterlife, appearing in such diverse contexts as *The Maltese Falcon* [dir. John Huston, 1941], Carly Simon's song "The Stuff that Dreams are Made of" [sic, 1987], and the documentary *Looking for Richard* [dir. Al Pacino, 1996].) Theatrical adaptations of Shakespeare's play have taken myriad forms over time. Written in the midst of nineteenth-century bardolatry and burgeoning stage performances, earlier adaptations tended to take the form of affectionate burlesques or loving tributes. A. H. O.'s *The Tempest, or the Wily Wizard, the Winsome Wench, and the Wicked Willain*, a Victorian lampoon, is a good example of the former; Percy MacKaye's lavish *Caliban by the Yellow Sands* (1916), a masque that identifies Shakespeare with Prospero and celebrates his civilizing power, exemplifies the latter. By contrast, adaptations from the mid-twentieth century onward often have a satirical edge or spring from oppositional politics.

CONTEMPORARY STAGE ADAPTATIONS OF THE TEMPEST

John Murrell's *New World* (1985)	portrays a comic and poignant family reunion of British emigrés to Canada struggling to assimilate
Philip Osment's *This Island's Mine* (1988)	uses loose connections to *The Tempest* to explore contemporary gay life in Britain
Rex Obano's *Play for England* (1997)	merges characters from *The Tempest* with contemporary British characters to offer social commentary

Continued...

Continued...

Brendan Byrnes's Lizzie Borden's Tempest (1998)	develops the historical fact that murderer Lizzie Borden played Miranda in a local production to meld her reading of the play with elements of her biography
Frank Bramwell's Tempus Fugit: Prospero's Will (2006)	provides a sequel in which Miranda returns to Prospero's island many years later to observe its decline

Other than the sonnets and *Hamlet*, few Shakespearean works have inspired more response from poets than *The Tempest*. One of the most famous, Robert Browning's "Caliban upon Setebos" (1864), imagines Caliban reflecting upon the nature of his brutal pagan god Setebos, a meditation that engages Victorian controversies about the effects of Darwinism upon religious belief. W. H. Auden's *The Sea and the Mirror* (1944) offers a series of poetic monologues by various characters, given after the play has ended. Its subtitle, "A Commentary on Shakespeare's *The Tempest*," captures the didactic quality of much of the sequence, though many critics have praised the emotional depth of the opening piece, Prospero's extended farewell to Ariel. Tellingly, Auden chooses Caliban as his primary mouthpiece for ideas about art. Sylvia Plath's "Ariel" (1963), a poem about female transformation and liberty written for her thirtieth birthday, alludes not only to the name of a beloved horse but also to Shakespeare's character who, released from the cloven pine, still longs for freedom. "Ariel" became the title poem of Plath's most famous poetic collection, *Ariel and other Poems* (1965, published posthumously). Ted Hughes's poems "Crow's Song about Prospero and Sycorax" (1971, in *Shakespeare's Poem*) and "Setebos" (1998, from *Birthday Letters*) address the play from quite different angles, in the first suggesting an uneasy parity between the male and female principles Prospero and Sycorax represent, in the second, recasting Hughes's stormy relationship with Sylvia Plath allegorically in terms of *The Tempest*. In *Highlife for Caliban* (1973, the third volume of a poetic trilogy), Sierra Leonean poet Lemuel Johnson uses several allusions to Caliban and *The Tempest* to confront Western attitudes toward third-world artists and peoples. Johnson's oppositional attitude marks a decisive shift in how non-Anglo-American poets have tended to reference the play in their verse. For example, Kamau Brathwaite, the renowned Caribbean poet, has often alluded to *The Tempest* in his work and even created "Sycorax's book" in his *Barabajan Poems* (1994) in answer to Prospero's magical tome.

DESERTED ISLES AND FAR-FLUNG PLANETS

An influential template for the durable genre of the castaway tale, *The Tempest* has provided building blocks for works as different as Daniel Defoe's classic *Robinson Crusoe* (1719) and the TV series *Gilligan's Island, Fantasy Island* and *Lost*. Two notable film adaptations offer a variation on this genre, the tale of male mid-life escape to a pastoral isle. Michael Powell's *Age of Consent* (1969) focuses on Bradley Morahan, an irascible Australian painter discontented with his life in New York City. To escape his uninspired though successful city life, he moves to an island in Queensland where he meets Cora Ryan, the beautiful young daughter of a local hag. Cora soon becomes his occasional servant and muse; her agreement to pose nude allows Bradley to recapture his lost creativity. Cora combines elements of Ariel's and Miranda's character. At first she works for Bradley only so that she can get her own freedom (in the form of a hairdressing job in Brisbane), but she also exudes the innocence and romantic appeal of Miranda. The film's provocative title teases out the erotic, even incestuous subtext of Prospero's fascination with Miranda's sexuality implicit in Morahan's desire for Cora, and indeed the two consummate their relationship in the final reel. The way the camera fastens upon the physical beauty of Cora (played by a young Helen Mirren) encourages the viewer to identify with rather than condemn Morahan. Paul Mazursky's *Tempest* (1982) explores similar themes, following Shakespeare's text somewhat more closely than does Powell. His Prospero figure is Philip Dimitrios, a New York developer whose mid-life crisis leads to dissatisfaction with his career and marriage. After his wife Antonia takes up with developer Alonzo, Philip leaves with his daughter Miranda for Greece where he takes up with a free-spirited singer Aretha. As Philip follows his dream of creating an amphitheater on an island inhabited only by Kalibanos, a zany goat-herd, Antonia and her retinue try to track down Philip in hopes of getting custody of Miranda. In a moment of magic realism toward the film's end, Philip conjures up a storm which brings the principal characters together on his island and sparks the beginnings of a romance between Miranda and Freddy, Alonzo's son. Mazursky's *Tempest* might best be seen as the masculine counterpart of his more famous film *An Unmarried Woman* (1978), about a woman's mid-life crisis.

Adaptors have found *The Tempest* amenable for transposition into a surprising number of other popular genres. For example, the play's isolated island setting, strange non-human inhabitants, and supernatural powers have suggested affinities with science fiction scenarios that several writers have explored. Veteran SF writer Poul Anderson makes recovery of Prospero's "drowned" book of magic the centerpiece of his *A Midsummer Tempest* (1974); aided by Oberon and Titania from *A Midsummer Night's Dream*, Prince Rupert, hero of the tale, uses Prospero's book to protect King Charles during an alternate universe version of the English Civil War. The classic *Star Trek* episode "Requiem for Methuselah" (broadcast 1967) concerns a lonely immortal not unlike Prospero who controls remarkable technological powers and creates an android daughter-consort for himself. "Emergence," an episode of *Star Trek: The Next Generation* (1994), opens with resident android Data playing Prospero and offering a portion of his "Ye elves of hills, brooks, standing lakes and groves" speech; the speech becomes yet another occasion for Data to learn about what it means to be human, but it also uses Prospero's words to anticipate the final show of the series, then in its last season. Aldous Huxley's *Brave New World* (1932) takes a far darker view. This classic novel portrays a technological future in which the population has been divided into castes and pacified by recreational sex, drugs and social

Anne Francis as Altaira and Robby the Robot in the 1956 film *Forbidden Planet* directed by Fred M. Wilcox
Courtesy of Douglas Lanier

engineering. The plot pits the "savage" John against various representatives of the dystopian World State, with the twist that John, ostensibly a Caliban-like rebel, is in fact humane and cultured (he often references Shakespeare) and the "utopian" World State repressive and cruel. The novel's title, taken from Miranda's exclamation of naive wonder at Alonso and his treacherous compatriots, reflects Huxley's deeply sardonic tone.

Interestingly, many adaptors of *The Tempest* to science fiction have followed Huxley's lead in reversing Shakespeare's utopian vision of Prospero's island. Two examples are noteworthy. One of the finest science fiction movies of its day, *Forbidden Planet* (1956) reimagines Shakespeare's tale from the perspective of Ferdinand, in this case J. J. Adams, commander of a spaceship sent to find settlers left on the planet Altair years earlier. Upon his arrival Adams discovers only Dr. Edward Morbius and his daughter Altaira. Like Prospero, Morbius, an irascible scientist, wields great power, not in the form of magic but rather the apparatus of an ancient, now vanished alien race, the Krell. His Ariel-like helpmate is Robby the Robot, capable of amazing technological feats. Like Miranda, Altaira quickly falls in love with the handsome Captain Adams, much to her father's disapproval. The Caliban of the piece is a mysterious monstrous force which attacks Adams' crew. Eventually we learn that this force is a projection of Morbius's unconscious thoughts which have been amplified by the Krell technology. In effect this revelation recasts Prospero's observation "this thing of darkness I / Acknowledge mine" in Freudian terms, and it leads Morbius to destroy the Krell's apparatus (just as Prospero destroys his staff and book) so that Adams, Altaira and crew can escape. If *The Tempest* presents a humanist fantasy of benevolent power wielded by an intellectual-king, *Forbidden Planet* expresses anxieties about the rising power of technocrats in the mid-twentieth-century, even as it plays to our fascination with technology with its gee-whiz gadgetry and state-of-the-art special effects.

Less well-known is Dan Simmons' paired novels *Ilium* (2003) and *Olympos* (2005), which present a dystopian vision of the future filtered through two master texts, Homer's *Iliad* and Shakespeare's *Tempest*. In *Ilium*, one plotline concerns the quest of Harman and his companions, decadent future humans, to discover the mystery of their race's long forgotten origins. In the process they fall victim to Caliban, a monster who seeks to kill the humans and delights in quoting Browning's poem "Caliban upon Setebos." Harman and company are protected from Caliban by Prospero, a sentient hologram which evolved out of the Internet; we later learn that Prospero and Ariel, the sentient biosphere of Earth, are the parents of Caliban. *Olympos* extends this *Tempest*-flavored plotline by eventually revealing that much of future history is shaped by a secret war between Prospero and Setebos, a monster from an alternate universe who allies with Caliban. Throughout both novels Simmons emphasizes the archetypal qualities of Shakespeare's characters, amplifying the conflict between their mythic natures to literally universal scope.

"A MOST STRANGE STORY": *The Tempest* , FANTASY, AND CHILDREN'S LITERATURE

The Tempest's fairies, monsters, wizards, and magic have remained popular fodder for adaptation and elaboration since the Victorian fairy craze of the nineteenth century. Indeed, many illustrations from this period have become part of the play's visual legacy alluded to by later artists, most notably Richard Dadd's "Come unto these yellow sands" (1842, referred to in Max Reinhardt and William Dieterle's 1935 film adaptation of *A Midsummer Night's Dream*) and John Waterhouse's "Miranda" (1916). Virginia and Alden Vaughan's *Shakespeare's Caliban: A Cultural History* (1991) provides an excellent overview of how illustrations of Caliban have reflected and in turn influenced different conceptions of the character over time. The prominence of fairy tale elements may explain why *The Tempest* is a popular source for adaptations directed at youth audiences, adaptations that often emphasize Prospero's benevolent parental qualities. In addition to being the basis for many children's play and picture adaptations, elements from *The Tempest* figure prominently in such young adult novels as Madeleine L'Engle's *A Wrinkle in Time* (1962), Zibby Oneal's *In Summer Light* (1985), Dennis Covington's *Lizard* (1991), and Jan Siegel's *Prospero's Children* (1999), Robin Kingsland's play *Prospero's Children* (1998), the musical *The Prairie* (Renee Enna, Mark Adamczyk, and Marianne Kallen, 2004), and "Shakespaw," an episode of the educational TV series *Wishbone* (1996). Animated and comic book adaptations also testify to the play's fantasy appeal. Though there was never a *Classics Illustrated* version, comic book adaptations have been created by Gareth Ewing (1994), Hillary Burningham (1999), David Messer (2005), and Paul Duffield (in Self Made Hero's Shakespeare manga series, 2007). Caliban is the name of a recurring character in *The X-Men*, the long-running Marvel comic series; like Shakespeare's character, Caliban enters the series as a despised mutant monster, though he has undergone several transformations over time. *Resan till Melonia* (*Journey to Melonia*, dir. Per Åhlin, 1989), an animated feature-length film, grafts characters and relationships from *The Tempest* onto a cautionary fable about militaristic capitalism and industrial pollution. In this version,

Caliban is a comic character made entirely of vegetables who saves the day. His heroic triumph is nearly undermined by an impromptu performance of *The Tempest* directed by a Shakespeare-obsessed dog named William.

The link between *The Tempest* and fantasy writing is explored in some detail in Neil Gaiman's comic book story "The Tempest" (appearing in *The Sandman*, 1996), the last of a trio of *Sandman* tales concerned with Shakespeare. Gaiman depicts the playwright at the end of his life, writing his final play as he contemplates retirement. The juxtaposition of scenes from *The Tempest* with vignettes of Shakespeare's life in Stratford clarifies that his fantastic tale has its roots in mundane reality. Prospero's concern with Miranda's chastity springs from his disapproval of his daughter Judith's courtship with neighbor Tom Quine, and Caliban's curse upon Prospero for teaching him language mirrors his conversation with waspish wife Anne about the value of his playwriting. Shakespeare meditates upon his deepening regret about how writing imaginative fiction has divided him from experiencing life directly and fully, a regret he feels most sharply with the death of his young son Hamnet, the child who in life Shakespeare did not appreciate. Through Shakespeare's discussions with the Sandman, an aloof embodiment of myth itself, Gaiman presents Shakespeare's writing of fantasy as a quietly heroic activity filled with self-sacrifice. In Gaiman's tale Shakespeare's developing script of *The Tempest* comes to reflect the playwright's growing recognition of the power and the limits of fantasy authorship. Gaiman cleverly uses the familiar autobiographical link between Shakespeare and Prospero to refute negative assumptions about fantasy writing–that it is merely crassly commercial, escapist, and derivative–and to claim the Bard as his own generic forebear. The notion of Prospero / Shakespeare as master mythmaker also undergirds Peter Greenaway's dazzling film *Prospero's Books* (1991), which uses the idea of Prospero as author to show the viewer the full array of mythic books and images upon which *The Tempest* draws.

"O BRAVE NEW WORLD": WESTERN TEMPESTS

Though at first glance the connection between a self-contained island and the expansive American landscape seems unlikely, *The Tempest* has twice been recast as a Western. William Wellman's *Yellow Sky* (1948) retells Shakespeare's narrative from the unusual perspective of "Stretch" Dawson, a character who combines elements of Alonso, Gonzalo and Ferdinand. Dawson is the leader of a group of bank robbers who, taking refuge in a ghost town on the salt flats, encounter an old prospector and his tomboy granddaughter,

Constance Mae. When Dawson's men learn that the prospector has stock-piled a fortune in gold, they resolve to steal it, but Stretch, having fallen in love with Constance, sides with her and her father, leading to a showdown. In this version, the role of Caliban is not filled, as one might expect, by the Apaches who visit the town, but rather by Dude, one of Dawson's men. Dude, a ruthless outlaw who lusts after Constance, has no problem with killing the prospector, and longs for Stretch's position as leader of the gang. In 1967, the film was remade as *The Jackals* (dir. Robert D. Webb), with the action resituated to the nineteenth-century South African Transvaal. In this version, Vincent Price played the prospector, bringing a wry campiness to the role.

Distantly related to these adaptations is Jack Bender's TV movie adaptation of *The Tempest* (first broadcast 1998), which transposes the plot to the Mississippi bayous during the American Civil War. In this version the conflict between Prospero and Antonio over ownership of a plantation has its ultimate source in differing views of slavery. Gideon Prosper is respectful to his slaves and even studies voodoo magic from Mambo Azaleigh, a black conjure woman with resemblances to Sycorax, whereas Anthony his brother has nothing but contempt for them, seeing his brother's attitude as a threat to the family plantation. This recasting of the racial politics of Shakespeare's play extends to Caliban and Ariel. The Caliban figure is filled by the Gator Man, a white trader in alligator hides played mostly for comedy, and the Ariel role by a black slave, Azaleigh's son who has mastered his mother's magical powers. This change gives new resonance to Ariel's oft-repeated desire to be free. Accordingly, the film's turning point comes when Ariel reminds Prosper of Lincoln's Emancipation Proclamation, leading Prosper to convert his desire for revenge upon his brother into a commitment to social justice. By freeing Ariel, Prosper allows him to join the Union forces and win the Battle of Vicksburg. The marriage between Ferdinand and Miranda, so crucial to Prospero's recovery of his Milanese dynasty in Shakespeare's play, fades into the background, here reduced to a romance between Miranda and Frederick, a Union soldier.

"MOST RARE AFFECTIONS": *The Tempest* AND ROMANCE

However, Miranda's love life does figure prominently in several adaptations of *The Tempest* which owe in various ways to the Gothic romance novel. Unlike Shakespeare's play, very few of these works concern themselves with Miranda's romance with Ferdinand. Rather, they find more interesting material in her tense, more complex relationships with Caliban and Prospero. Imagining a tortured romance between Miranda and Caliban, a version of the "beauty and the beast" motif, is a popular premise. Tad Williams' *Caliban's Hour* (1994), for example, offers an alternative chronicle of the events of *The Tempest* as retold by Caliban. Here he is not a monster but a sensitive innocent who genuinely loves Miranda. He becomes embittered when Miranda romantically betrays him and when Prospero treats him cruelly. Caliban reveals his tale of thwarted devotion to a much older Miranda, now unhappily married to an aloof Ferdinand and determined to force her daughter Giulietta into an arranged marriage. Elizabeth Nunez's *Prospero's Daughter* (2006) offers a post-colonial take on the Miranda-Caliban romance. The Prospero figure of the novel is Dr. Peter Gardner, a British scientist who relocates to Trinidad after botching an experiment. He falls into an emotional tempest when he learns of a romance between his daughter Virginia and his mixed-race house servant Carlos. Eventually the accusation of rape Gardner directs at Carlos becomes the catalyst for revealing Gardner's own sexual and racist crimes. Russell Hoban's "Some Episodes in the History of Miranda and Caliban," an experimental piece in his collection *The Moment behind the Moment* (1992), reconceives of Miranda and Caliban's relationship in archetypal terms, tracing their various reincarnations in myth and history across a dizzying array of eras. Rachel Ingalls's *Mrs. Caliban* (1983) offers a droll postmodern version of the Miranda-Caliban romance with its deadpan portrait of a bored housewife's affair with a muscle-bound, green marine mutant who has escaped from a science experiment, a creature who may or may not be a figment of her imagination.

Transcending the confines of the romance novel is Gloria Naylor's superb *Mama Day* (1988), a reimagination of *The Tempest* from an African-American perspective in which the romance between Miranda and Ferdinand is central. The novel features two intertwined plotlines. One is a history of Willow Springs, an island off the southern United States coast occupied by an independent black community governed by Miranda "Mama" Day, a powerful matriarch and conjure woman. The other narrative, told from alternating points of view, concerns the tempestuous love relationship between George, an orphaned New Yorker, and Cocoa (aka Ophelia), Mama Day's great niece who was raised in Willow Springs. George and Cocoa come to represent two poles of contemporary African-American experience—George the perspective of the modern black urban male, cut off from his past and drawn to logic and technology, and Cocoa the perspective of a black rural woman transplanted to the city, in danger of losing contact with her social and spiritual roots. When George and Cocoa visit Willow Springs, Cocoa falls victim to the spells of Ruby, a black magic practitioner reminiscent of Sycorax. As George searches for a cure to Cocoa's illness, his rational, individualist perspective is severely tested. In a magical tempest he confronts the mystical power of what Willow Springs represents—a legacy of African-American independence, matriarchy, spirituality, and community. Gloria Naylor's novel is a fine example of answering Shakespeare's play by rewriting it, in her case by transforming Prospero's patriarchal tyranny and racism into Mama Day's sternly benevolent matriarchalism and black pride.

"THIS THING OF DARKNESS": *The Tempest* AFTER COLONIALISM

An important group of adaptations spring from the perception that as one of the first plays to portray contact between Europe and the New World, *The Tempest* has provided an influential endorsement for colonialism. Nowhere has this endorsement been more powerful than in the play's portrayal of Caliban, the island's native rebel who, given his monstrous, uneducable, sexually unruly, and foolish nature, seems to deserve his rough treatment by Prospero and ultimately accepts his status as slave. Though Prospero's famous line, "This thing of darkness I / Acknowledge mine" (5.1.273-274), might be read as his acknowledgment of guilt, it can just as easily be read as a rather ugly revelation of his racism. Since the early twentieth century, several writers from Latin America, Africa and the Caribbean have written trenchant critiques of *The Tempest* as a colonial myth. Three of the most influential of these are José Enrique Rodó's *Ariel* (1900), which treats Ariel as a symbol of Latin American cultural achievement and Caliban of Anglo-American degradation, reversing the usual identifications; George Lamming's *The Pleasures of Exile* (1960), which uses Caliban as a sympathetic metaphor for the plight of colonial Caribbeans; and Fernández Retamar's "Caliban" (1971), which presents Caliban's revolutionary temperament as a model for Caribbean politics. The reconception of Caliban as a sympathetic, even heroic symbol of oppressed third-world peoples rather than a barbaric monster has been the hallmark of post-colonial adaptations of *The Tempest* of the past half-century.

Many artistic responses to the legacies of imperialism take the form of rewrites of *The Tempest*. One of the most noteworthy is Martinique writer Aimé Césaire's play *Une Tempête* (*A Tempest*), written for an all-black company in 1969. Césaire recasts portions of Shakespeare's play so that it addresses issues in black liberation and colonial politics of the period. Prospero is presented as a needy colonial tyrant, and Caliban and Ariel as black slaves with differing strategies of struggle against Prospero—Caliban advocates direct confrontation, while Ariel prefers to appeal to Prospero's reason and moral sensibilities. Mid-play, the African trickster god Eshu appears during the marriage masque to taunt Prospero and his conjured European goddesses. In the final scene, Césaire gives Caliban a powerful speech in which he directly confronts a now impotent Prospero about his enslavement. Two years earlier, Ngugi wa Thiong'o in his novel *A Grain of Wheat* (1967) offered a similarly withering portrait of a failed British colonial administrator, John Thompson, who even writes a chronicle of his experiences entitled *Prospero in Africa*.

Though Césaire was not the first to rewrite *The Tempest* in a post-colonial vein, his play influenced many later interpretations of the play as well as popular adaptations. Many recent adaptors have reoriented the play's characters, plotline and key speeches so that they speak more directly and critically to the experience of racism or colonial rule. Ironically *The Tempest*, once regarded by many as a defense of imperialism, has now become a popular vehicle for post-colonial critique, though, it should be added, adaptations which stress Prospero's benevolence and Caliban's monstrosity still find popular audiences as well. Indeed, the tension between these two *Tempests*—the charming fairy tale of magical forgiveness and the dark fable of political power and resistance—does much to explain the energy that continues to animate the play's life in worldwide popular culture.

SOME POST-COLONIAL ADAPTATIONS OF *THE TEMPEST*

George Lamming's novel *Water with Berries* (1971)	relates the dispiriting experience of three West Indian émigrés to London through the plot of *The Tempest*
Mulk Ray Anand's novel *Caliban and Gandhi* (1990)	addresses Gandhi's philosophy of non-violence in the context of the post-colonial experience
Marina Warner's novel *Indigo, or The Mapping of the Waters* (1992)	sympathetically reimagines Sycorax as a Caribbean islander
Romesh Gunesekera's novel *Reef* (1994)	concerns a Sri Lankan manservant who works for a tyrannical marine biologist

Continued...

Continued...

Raquel Carrió's play *Otra Tempestad (Another Tempest*, 1998)	Cuban production which adds a number of Shakespearean characters (Hamlet, Shylock, and Macbeth among them) to those who land on Prospero's island; they all proceed to fight over their various utopian visions
Kalyan Ray's postmodern novel *East-words* (2005)	mashes up traditional Indian mythic characters and characters from *The Tempest* (and other plays) as Shakespeare is reimagined as an Indian writer, Sheikh Piru

Dramatis Personae

ALONSO, King of Naples

SEBASTIAN, his brother

PROSPERO, the rightful Duke of Milan

ANTONIO, his brother, the usurping Duke of Milan

FERDINAND, son to the King of Naples

GONZALO, an honest old councilor

ADRIAN and FRANCISCO, lords

CALIBAN, a savage and deformed slave

TRINCULO, a jester

STEPHANO, a drunken butler

MASTER OF A SHIP
BOATSWAIN
MARINERS
COURTIERS

MIRANDA, daughter to Prospero

ARIEL, an airy spirit

Personated by spirits:
IRIS
CERES
JUNO
NYMPHS
REAPERS

[The Tempest

Act 1

0: Scene: **A tempestuous...heard**: The first scene takes place on the deck of a ship at sea, the rest on the island. Stage directions in *The Tempest* are often more descriptive than practical, as if recorded by a spectator rather than explained for the benefit of the playing company that would have to realize them; for instance, "noise" relates to thunder, not lightning, but this does not mean that visual effects were not also used in the original production. The thunder was probably simulated by rolling a metal ball down a metal trough, and by loud drums; lightning was achieved with fireworks, more feasible at the outdoor Globe than at the indoor Blackfriars Theatre, where the smell would not have dissipated. It is believed that the Folio text's directions were written (or at least altered) by Ralph Crane, the scribe who prepared Shakespeare's manuscripts for performance and publication.

3: **good**: probably not sarcastic; either an expression of satisfaction with the Boatswain's readiness, or a clipped form of address (e.g., "good fellow"); **yarely**: quickly

4: Stage Direction: ***Enter MARINERS***: The Folio prescribes no exit for them, though they re-enter at line 50; presumably they come and go individually throughout this chaotic scene, and reappear as a group only when the ship is about to wreck.

5-6: "Heigh, my hearts! Cheerly, cheerly, my hearts! Yare, yare! Take in / the topsail! Tend to th'master's whistle!": The Ensemble in the 1995 Joseph Papp Public Theater production directed by George C. Wolfe

Photo: Michal Daniel

5–6: Scene: **Take...topsail!**: the first in a series of attempts to reduce speed; since this requires ropes, the line may be delivered to mariners offstage

6: **Tend**: heed (maneuvers were signaled with a whistle; even though the Master has exited and does not return, his whistle can still be heard)

6–7: **Blow...enough!**: i.e., Do your worst, as long as there is room for the ship between sea and land.

9: **Play the men**: act like men

Act 1, Scene 1]

A tempestuous noise of thunder and lightning heard.
Enter a SHIP-MASTER and a BOATSWAIN.

MASTER
Boatswain!

BOATSWAIN
Here, master. What cheer?

MASTER
Good—speak to th' mariners. Fall to't, yarely, or we run
ourselves aground. Bestir, bestir!

Exit
Enter MARINERS

BOATSWAIN
Heigh, my hearts! Cheerly, cheerly, my hearts! Yare, yare! Take in   5
the topsail! Tend to th'master's whistle! [*To the storm*] Blow till
thou burst thy wind, if room enough!

Enter ALONSO, SEBASTIAN, ANTONIO,
FERDINAND, GONZALO, and others

ALONSO
Good boatswain, have care! Where's the master? [*To
MARINERS*] Play the men.

BOATSWAIN
I pray now, keep below.   10

ANTONIO
Where is the master, bos'n?

BOATSWAIN
Do you not hear him? You mar our labor. Keep your cabins! You
do assist the storm.

15: **cares**: (plural subjects often took singular verb-forms in the period); **roarers**: 1) crashing waves and winds, and 2) rioting people, i.e., the mariners

20: **hand**: handle

26: **complexion**: indication of one's nature in one's physical appearance, or "character"; here, in the face

25–26: **he...gallows**: from the proverb, "he that is born to be hanged need never fear drowning"

28: **cable**: anchor cable; **doth little advantage**: i.e., is not helping

30-31: "Down with the topmast! Yare! Lower, lower! Bring her to try with / main-course": The Ensemble in the 2000 production at Shakespeare's Globe directed by Lenka Udovicki
Photo: Donald Cooper

30: **Bring her to try**: variant nautical term for lying "hove-to," using only the mainsail ("main-course") to stay close to the wind and avoid landfall

31: Stage Direction: *A cry within*: The Folio runs this stage direction together with the courtiers' entrance, after "a plague upon this howling," but the Boatswain's impatience is clearly with them, not the storm; some directors introduce a line like "look to the King!" to identify the offstage screams as theirs rather than the mariners'.

32: **plague**: this word is followed in the Folio by a long dash, possibly to suggest a string of improvised expletives

33: **office**: labor

GONZALO
  Nay, good, be patient.

BOATSWAIN
  When the sea is. Hence, what cares these roarers for the name of   15
  king? To cabin. Silence! Trouble us not.

GONZALO
  Good, yet remember whom thou hast aboard.

BOATSWAIN
  None that I more love than myself. You are a councilor. If you can
  command these elements to silence, and work the peace of the
  present, we will not hand a rope more; use your authority! If you   20
  cannot, give thanks you have lived so long, and make yourself
  ready in your cabin for the mischance of the hour, if it so hap. [*To
  the MARINERS*] Cheerly, my good hearts! [*To the COURTIERS*]
  Out of our way, I say!

                                                                    Exit

GONZALO
  I have great comfort from this fellow. Methinks he hath no   25
  drowning mark upon him; his complexion is perfect gallows.
  Stand fast, good Fate, to his hanging! Make the rope of his destiny
  our cable, for our own doth little advantage. If he be not born to
  be hanged, our case is miserable.

                                                                  Exeunt
                                                          Enter BOATSWAIN

BOATSWAIN
  Down with the topmast! Yare! Lower, lower! Bring her to try with   30
  main-course.
                                                            A cry within
  A plague upon this howling! They are louder than the weather or
  our office.
                                Enter SEBASTIAN, ANTONIO, and GONZALO
  Yet again? What do you here? Shall we give o'er and drown?
  Have you a mind to sink?   35

40: **warrant**: guarantee

41: **as leaky...wench**: comparison to a menstruating woman without any absorbent padding, or possibly to a woman sexually aroused but unsatisfied

42: **Lay her ahold**: bring the ship close to the wind so as to hold it away from the rocks; this technique requires setting more sail than hove-to, and thus the subsequent comma; **her two courses**: the ship's two sails, mainsail and foresail

42-43: "Lay her ahold, ahold! Set her two courses off to sea again! Lay/ her off!": The Ensemble in the 1995 Joseph Papp Public Theater production directed by George C. Wolfe

Photo: Michal Daniel

42–43: **Lay her off!**: take the ship out to sea

45: **mouths be cold**: from the expression "to be cold in the mouth," i.e., dead. If the line is interpreted as fatalistic resignation, the Boatswain may at this point take a swig of liquor, thus justifying Antonio's subsequent remark about drunkards.

48: **merely**: completely

49: **wide-chopped**: big-mouthed

50: **washing of ten tides**: pirates were hanged at the sea-shore and left until three tides had washed over their corpses; Antonio thinks the Boatswain deserves ten

SEBASTIAN
A pox o' your throat, you bawling, blasphemous, incharitable dog!

BOATSWAIN
Work you, then.

ANTONIO
Hang, cur, hang, you whoreson insolent noisemaker! We are less
afraid to be drowned than thou art.

GONZALO
I'll warrant him for a drowning, though the ship were no stronger   40
than a nutshell, and as leaky as an unstanched wench.

BOATSWAIN
Lay her ahold, ahold! Set her two courses off to sea again! Lay
her off!

Enter MARINERS, wet

MARINERS
All lost! To prayers, to prayers! All lost!

[Exit MARINERS]

BOATSWAIN
What, must our mouths be cold?   45

GONZALO
The King and Prince at prayers! Let's assist them,
For our case is as theirs.

SEBASTIAN
                            I am out of patience.

ANTONIO
We are merely cheated of our lives by drunkards.
This wide-chopped rascal—would thou mightst lie drowning
The washing of ten tides!   50

[Exit BOATSWAIN]

52: **glut**: swallow

52: Stage Direction: ***split***: break in two upon the rocks

55: **thousand furlongs**: 1 furlong = 220 yards, so Gonzalo offers roughly a hundred mile stretch of sea

56: **long heath, brown furze**: heather and gorse, shrubs connotative of bad, uncultivated soil

"The Magic Grottoes": 1870 rendering by Currier & Ives
Courtesy of the Library of Congress

57: Stage Direction: ***Exit***: Even with continued lightning and thunder, on the bare Jacobean stage, the wreck would have been implicit by this point; later productions have needed more action to complete the scene. Depending on the degree of realism in the set design, the ship may appear to split or sink, through a combination of lighting effects, simulated noises of cracking, leaking and crashing, or the actual fracturing of the set; the mariners may come back onstage after the "confused noise" to scatter and fall overboard. Hall's productions (1974, 1988) used the disintegration of the ship (symbolized by a billowing, falling sail) to form a seamless transition to 1.2. Some directors have also used this ending to introduce material. Ariel was revealed by Burton in 1854, Norman Wright in 1946, Michael Benthall in 1951 and Brook in 1990; Jennifer Tipton in 1991 showed Ferdinand—even though he does not appear above deck in the scene—leaping from a burning chair and presumably into the water.

GONZALO
                          He'll be hanged yet,   50
  Though every drop of water swear against it,
  And gape at wid'st to glut him.

                                    A confused noise within:
                                          "Mercy on us!"
                                       "We split, we split!"
                              "Farewell my wife and children!"
                                        "Farewell brother!"
                                   "We split, we split, we split!"

ANTONIO
  Let's all sink with the King.

SEBASTIAN
  Let's take leave of him.

                                         Exit [with ANTONIO]

GONZALO
  Now would I give a thousand furlongs of sea for an acre of   55
  barren ground—long heath, brown furze, anything! The wills
  above be done, but I would fain die a dry death.

                                                            Exit

0: Location: *[The island]*: The Folio specifies no setting, but in production, directors traditionally localized to a rocky seacoast—which would have afforded Miranda her view of the ship—either just outside of, or within, Prospero's cell. The cell itself has been imagined as variously homely or forbidding. Tree (1904) was the first to depict it as a study, piled with books and outfitted with a simple rocking chair and table.

0: Stage Direction: *Enter*: Although actors had to enter on Shakespeare's stage, modern productions often use curtains to discover them. Kean (1857) revealed Prospero atop a high promontory, "superintending the effect of his art," while a more dynamic transition was achieved by Ron Daniels (1982), in which the audience's first glimpses of Prospero came during the intermittent lightning flashes of a blackout that followed the storm, his cloak swirling as he commanded the elements.

1-2: "If by your art, my dearest father, you have / Put the wild waters in this roar, allay them": "Miranda"; painting ca. 1916
John William Waterhouse (1849-1917)

1: **art**: science, learning, skill; used throughout to refer to Prospero's magic, and its tools
4: **welkin's cheek**: sky's face
11: **or ere**: before
13: **fraughting**: forming the cargo, as in "freight"; **collected**: composed
14: **amazement**: overwhelming mixture of fear and wonder (together with pity, exactly the complex emotional response Aristotle assigned to tragedy); "Miranda" itself means "wonderful" or "to be wondered at," related to the word "admire"; **piteous**: pitying
20: **full poor**: extremely humble; **cell**: an isolated, one-room dwelling (e.g., a hut, cottage or cave) appropriate to a hermit, monk or poor person; not a prison cell, which is an eighteenth century usage of the word
22: **meddle**: mingle, contaminate; interestingly, Miranda soon contradicts herself, recalling her prior "bootless inquisition" of Prospero for more information

Act 1, Scene 2]

[The island.] Enter PROSPERO and MIRANDA.

MIRANDA
   If by your art, my dearest father, you have
   Put the wild waters in this roar, allay them.
   The sky, it seems, would pour down stinking pitch
   But that the sea, mounting to th' welkin's cheek,
   Dashes the fire out. O, I have suffered   5
   With those that I saw suffer! A brave vessel—
   Who had no doubt some noble creature in her—
   Dashed all to pieces! O, the cry did knock
   Against my very heart! Poor souls, they perished.
   Had I been any god of power, I would   10
   Have sunk the sea within the earth, or ere
   It should the good ship so have swallow'd, and
   The fraughting souls within her.

PROSPERO
                     Be collected.
   No more amazement. Tell your piteous heart
   There's no harm done.

MIRANDA
              O, woe the day!

PROSPERO
                    No harm.   15
   I have done nothing but in care of thee,
   Of thee, my dear one, thee my daughter, who
   Art ignorant of what thou art; naught knowing
   Of whence I am, nor that I am more better
   Than Prospero, master of a full poor cell,   20
   And thy no greater father.

MIRANDA
             More to know
   Did never meddle with my thoughts.

22–24: Scene: **'Tis time...from me**: Some productions add additional magic here, to suggest from the start Prospero's compulsion to perform, and the reluctance with which he yields his powers. In Burton (1854), a final wave of Prospero's staff caused a seemingly inert tree on the right front wing to topple gently, its branches forming a natural hanger on which to lay his robe; this also solved the problem of where exactly he is to set down his accessories, other than the ground.

25: **lie...art**: i.e., Prospero's robe, which he has just put off; possibly also his staff and book(s)

28: **provision**: foresight

31: **Betid**: befell

32: Scene: **Sit down**: Garrick (1757) substituted "attend," wishing the actors to remain standing. Modern productions vary in the degree of physicality Prospero adds to this request—he may gently lower her, forcibly seat her, or do nothing—depending on the level of tension desired from the paternal relationship in the rest of the scene.

35: **bootless inquisition**: fruitless interrogation

36-37: "The hour's now come; / The very minute bids thee ope thine ear": Kananu Kirimi as Miranda and Vanessa Redgrave as Prospero in the 2000 production at Shakespeare's Globe directed by Lenka Udovicki

Photo: Donald Cooper

 tracks 2-4

38–89:
William Hutt as Prospero and Jennifer Gould as Miranda
Ian McKellen as Prospero and Emilia Fox as Miranda

41: **Out**: fully

42: **By what**: by means of what image in your memory

43: **tell me that**: tell me that which

PROSPERO
                              'Tis time
I should inform thee farther. Lend thy hand
And pluck my magic garment from me.
                    [MIRANDA helps PROSPERO remove his robe]
                        So,
Lie there, my art. *[To MIRANDA]* Wipe thou thine eyes;
    have comfort.   25
The direful spectacle of the wreck, which touched
The very virtue of compassion in thee,
I have with such provision in mine art
So safely ordered that there is no soul,
No, not so much perdition as an hair   30
Betid to any creature in the vessel
Which thou heard'st cry, which thou saw'st sink. Sit down,
For thou must now know farther.

MIRANDA
                            You have often
Begun to tell me what I am, but stopped
And left me to a bootless inquisition,   35
Concluding, "Stay. Not yet."

PROSPERO
                        The hour's now come;
The very minute bids thee ope thine ear.
Obey, and be attentive. Canst thou remember
A time before we came unto this cell?
I do not think thou canst, for then thou wast not   40
Out three years old.

MIRANDA
                Certainly, sir, I can.

PROSPERO
    By what? By any other house or person?
    Of anything the image tell me that
    Hath kept with thy remembrance.

38–89:
William Hutt as Prospero and Jennifer Gould as Miranda
Ian McKellen as Prospero and Emilia Fox as Miranda

46: **remembrance warrants**: memory guarantees
50: **backward**: past
54: **Milan**: accented on the first syllable (like "Dylan") in Shakespeare's English
57–60: Scene: **Sir, are not...worse issued**: This exchange has historically inspired unease, and thus, a range of creative readings. Davenant (1667), sensing sarcasm in "a piece of," changed it to "all"; later producers like Kean (1857) cut the entire passage, bothered by Miranda's doubting her paternity. Macready (1838), however, kept it and inserted a heavy pause in Prospero's reply: "thy mother was a piece of virtue, and she said—thou wast my daughter..." Until the mid 1900s Prospero's lines were often omitted, but recent productions have tried to play up their misogynistic subtext, inflecting Prospero's only mention of his wife with a note of disdain. Still others have rejected this as overly literal, passing off his odd reference to paternal anxiety as a joke.
57: **piece**: model of, i.e., masterpiece

60-62: "O the heavens! What foul play had we that we came from thence?/ Or blessed was't we did?": Alice Krige as Miranda and Derek Jacobi as Prospero in the 1982 Royal Shakespeare Company production directed by Ron Daniels
Photo: Donald Cooper

60: **no worse issued**: no less nobly descended
64: **holp**: archaic form of "helped"

MIRANDA
                                        'Tis far off,
And rather like a dream than an assurance   45
That my remembrance warrants. Had I not
Four or five women once that tended me?

PROSPERO
Thou hadst, and more, Miranda. But how is it
That this lives in thy mind? What seest thou else
In the dark backward and abyss of time?   50
If thou rememb'rest aught ere thou cam'st here,
How thou cam'st here thou mayst.

MIRANDA
                                        But that I do not.

PROSPERO
Twelve year since, Miranda, twelve year since,
Thy father was the Duke of Milan, and
A prince of power.   55

MIRANDA
Sir, are not you my father?

PROSPERO
Thy mother was a piece of virtue, and
She said thou wast my daughter; and thy father
Was Duke of Milan, and his only heir
And princess no worse issued.

MIRANDA
                                        O the heavens!   60
What foul play had we that we came from thence?
Or blessèd was't we did?

PROSPERO
                        Both, both, my girl.
By foul play, as thou say'st, were we heav'd thence,
But blessedly holp hither.

tracks 2–4

38–89:
William Hutt as Prospero and Jennifer Gould as Miranda
Ian McKellen as Prospero and Emilia Fox as Miranda

65: teen: trouble; **turned you to**: 1) put you in mind of, 2) made you recall
66: from: away from, beyond

67–169: Scene: My brother and thy uncle...my dukedom: Prospero embarks on an extremely long narration that raises both internal and contingent staging issues. At more than a hundred lines, broken up only by perfunctory responses from Miranda, the passage requires an oratorically gifted actor to render its complex grammar vivid; it has often been shortened as a result—which can in turn weaken it—and some productions introduce props or even dramatizations of Prospero's flashback. He frequently interrupts himself to renew Miranda's attention, suggesting many possibilities: a testy, pedantic Prospero who lectures his daughter; a Prospero who gently condescends to her, believing his own account tedious; a Miranda who, rapt by the disclosure of their family history, lovingly obliges; or even a sarcastic Miranda who really is bored, which some productions have used to render comic the fact that he ends by putting her to sleep.

70–71: put / The manage: entrusted the administration
72: Through all the signories: among all the city-states (of northern Italy)
74: liberal arts: the seven disciplines studied at universities, comprised of logic, rhetoric, grammar (the *trivium*), mathematics, geometry, music, astronomy (the *quadrivium*); thus appropriate to a free man ("liberal"), unlike the indentured mechanical trades
80: perfected: practiced in, expert at
82: trash: from hounding, to leash; to restrain or rein in; **over-topping**: over-reaching, showing undue ambition
87: ivy...trunk: a metaphor for symbiotic relationships turned parasitic, as in a weed that encircles and chokes a tree
88: verdure: vitality, power

MIRANDA

                     O, my heart bleeds
To think o' th' teen that I have turned you to,   65
Which is from my remembrance. Please you, farther!

PROSPERO

My brother and thy uncle, called Antonio—
I pray thee, mark me, that a brother should
Be so perfidious!—he, whom next thyself
Of all the world I lov'd, and to him put   70
The manage of my state, as at that time
Through all the signories it was the first,
And Prospero the prime duke, being so reputed
In dignity, and for the liberal arts
Without a parallel; those being all my study,   75
The government I cast upon my brother,
And to my state grew stranger, being transported
And rapt in secret studies. Thy false uncle—
Dost thou attend me?

MIRANDA

                Sir, most heedfully.

PROSPERO

Being once perfected how to grant suits,   80
How to deny them, who t'advance, and who
To trash for over-topping, new created
The creatures that were mine, I say, or changed 'em,
Or else new formed 'em; having both the key
Of officer and office, set all hearts i' th' state   85
To what tune pleased his ear, that now he was
The ivy which had hid my princely trunk,
And sucked my verdure out on't—thou attend'st not?

MIRANDA

O, good sir, I do.

PROSPERO

              I pray thee mark me.
I thus neglecting worldly ends, all dedicated   90

91: **closeness**: privacy, seclusion

93: **O'er-prized all popular rate**: surpassed common understanding ("by being so retired" implies that it was Prospero's secrecy, not the arts themselves, that confused and alienated his subjects)

98: **sans**: French for "without"

99: **revenue**: accented on the second syllable

101–103: **Who...lie**: i.e., "who, having made his memory such a sinner against truth as to validate his own lie simply by telling it"

104: **out o' th' substitution**: by virtue of having been deputized

105: **executing**: performed

108: **screen**: barrier

110: **Absolute**: self-sufficient, totally; **Me**: as for me

111: **temporal royalties**: practical duties of rule, as opposed to its spiritual/intellectual rewards

112: **confederates**: forms an alliance with (a verb)

113: **dry...sway**: thirsty for, hence 1) eager for, 2) needful of influence; the second implies that Antonio, despite Prospero's negligence, still lacked popular support for his coup

115: **his coronet to his crown**: i.e., Antonio's (lesser) power to Alonso's (greater) one

118-119: "Mark his condition, and th' event; then tell me / If this might be a brother": Philip Voss as Prospero and Nikki Amuka-Bird as Miranda in the 2000 Royal Shakespeare Company production directed by James Macdonald
Photo: Donald Cooper

118: **condition...event**: the terms of his agreement with Naples and its consequences

To closeness, and the bettering of my mind
With that which, but by being so retired,
O'er-prized all popular rate, in my false brother
Awaked an evil nature, and my trust,
Like a good parent, did beget of him   95
A falsehood in its contrary as great
As my trust was, which had indeed no limit,
A confidence sans bound. He being thus lorded—
Not only with what my revenue yielded,
But what my power might else exact—like one   100
Who, having into truth by telling of it,
Made such a sinner of his memory
To credit his own lie, he did believe
He was indeed the duke, out o' th' substitution
And executing th' outward face of royalty   105
With all prerogative. Hence his ambition growing—
Dost thou hear?

MIRANDA
                    Your tale, sir, would cure deafness.

PROSPERO
To have no screen between this part he played
And him he played it for, he needs will be
Absolute Milan. Me, poor man, my library   110
Was dukedom large enough. Of temporal royalties
He thinks me now incapable; confederates—
So dry he was for sway—with King of Naples
To give him annual tribute, do him homage,
Subject his coronet to his crown, and bend   115
The dukedom yet unbowed (alas, poor Milan!)
To most ignoble stooping.

MIRANDA
                    O the heavens!

PROSPERO
Mark his condition, and th' event; then tell me
If this might be a brother.

124: **in lieu o' th' premises**: in exchange for the promises

126: **extirpate**: remove

132: **ministers**: agents

135: **hint**: trigger

136-138: "Hear a little further, / And then I'll bring thee to the present business / Which now's upon's": Philip Goodwin as Prospero and Samantha Soule as Miranda in the 2005 Shakespeare Theatre Company production directed by Kate Whoriskey
Photo: Richard Termine

139: **impertinent**: irrelevant, superfluous

140: **wench**: not derogatory, but a familiar term of endearment for a young woman

MIRANDA
                    I should sin
To think but nobly of my grandmother.   120
Good wombs have borne bad sons.

PROSPERO
                         Now the condition.
This King of Naples, being an enemy
To me inveterate, hearkens my brother's suit;
Which was that he, in lieu o' th' premises
Of homage and I know not how much tribute,   125
Should presently extirpate me and mine
Out of the dukedom, and confer fair Milan,
With all the honors, on my brother; whereon,
A treacherous army levied, one midnight
Fated to th' purpose, did Antonio open   130
The gates of Milan, and i' th' dead of darkness
The ministers for th' purpose hurried thence
Me and thy crying self.

MIRANDA
                    Alack, for pity!
I not remembr'ing how I cried out then
Will cry it o'er again; it is a hint   135
That wrings my eyes to 't.

PROSPERO
                    Hear a little further,
And then I'll bring thee to the present business
Which now's upon's; without the which this story
Were most impertinent.

MIRANDA
                    Wherefore did they not
That hour destroy us?

PROSPERO
                    Well demanded, wench.   140
My tale provokes that question. Dear, they durst not,

145: In few: i.e., in few words; **bark**: small ship (Shakespeare apparently forgets that Milan is not a deepwater port and thus can not accommodate a ship, an error he sometimes makes with other cities in his plays)

147: butt: 1) literally, a tub or a barrel (compare with Stephano's use of the term as a wine-cask); also 2) slang coinage here for a sloop or rudimentary floating vessel

152-153: "Alack, what trouble / Was I then to you!": Ted van Griethuysen as Prospero and Ana Reeder as Miranda in the 1997 Shakespeare Theatre Company production directed by Garland Wright

Photo: Carol Rosegg

153: cherubin: cherub, or little angel; the use of the Hebrew plural "cherubin" as a singular was common. (At this point, many a Prospero embraced Miranda or extended a sign of affectionate reassurance, such as taking her hand.)

156: decked: adorned

157: which: i.e., Miranda's smile

157–158: burden...stomach: a metaphor of (re-)birth; "burden" refers to the contents of the womb and "groaned" to labor pains; "An undergoing stomach" means the courage to endure (or undergo) suffering

164: Master of this design: architect of this plot. It is unclear whether Prospero means the plot to depose him or the plot to help him into exile, but one is an extension of the other, and since Gonzalo is a Neapolitan the former is the only "design" to which he could have been "appointed"; nevertheless, the act Prospero stresses here is Gonzalo's "charity," not his offense in collaborating.

165: stuffs: foodstuffs

166: steaded: been of use

So dear the love my people bore me, nor set
A mark so bloody on the business; but
With colors fairer painted their foul ends.
In few, they hurried us aboard a bark,   145
Bore us some leagues to sea, where they prepared
A rotten carcass of a butt, not rigged,
Nor tackle, sail, nor mast—the very rats
Instinctively have quit it. There they hoist us
To cry to th' sea that roared to us; to sigh   150
To th' winds, whose pity, sighing back again,
Did us but loving wrong.

MIRANDA
                                    Alack, what trouble
Was I then to you!

PROSPERO
                            O, a cherubin
Thou wast that did preserve me. Thou didst smile,
Infusèd with a fortitude from heaven,   155
When I have decked the sea with drops full salt,
Under my burden groaned, which raised in me
An undergoing stomach, to bear up
Against what should ensue.

MIRANDA
                                How came we ashore?

PROSPERO
By providence divine;   160
Some food we had, and some fresh water, that
A noble Neapolitan, Gonzalo,
Out of his charity—who being than appointed
Master of this design—did give us, with
Rich linens, garments, stuffs, and necessaries,   165
Which since have steaded much; so, of his gentleness,
Knowing I loved my books, he furnished me
From mine own library with volumes that

170: Scene: **Now I arise**: meant both figuratively, as Prospero prepares to reverse his fortunes, and literally, if he and Miranda have been seated until now. He may at this point don his magic robe and staff again, although he can also do so after line 1.2.188 ("I am ready now"), after he has put Miranda to sleep and before he calls Ariel.

174: **princes**: royal children, irrespective of gender

175: **careful**: 1) caring, and 2) watchful

180: **dear lady**: not Miranda but Fortune, now Prospero's benefactor rather than tormenter; "Lady Fortune" was a commonplace for the fickleness of chance

182: **zenith**: apex of fortune

183: **influence**: astrological power over worldly events; Prospero uses the star as a metaphor for his window of opportunity

185–187: Scene: **Here cease...choose**: Productions almost universally indicate some action by which Prospero puts Miranda into her swoon, such as a wave of his staff or holding out his arm to lower her to the ground; Miranda is certainly asleep by the following line, but may already be so by "I know thou canst not choose," sometimes delivered as an aside.

186: **dullness**: drowsiness

188-189: "Come away, servant, come! I am ready now. / Approach, my Ariel. Come": Bonnie Engstrom as Ariel in the 1995 Royal Shakespeare Company production directed by David Thacker

Photo: Donald Cooper

189: **Ariel**: from the Hebrew, "lion of god"; a frequent name for spirits in magical texts

189: Stage Direction: ***Enter ARIEL***: Depending on the production, Ariel's entrance has ranged from meek and submissive to breathtakingly exuberant; in the nineteenth century, he began as a ball of fire.

193: **task**: charge, commit (a verb)

I prize above my dukedom.

MIRANDA

                         Would I might
But ever see that man!

PROSPERO

                         Now I arise.   170
Sit still, and hear the last of our sea-sorrow.
Here in this island we arrived, and here
Have I, thy schoolmaster, made thee more profit
Than other princes can, that have more time
For vainer hours, and tutors not so careful.   175

MIRANDA

Heavens thank you for't. And now I pray you, sir—
For still 'tis beating in my mind—your reason
For raising this sea-storm?

PROSPERO

                         Know thus far forth:
By accident most strange, bountiful Fortune,
Now my dear lady, hath mine enemies   180
Brought to this shore; and by my prescience
I find my zenith doth depend upon
A most auspicious star, whose influence
If now I court not, but omit, my fortunes
Will ever after droop. Here cease more questions.   185
Thou art inclined to sleep. 'Tis a good dullness,
And give it way. I know thou canst not choose.

                                        [MIRANDA sleeps]

Come away, servant, come! I am ready now.
Approach, my Ariel. Come.

                                        Enter ARIEL

ARIEL

All hail, great master, grave sir, hail! I come   190
To answer thy best pleasure. Be't to fly,
To swim, to dive into the fire; to ride
On the curled clouds; to thy strong bidding task

194: **quality**: either the order of spirits Ariel leads, or his own capabilities

195: **to point**: to exact detail

196: **To every article**: to the letter (a legalism)

197–198: **beak...deck**: following an anatomical metaphor, the beak of a ship is the prow, the waist its midships, and the deck (or poop-deck) its stern

199: **flamed amazement**: Ariel's description parallels sailors' accounts of St. Elmo's Fire (a mysterious glow aboard oceangoing vessels), here enacted as a terrifying blaze rather than, as was more common, a good omen; compare with Miranda's "amazement" in 1.2.1-14

201: **yards**: crossbars on the masts; **bowsprit**: base pole of the sail; **distinctly**: separately

202: **Jove's lightning**: Jove (or Jupiter, in Roman mythology), the god of the sky and thunder, traditionally pictured with lightning bolts

204: **sight-outrunning**: faster than the eye can follow

205: **Neptune**: Roman god of the sea, traditionally pictured with a trident

206–207: **Seem...shake**: Ariel explains the sea's upheaval as merely an optical illusion of his violent display.

208: **coil**: tumult, uproar

210: **of the mad**: such as madmen have

213: **Then all afire with me**: The Folio's punctuation suggests this phrase describes Ferdinand, but editors have preferred the reading that fits with Ariel's previous lines, which seems to limit his pyrotechnics to the ship, not its specific passengers.

214: **up-staring**: standing on end

Ariel, and all his quality.

PROSPERO

                        Hast thou, spirit,
Performed to point the tempest that I bade thee?   195

ARIEL

To every article.
I boarded the king's ship. Now on the beak,
Now in the waist, the deck, in every cabin,
I flamed amazement. Sometime I'd divide
And burn in many places. On the topmast,   200
The yards, and bowsprit would I flame distinctly,
Then meet and join. Jove's lightning, the precursors
O' th' dreadful thunderclaps, more momentary
And sight-outrunning were not; the fire and cracks
Of sulphurous roaring the most mighty Neptune   205
Seem to besiege and make his bold waves tremble,
Yea, his dread trident shake.

PROSPERO

                        My brave spirit!
Who was so firm, so constant, that this coil
Would not infect his reason?

ARIEL

                        Not a soul
But felt a fever of the mad, and played   210
Some tricks of desperation. All but mariners
Plunged in the foaming brine and quit the vessel,
Then all afire with me; the king's son Ferdinand,
With hair up-staring (then like reeds, not hair),
Was the first man that leapt, cried "Hell is empty,   215
And all the devils are here!"

PROSPERO

                        Why, that's my spirit!
But was not this nigh shore?

219: **sustaining garments**: clothes that buoyed them up long enough to swim to shore

224: **angle**: corner

225: **this sad knot**: conventional gesture of melancholy; Ariel presumably demonstrates Ferdinand's dejection by folding his arms, possibly sitting down as well

229: **fetch dew**: gathered at night, dew was thought to be an ingredient of magic: compare Caliban's reference to Sycorax at 1.2.323-324

230: **still-vexed Bermudas**: The as-yet uncolonized Bermuda islands—"Bermoothes" in the Folio—were feared for their treacherous reefs, and were reputedly always stormy (perhaps making Ariel's feat of gathering dew sound all the more remarkable).

232: **charm...labor**: with a spell added to the ordeal they had undergone

235: **float**: sea

238-239: "Ariel, thy charge / Exactly is performed; but there's more work": "Prospero and Ariel" by William Hamilton (1787)

William Hamilton (1751-1801)

240: Scene: **What is...day?**: Prospero obviously knows the answer better than Ariel does, but this question begins a tense exchange in which Prospero asks similarly leading questions to make Ariel recall his former captivity and honor his debt; directors sometimes prepare for this darker shift in mood by having Ariel start to leave at "exactly is performed," only to halt, glare, or be detained by Prospero at "but there's more work".

ARIEL
                    Close by, my master.

PROSPERO
  But are they, Ariel, safe?

ARIEL
                    Not a hair perished.
  On their sustaining garments not a blemish,
  But fresher than before; and as thou bad'st me,   220
  In troops I have dispersed them 'bout the isle.
  The King's son have I landed by himself,
  Whom I left cooling of the air with sighs
  In an odd angle of the isle, and sitting,
  His arms in this sad knot.

PROSPERO
                    Of the King's ship   225
  The mariners say how thou hast disposed,
  And all the rest o' th' fleet.

ARIEL
                    Safely in harbor
  Is the King's ship, in the deep nook where once
  Thou call'dst me up at midnight to fetch dew
  From the still-vexed Bermudas, there she's hid;   230
  The mariners all under hatches stowed,
  Who, with a charm joined to their suffered labor,
  I have left asleep. And for the rest o' th' fleet,
  Which I dispersed, they all have met again,
  And are upon the Mediterranean float   235
  Bound sadly home for Naples,
  Supposing that they saw the king's ship wrecked,
  And his great person perish.

PROSPERO
                    Ariel, thy charge
  Exactly is performed; but there's more work.
  What is the time o' th' day?   240

240: **midseason**: noon

241: **glasses**: hours, hence "two glasses" is 2 p.m.

243–301:
Bob Peck as Prospero and Adrian Lester as Ariel
Ian McKellen as Prospero and Scott Handy as Ariel

tracks 5-7

244: **remember**: remind

245-246: "How now? Moody? / What is't thou canst demand?": Wallace Acton as Ariel and Ted van Griethuysen as Prospero in the 1997 Shakespeare Theatre Company production directed by Garland Wright
Photo: Carol Rosegg

247: **time**: allotted period (of Ariel's indenture)

251: **bate...year**: abate or shorten by one year my term of service

ARIEL

                    Past the midseason.   240

PROSPERO

  At least two glasses. The time 'twixt six and now
  Must by us both be spent most preciously.

ARIEL

  Is there more toil? Since thou dost give me pains,
  Let me remember thee what thou hast promised,
  Which is not yet performed me.

PROSPERO

                              How now? Moody?   245
  What is't thou canst demand?

ARIEL

                          My liberty.

PROSPERO

  Before the time be out? No more.

ARIEL

                              I prithee,
  Remember I have done thee worthy service,
  Told thee no lies, made no mistakings, served
  Without or grudge or grumblings. Thou did promise   250
  To bate me a full year.

PROSPERO

                        Dost thou forget
  From what a torment I did free thee?

ARIEL

                              No.

PROSPERO

  Thou dost; and think'st it much to tread the ooze
  Of the salt deep,
  To run upon the sharp wind of the north,   255

243–301:
Bob Peck as Prospero and Adrian Lester as Ariel
Ian McKellen as Prospero and Scott Handy as Ariel

256: **veins:** 1) underground streams, or 2) seams of mineral deposits

257: **baked:** hardened

259: **Sycorax:** Shakespeare's invention; the name appears to derive from the Greek *korax*, meaning both "raven" and "curved"—perhaps explaining the reference to "hoop" in the following line

260: **grown into a hoop:** progressively bent into a hunchback

263: **Argier:** Algiers, in North Africa; **was she so:** Prospero is probably not disputing Ariel (since he can only have learned this fact from him), but rather expressing sarcastic impatience with his answers.

268: **one thing she did:** generally assumed to be copulation; because she was pregnant, her sentence was commuted from death to exile (a common mitigation)

271: **blue-eyed hag:** blue eyelids were thought to be a sign of pregnancy; also associated with malevolent women

274: **for:** because

275: **earthy:** 1) lewd, but also 2) the element antithetical to Ariel's airy nature

276: **hests:** behests, commands

To do me business in the veins o' th' earth
When it is baked with frost.

ARIEL
                    I do not, sir.

PROSPERO
Thou liest, malignant thing! Hast thou forgot
The foul witch Sycorax, who with age and envy
Was grown into a hoop? Hast thou forgot her?   260

ARIEL
No, sir.

PROSPERO
Thou hast. Where was she born? Speak. Tell me!

ARIEL
Sir, in Argier.

PROSPERO
                    O, was she so! I must
Once in a month recount what thou hast been,
Which thou forget'st. This damned witch Sycorax,   265
For mischiefs manifold, and sorceries terrible
To enter human hearing, from Argier,
Thou know'st, was banished. For one thing she did
They would not take her life. Is not this true?

ARIEL
Ay, sir.   270

PROSPERO
This blue-eyed hag was hither brought with child,
And here was left by th' sailors. Thou, my slave,
As thou report'st thyself, was then her servant;
And for thou wast a spirit too delicate
To act her earthy and abhorred commands,   275
Refusing her grand hests, she did confine thee,

tracks 5-7

243–301:
Bob Peck as Prospero and Adrian Lester as Ariel
Ian McKellen as Prospero and Scott Handy as Ariel

283: **as mill-wheels strike**: as fast as the blades of a water-wheel strike the water

290: **penetrate the breasts**: arouse sympathy

297: **his**: its

299: **correspondent**: responsive, compliant

300: **do my spiriting gently**: graciously perform the work of a spirit

By help of her more potent ministers,
And in her most unmitigable rage,
Into a cloven pine, within which rift
Imprisoned thou didst painfully remain   280
A dozen years; within which space she died
And left thee there, where thou didst vent thy groans
As fast as mill-wheels strike. Then was this island—
Save for the son that she did litter here,
A freckled whelp, hag-born—not honored with   285
A human shape.

ARIEL
                        Yes, Caliban her son.

PROSPERO
Dull thing, I say so; he, that Caliban
Whom now I keep in service. Thou best know'st
What torment I did find thee in. Thy groans
Did make wolves howl, and penetrate the breasts   290
Of ever-angry bears; it was a torment
To lay upon the damned, which Sycorax
Could not again undo. It was mine art,
When I arrived and heard thee, that made gape
The pine, and let thee out.

ARIEL
                        I thank thee, master.   295

PROSPERO
If thou more murmur'st, I will rend an oak
And peg thee in his knotty entrails, till
Thou hast howl'd away twelve winters.

ARIEL
                        Pardon, master.
I will be correspondent to command
And do my spriting gently.   300

303: Scene: **nymph o' th' sea**: The nymph costume is a seemingly pointless disguise if Ariel is to be invisible to all but Prospero; but the audience can see him, and in the context of luring Ferdinand from the shore, this disguise is mythologically appropriate. Nevertheless, many productions omit the detail.

303–306: Scene: **Go make...diligence!**: Ariel is not necessarily reluctant to depart, since Prospero has not yet finished his instructions, but some actors interpret Prospero's reiteration that way; it is also, however, consistent with his bossiness.

309-311: "Come on, / We'll visit Caliban, my slave, who never / Yields us kind answer": Philip Goodwin as Prospero and Samantha Soule as Miranda in the 2005 Shakespeare Theatre Company production directed by Kate Whoriskey
Photo: Richard Termine

313: **miss**: do without

316: **earth**: base element (in contrast to Ariel, perhaps)

316: Stage Direction: ***Within***: As opposed to the mariners' offstage "cry within," here Caliban was probably concealed in the discovery place at the back of the stage in Jacobean theaters, but it has also been suggested he climbs out from the trapdoor.

PROSPERO

                    Do so;   300
And after two days, I will discharge thee.

ARIEL

                            That's my noble master!
What shall I do? Say what? What shall I do?

PROSPERO

Go make thyself like a nymph o' th' sea. Be subject
To no sight but thine, and mine, invisible
To every eyeball else. Go take this shape   305
And hither come in't. Go! Hence, with diligence!

                                    Exit [ARIEL]
[*To MIRANDA*] Awake, dear heart, awake; thou hast slept well.
Awake.

MIRANDA

                The strangeness of your story put
Heaviness in me.

PROSPERO

                    Shake it off. Come on,
We'll visit Caliban, my slave, who never   310
Yields us kind answer.

MIRANDA

                    'Tis a villain, sir,
I do not love to look on.

PROSPERO

                  But as 'tis,
We cannot miss him. He does make our fire,
Fetch in our wood, and serves in offices
That profit us. What ho, slave! Caliban!   315
Thou earth, thou, speak!

CALIBAN

                [*Within*] There's wood enough within.

318: **When**: what's keeping you?

319: **quaint**: ingenious, fine

320: Stage Direction: ***Whispers***: Since the First Folio provides no subsequent information for Prospero to impart, "in thine ear" and Ariel's immediate response imply a whisper. A production must at this point decide how candid Prospero is about Ariel's existence, especially if concealing it from Miranda were the reason he put her to sleep earlier. Most treat this and subsequent conferences as conventional asides—spoken in close proximity yet unnoticed by others; Hytner's (RSC, 1988) Prospero and Ariel stood far apart, but appeared to communicate privately in their normal voices, as if telepathic.

321: **got**: begot, conceived

322: **dam**: mother

322: Scene: ***Enter Caliban***: Macready (1838) began the tradition of having Caliban enter crawling on all fours, then rising to his feet to rush at Prospero; Prospero checked him with a spell. Many productions have since stressed Caliban's connection to the earth by integrating him with the scenery: in Tree's production (1904), a rock opened to let him out; Neville Coghill (1949) has Caliban climb out of a tank submerged in an onstage lake; in Hytner's production (RSC, 1988), he remained onstage the whole time, camouflaged against a rock, from which he appeared to peel himself off.

323: **dew**: associated with magic potions; see 1.2.229; **brushed**: gathered

325: **southwest**: southerly winds brought warm, damp air, considered unwholesome

328: **Urchins**: not sea creatures here, but goblins (in the shape of spiny hedgehogs)

329: **vast...thee**: for that period of nighttime when they are active, (shall) torture you

330–331: **pinched...honeycomb**: covered with pinches as thoroughly as honeycombs have cells

332: Scene: **I must...dinner**: Sometimes Caliban takes this line as a cue for his attempt to exit, only to be restrained by Prospero; in productions by Benson (1891) and by Tree (1904), Caliban gnawed at a fish he entered carrying.

333-376:
Denis Shaw as Caliban, Donald Wolfit as Prospero, Rosalind Iden as Miranda
Wayne Best as Caliban, William Hutt as Prospero, Jennifer Gould as Miranda

337: **bigger...less**: the sun and the moon

PROSPERO
    Come forth I say! There's other business for thee.
    Come thou, tortoise! When?

                         Enter ARIEL like a water-nymph
    [*To Ariel*] Fine apparition! My quaint Ariel,
    Hark in thine ear.

                              [Whispers to ARIEL]

ARIEL
                My lord, it shall be done.   320
                                    Exit

PROSPERO
    [*To CALIBAN*] Thou poisonous slave, got by the devil himself
    Upon thy wicked dam, come forth!

                                Enter CALIBAN

CALIBAN
    As wicked dew as e'er my mother brushed
    With raven's feather from unwholesome fen
    Drop on you both! A southwest blow on ye   325
    And blister you all o'er!

PROSPERO
    For this, be sure, tonight thou shalt have cramps,
    Side-stitches that shall pen thy breath up. Urchins
    Shall, for that vast of night that they may work,
    All exercise on thee; thou shalt be pinched   330
    As thick as honeycomb, each pinch more stinging
    Than bees that made 'em.

CALIBAN
                I must eat my dinner.
    This island's mine by Sycorax my mother,
    Which thou tak'st from me. When thou cam'st first,
    Thou strok'st me, and made much of me; wouldst give me   335
    Water with berries in't; and teach me
    How to name the bigger light, and how the less,
    That burn by day and night; and then I loved thee,
    And showed thee all the qualities o' th' isle,

Costume rendering for Caliban by Deborah M. Dryden from the 2007 Oregon
Shakespeare Festival production directed by Libby Appel
Courtesy of Oregon Shakespeare Festival

tracks 8-10

333-376:
Denis Shaw as Caliban, Donald Wolfit as Prospero, Rosalind Iden as Miranda
Wayne Best as Caliban, William Hutt as Prospero, Jennifer Gould as Miranda

344: **sty me**: pen me up (e.g., like a pig)
347: **stripes**: whiplashes (some productions have Prospero picking up a whip by this point)
348: **humane**: synonymous with (and pronounced similarly to) "human"
349-353: Scene: **till thou didst seek...with Calibans**: Until the late nineteenth century the lines referring to Caliban's attempted rape were habitually cut or altered.
353-364: **Abhorrèd slave...than a prison**: Early editors reassigned this speech to Prospero, believing it unfit for Miranda's demure nature, and a surprising number of modern productions still adopt the transposition.
354: **print**: imprint
355: **capable of**: susceptible to
360: **race**: natural disposition (Caliban does not have, so far as the play indicates, a classifiable or recognizably race or human ethnicity)
364: **more**: worse
366: **red plague**: any number of diseases producing lesions or bleeding sores; **rid**: kill

The fresh springs, brine pits, barren place and fertile;   340
Curs'd be I that I did so! All the charms
Of Sycorax—toads, beetles, bats, light on you!
For I am all the subjects that you have,
Which first was mine own king; and here you sty me
In this hard rock, whiles you do keep from me   345
The rest o' th' island.

PROSPERO
                         Thou most lying slave,
Whom stripes may move, not kindness! I have used thee—
Filth as thou art—with humane care, and lodged thee
In mine own cell, till thou didst seek to violate
The honor of my child.   350

CALIBAN
Oh ho, oh ho! Would't had been done!
Thou didst prevent me; I had peopled else
This isle with Calibans.

MIRANDA
                       Abhorrèd slave,
Which any print of goodness wilt not take,
Being capable of all ill! I pitied thee,   355
Took pains to make thee speak, taught thee each hour
One thing or other. When thou didst not, savage,
Know thine own meaning, but wouldst gabble like
A thing most brutish, I endowed thy purposes
With words that made them known. But thy vile race—   360
Though thou didst learn—had that in't which good natures
Could not abide to be with; therefore wast thou
Deservedly confined into this rock,
Who hadst deserved more than a prison.

CALIBAN
You taught me language, and my profit on't   365
Is I know how to curse. The red plague rid you
For learning me your language.

tracks 8-10

333-376:
Denis Shaw as Caliban, Donald Wolfit as Prospero, Rosalind Iden as Miranda
Wayne Best as Caliban, William Hutt as Prospero, Jennifer Gould as Miranda

368: **thou'rt best**: you would be best advised

369: **answer other business**: perform future tasks

371: **old**: of old age

372: **aches**: pronounced "aitches" (with two syllables)

375: **Setebos**: according to sixteenth century translations of Magellanic travel accounts, a devil in the pagan religion of Patagonian natives in South America

376: Stage Direction: ***Exit Caliban***: (the adjacency of Caliban's exit and Ariel's entrance leads some directors to overlap them; Tree's (1904) Caliban, left alone onstage and skulking menacingly back toward Prospero's cell, could hear Ariel's music and became entranced by it, trying to dance and singing inarticulately. Productions that want Miranda ignorant of Ariel, meanwhile, such as Benthall (1951) and Hall (1988), have Prospero charm her eyes shut)

376: Stage Direction: ***invisible***: Ariel's invisibility has already been established for the audience by Prospero's earlier instructions, and is reinforced by Ferdinand's inability to see him; invisibility did not require any special stage effects, especially since Ariel is dressed as a sea-nymph; ***playing and singing***: In Shakespeare's original staging, Ariel probably played a lute, and accompanied himself with song.

379–380: **kissed...whist**: a notoriously obscure passage, but either "kissed the wild waves into silence" or "kissed the wild waves' lips"

384: Stage Direction: ***Burden***: refrain (sung by other spirits, probably unseen within, though some modern productions choose to make them visible, often crowding behind Ferdinand and impelling him forward with their voices); ***dispersedly***: 1) not in unison, or 2) emanating from several different directions

388: **chanticleer**: folk-name for any rooster

390: **Cock-a-diddle dow**: The Folio text of the song—lineated and typeset very confusingly—ends at Ariel's "Cry cock-a-diddle dow," but its verse form implies a final refrain from the Burden, and Ariel's line seems to invite one; most editors silently complete it.

392: **waits**: attends

PROSPERO

                    Hag-seed, hence!
Fetch us in fuel; and be quick, thou'rt best,
To answer other business. Shrug'st thou, malice?
If thou neglect'st or dost unwillingly   370
What I command, I'll rack thee with old cramps,
Fill all thy bones with aches, make thee roar,
That beasts shall tremble at thy din.

CALIBAN

                    No, pray thee.
[*Aside*] I must obey. His art is of such power
It would control my dam's god Setebos,   375
And make a vassal of him.

PROSPERO

                    So, slave, hence!

                                            Exit CALIBAN
        Enter FERDINAND, and ARIEL invisible, playing and singing

ARIEL

        [*Sings*]
        Come unto these yellow sands,
            And then take hands;
        Curtsied when you have, and kist
            The wild waves whist,   380
        Foot it featly here and there,
            And sweet sprites bear the burden.
        Hark, hark!
    (*Burden, dispersedly.*) Bow-wow.
        The watch-dogs bark!   385
    [*Burden, dispersedly.*] Bow-wow.
        Hark, hark! I hear
        The strutting strain of chanticleer
            Cry cock-a-diddle dow.
    [*Burden, dispersedly.*] Cock-a-diddle dow.   390

FERDINAND

    Where should this music be? I' th' air or th' earth?
    It sounds no more; and sure it waits upon

Costume rendering for Miranda by Deborah M. Dryden from the 2007 Oregon Shakespeare Festival production directed by Libby Appel

Courtesy of Oregon Shakespeare Festival

393: **Sitting...weeping**: the subject of these actions is supposed to be Ferdinand, but his failure to complete the sentence may underscore his disorientation

396: **passion**: suffering

399: Scene: **begins again**: The lag between Ferdinand's remark and the resumption of Ariel's singing calls for music, and productions universally provide it.

400: **Full fathom five**: five fathoms, or thirty feet deep

407: Stage Direction: ***Burden*. Ding dong**: In the First Folio, this line is set in roman type while the rest of the song is in italic, possibly indicating a stage direction for a sound effect rather than speech.

409: **remember**: commemorate

410-411: **no sound / That the earth owes**: owes = owns; thus, "unearthly"; **above me**: may indicate either that Ariel moves upstage (and possibly continues singing), or refer to musicians playing in an upper room of the stage

412: **advance**: rise; possibly Miranda has been averting her eyes until now—though he may have charmed her—or Prospero is simply telling her to move closer

415: **brave form**: noble shape

416: Scene: **such**: Prospero here gestures to demonstrate his point

418: **but**: except; **stained**: disfigured

419: **canker**: infection

Some god o' th' island. Sitting on a bank,
Weeping again the king my father's wreck,
This music crept by me upon the waters,   395
Allaying both their fury and my passion
With its sweet airs. Thence I have followed it,
Or it hath drawn me rather; but 'tis gone.
No, it begins again.

ARIEL
　　　[*Sings*]
　　　Full fathom five thy father lies,   400
　　　　　Of his bones are coral made;
　　　Those are pearls that were his eyes;
　　　　　Nothing of him that doth fade,
　　　　　But doth suffer a sea-change
　　　Into something rich and strange.   405
　　　Sea-nymphs hourly ring his knell

　　　　　　　　　　　　　　　　　(*Burden*.) Ding dong.

　　　Hark now, I hear them, ding dong bell.

FERDINAND
The ditty does remember my drowned father.
This is no mortal business, nor no sound   410
That the earth owes; I hear it now above me.

PROSPERO
[*To MIRANDA*] The fringèd curtains of thine eye advance
And say what thou seest yond.

MIRANDA
　　　　　　　　　　　What is't, a spirit?
Lord, how it looks about! Believe me, sir,
It carries a brave form. But 'tis a spirit.   415

PROSPERO
No, wench, it eats, and sleeps, and hath such senses
As we have—such. This gallant which thou seest
Was in the wreck; and but he's something stained
With grief—that's beauty's canker—thou mightst call him

423-424: "[Aside] It goes on, I see, / As my soul prompts it. Spirit, fine spirit, I'll free thee / Within two days for this": Philip Goodwin as Prospero, Samantha Soule as Miranda, and Duane Boutté as Ferdinand in the 2005 Shakespeare Theatre Company production directed by Kate Whoriskey

Photo: Richard Termine

424: Scene: **Spirit, fine spirit**: Prospero refers to Ariel, but need not be addressing him directly; the text leaves open what Ariel does for the remainder of the scene, until Prospero calls on him again. If he does not exit and reappear later, a playful Ariel can create meaningful (if potentially disruptive) stage business: Miller's 1970 Ariel mirrored Ferdinand's gestures while Miranda questioned his nature as man or spirit—producing provocative confusion about which she meant, since audiences can see Ariel but may not know if Miranda can.

425–431: Scene: **Most sure...no?**: Since after Miranda's reply Ferdinand exclaims that he had not expected her to understand him, actors often deliver this speech with over-pronounced body language and gestures.

427: **remain**: dwell

429: **bear me**: conduct myself

431: **maid**: an unmarried girl (as opposed to someone's wife, or a goddess)

433: **best...speech**: Ferdinand is not boasting of his linguistic skills, but assuming that he has succeeded his father's throne—thus, socially "the best of them" that speak his language.

434: Stage Direction: *[Emerging]*: Prospero's sudden challenge does not seem to elicit from Ferdinand a request for introduction, or prevent Prospero from once again withdrawing to a stage position from which he can comment on their exchange.

436: **A single thing**: 1) just a man, or 2) the same as what I claim to be, the King of Naples (in answer to Prospero's insinuation to the contrary)

437: **He does hear me**: Ferdinand believes he is the King of Naples, and he can hear himself

A goodly person. He hath lost his fellows,   420
And strays about to find 'em.

MIRANDA
                          I might call him
A thing divine, for nothing natural
I ever saw so noble.

PROSPERO
                    [*Aside*] It goes on, I see,
As my soul prompts it. Spirit, fine spirit, I'll free thee
Within two days for this.

FERDINAND
                        [*Seeing MIRANDA*] Most sure, the goddess   425
On whom these airs attend! Vouchsafe my prayer
May know if you remain upon this island,
And that you will some good instruction give
How I may bear me here. My prime request,
Which I do last pronounce, is—O, you wonder!—   430
If you be maid or no?

MIRANDA
                      No wonder, sir,
But certainly a maid.

FERDINAND
                  My language? Heavens!
I am the best of them that speak this speech,
Were I but where 'tis spoken.

PROSPERO
                      [*Emerging*] How? The best?
What wert thou if the King of Naples heard thee?   435

FERDINAND
A single thing, as I am now, that wonders
To hear thee speak of Naples. He does hear me,
And that he does I weep; myself am Naples,

439: **never...ebb**: crying ever since
442: **twain**: two (among them); Antonio, whom Ferdinand considers Duke of Milan, evidently had a son also on board, whom Ferdinand believes must likewise have drowned; this son—not implausible, since Antonio's brother Prospero has a teenage daughter—is nowhere mentioned in the rest of the play.
443: **control**: refute
445: **changed eyes**: exchanged amorous looks

446: Scene: **A word**: Prospero formally calls Ferdinand over, but the ensuing dialogue makes it unclear how much he obeys. In some cases, during Prospero's aside Ferdinand and Miranda begin to exchange amorous caresses, giving Prospero a different reason, and more urgency, to interrupt; a similar sequence recurs ten lines later.

447: **done...wrong**: dishonored yourself (by lying about his newfound title, or perhaps in Prospero's mind, by being too forward with Miranda)

448: "Why speaks my father so urgently?": Claudie Blakely as Miranda and Sir Ian McKellen as Prospero in the 1999 West Yorkshire Playhouse production directed by Jude Kelly
Photo: Donald Cooper

452: **affection...forth**: love not already pledged to someone else
455: **uneasy**: difficult, complicated;
455–456: **light...light**: a pun: too easy a courtship can make the prize either 1) cheap, or 2) promiscuous (curiously, Prospero never mentions these paternalistic motives again, and productions must decide whether it is his jealousy or his rationale for acting jealous that is feigned)
458: **ow'st**: own'st

Who with mine eyes, never since at ebb, beheld
The king my father wrecked.

MIRANDA
                    Alack, for mercy!   440

FERDINAND
    Yes, faith, and all his lords, the Duke of Milan
    And his brave son being twain.

PROSPERO
                    [*Aside*] The Duke of Milan
    And his more braver daughter could control thee,
    If now 'twere fit to do it. At the first sight
    They have changed eyes. Delicate Ariel,   445
    I'll set thee free for this.—A word, good sir;
    I fear you have done yourself some wrong. A word!

MIRANDA
    Why speaks my father so ungently? This
    Is the third man that e'er I saw; the first
    That e'er I sighed for. Pity move my father   450
    To be inclined my way!

FERDINAND
                    O, if a virgin,
    And your affection not gone forth, I'll make you
    The Queen of Naples.

PROSPERO
                    Soft, sir! One word more.
    [*Aside*] They are both in either's powers. But this swift business
    I must uneasy make, lest too light winning   455
    Make the prize light.—One word more! I charge thee
    That thou attend me. Thou dost here usurp
    The name thou ow'st not, and hast put thyself
    Upon this island as a spy, to win it
    From me, the lord on't.

461: **temple**: i.e., body; (the moral equivalence of exterior and interior is a standard point of Renaissance philosophy, but in the context of the play, a questionable one)
467: **fresh-brook mussels**: (freshwater mussels are inedible, thus supporting Prospero's point)
469: **entertainment**: treatment

470: Scene/Stage Direction: ***charmed from moving***: This is a passive stage direction with multiple realizations, which Prospero's subsequent mocks can locate anywhere in the next twenty lines. Ferdinand may find his sword impossible to raise or wield: Bill Alexander's (1994) production stuck it in the ground, while Brook (1990) had Ariel physically bending back the blade from striking. More conventionally, Prospero freezes and/or neutralizes Ferdinand with a wave of his staff.

471: **trial**: judgment
472: **gentle...fearful**: noble, and thus not cowardly

473-474: "Put thy sword up, traitor, / Who mak'st a show but dar'st not strike": Raul Julia as Prospero, Jessica Nelson as Miranda, and Barry Miller as Ferdinand in the 1981 New York Shakespeare Festival production directed by Lee Breuer
Photo: George Joseph

473: **My foot my tutor?**: i.e., Shall I be instructed by my subordinate?
475: **ward**: defensive fighting posture (a taunt, since Ferdinand cannot move)

FERDINAND
No, as I am a man! 460

MIRANDA
There's nothing ill can dwell in such a temple.
If the ill spirit have so fair a house,
Good things will strive to dwell with't.

PROSPERO
Follow me.—
Speak not you for him, he's a traitor! [*To FERDINAND*] Come,
I'll manacle thy neck and feet together. 465
Seawater shalt thou drink; thy food shall be
The fresh-brook mussels, withered roots, and husks
Wherein the acorn cradled. Follow!

FERDINAND
No.
I will resist such entertainment till
Mine enemy has more power.
He draws, and is charmed from moving

MIRANDA
O dear father, 470
Make not too rash a trial of him, for
He's gentle, and not fearful.

PROSPERO
[*To MIRANDA*] What, I say?
My foot my tutor?—[*To FERDINAND*] Put thy sword up, traitor,
Who mak'st a show but dar'st not strike, thy conscience
Is so possessed with guilt. Come, from thy ward, 475
For I can here disarm thee with this stick
And make thy weapon drop.

MIRANDA
Beseech you, father—

PROSPERO
Hence! Hang not on my garments.

488: Thy nerves...infancy again: Ferdinand's muscles slacken, as they were in "infancy."

499-500: "Thou hast done well, fine Ariel. Follow me; / Hark what thou else shalt do me": Ted van Griethuysen as Prospero, Wallace Acton as Ariel, and William Hulings as Ferdinand in the 1997 Shakespeare Theatre Company production directed by Garland Wright
Photo: Carol Rosegg

499–500: Scene: Follow...do me: The Folio's punctuation leaves ambiguous which lines Prospero speaks to Ariel and which to Ferdinand. "Follow me" is sometimes delivered to Ferdinand; "hark what thou else shalt do me" may refer to Ferdinand's later manual labor. But this spray of instructions is confusing, since Prospero's next lines imply that he and Ariel have talked apart, which seems necessary to allow Miranda naturalistic space to address Ferdinand.

MIRANDA

                         Sir, have pity;
I'll be his surety.

PROSPERO

                Silence! One word more
Shall make me chide thee, if not hate thee. What,   480
An advocate for an impostor? Hush!
Thou think'st there is no more such shapes as he,
Having seen but him and Caliban. Foolish wench,
To th' most of men this is a Caliban,
And they to him are angels.

MIRANDA

                   My affections   485
Are then most humble. I have no ambition
To see a goodlier man.

PROSPERO

                [*To FERDINAND*] Come on, obey.
Thy nerves are in their infancy again,
And have no vigor in them.

FERDINAND

                 So they are;
My spirits, as in a dream, are all bound up.   490
My father's loss, the weakness which I feel,
The wreck of all my friends, nor this man's threats
To whom I am subdued, are but light to me,
Might I but through my prison once a day
Behold this maid. All corners else o' th' earth   495
Let liberty make use of—space enough
Have I in such a prison.

PROSPERO

[*Aside*] It works. [*To FERDINAND*] Come on.
[*To ARIEL*] Thou hast done well, fine Ariel. Follow me;
Hark what thou else shalt do me.   500

503-504: "Thou shalt be as free / As mountain winds": Aunjanue Ellis as Ariel and Patrick Stewart as Prospero in the 1995 Joseph Papp Public Theater production directed by George C. Wolfe

Photo: Michal Daniel

502: **unwonted**: unusual

504: **then**: until then

MIRANDA

                               [*To FERDINAND*] Be of comfort;   500
My father's of a better nature, sir,
Than he appears by speech. This is unwonted
Which now came from him.

PROSPERO

                            [*To ARIEL*] Thou shalt be as free
As mountain winds; but then exactly do
All points of my command.

ARIEL

                     To th' syllable.   505

PROSPERO

[*To FERDINAND*] Come, follow. [*To MIRANDA*] Speak not for him.
                                         Exeunt

[The Tempest

Act 2

0: Scene: ***Enter...and others***: The Folio here adds "*and others*" after the list of courtiers, and similarly adds an "*etc.*" to the opening stage directions of 3.3. Nothing prevents a production from including miscellaneous royal attendants in these scenes, but since the stage directions for the climactic 5.1 specify no such extras (who would also interfere with its spatial dynamics), editors usually delete them. Many productions furthermore collapse Adrian and Francisco, whom the text does not significantly differentiate. Some directors prefer an elaborate discovery, in order to establish plot, setting and character. Director Eric Crozier (1946) had Alonso lying on his cloak despondently, while offstage voices called out for Ferdinand; Antonio and Sebastian sat far from the king; Gonzalo entered, causing Alonso to sit up expectantly, then slump back in dejection. The costuming of the courtiers varies widely, but tends to emphasize sumptuousness and overcivilization.

1-3: "Beseech you, sir, be merry. You have cause— / So have we all—of joy; for our escape / Is much beyond our loss": The Ensemble in the 1992 Ninagawa Company production directed by Yukio Ninagawa
Photo: Donald Cooper

3: **beyond**: greater than; **hint**: occasion, cause
5: **masters...merchant**: the captain of a merchant's ship
10: **cold porridge**: 1) reluctantly, or 2) a pun on "peace," i.e., pease-porridge. Sebastian and Antonio here begin a vicious running commentary on their comrades' efforts at optimism
11: **visitor**: churchman who comforts the sick; **give him o'er**: leave him alone
14: **One. Tell**: the stroke of one; keep count; **entertained**: suffered

Act 2, Scene 1]

Enter ALONSO, SEBASTIAN, ANTONIO, GONZALO,
ADRIAN, FRANCISCO, and others

GONZALO
  [*To ALONSO*] Beseech you, sir, be merry. You have cause—
  So have we all—of joy; for our escape
  Is much beyond our loss. Our hint of woe
  Is common; every day some sailor's wife,
  The masters of some merchant, and the merchant,   5
  Have just our theme of woe; but for the miracle—
  I mean our preservation—few in millions
  Can speak like us. Then wisely, good sir, weigh
  Our sorrow with our comfort.

ALONSO
                              Prithee, peace.

SEBASTIAN
  [*Aside to ANTONIO*] He receives comfort like cold porridge.   10

ANTONIO
  The visitor will not give him o'er so.

SEBASTIAN
  Look, he's winding up the watch of his wit; by and by it will strike.

GONZALO
  Sir,—

SEBASTIAN
  One. Tell.

GONZALO
            When every grief is entertained
  That's offered, comes to the entertainer—   15

16: **dollar**: Sebastian cynically interprets "entertainer" as either "performer" or "innkeeper"; hence the need for payment

17: **Dolor**: grief (with Gonzalo's obvious attempt to pun in retaliation)

20: **spendthrift**: Antonio extends the monetary pun: Gonzalo dispenses grief in his very attempts to dispel it

24: **Which...crow?**: who will you bet blabs first?

25: **old cock**: i.e., Gonzalo

26: **cockerel**: a young rooster, i.e., Adrian

SEBASTIAN
  A dollar.

GONZALO
  Dolor comes to him indeed, you have spoken truer than you purposed.

SEBASTIAN
  You have taken it wiselier than I meant you should.

GONZALO
  Therefore, my lord—

ANTONIO
  Fie, what a spendthrift is he of his tongue!   20

ALONSO
  I prithee, spare.

GONZALO
  Well, I have done. But yet—

SEBASTIAN
  He will be talking.

ANTONIO
  Which, of he or Adrian, for a good wager, first begins to crow?

SEBASTIAN
  The old cock.   25

ANTONIO
  The cockerel.

SEBASTIAN
  Done! The wager?

ANTONIO
  A laughter.

29: **a match**: it is a deal

30: **desert**: deserted, uninhabited (not necessarily dry or barren)

32: Scene: **You're paid**: Since Sebastian chose Gonzalo as the first to continue speaking, it is actually he who has won the wager; the Folio may have accidentally switched speech prefixes, or "you've" may be a misprint for "you're." Some productions give the line to Antonio, and the preceding laugh to Sebastian; some give Gonzalo's line to Adrian. No standard solution exists, however, and the illogical order may work fine as it stands.

36: **He...miss't**: he doesn't miss a beat

37: **temperance**: climate

38: **Temperance**: Antonio's lewd pun on a girl's name; thus "delicate," or inclined to pleasure

39: **subtle**: crafty, (sexually) skilled

SEBASTIAN
  A match.

ADRIAN
  Though this island seem to be desert—   30

ANTONIO
  Ha, ha, ha!

SEBASTIAN
  So! You're paid.

ADRIAN
  Uninhabitable, and almost inaccessible—

SEBASTIAN
  Yet—

ADRIAN
  Yet—   35

ANTONIO
  He could not miss't.

ADRIAN
  It must needs be of subtle, tender, and delicate temperance.

ANTONIO
  Temperance was a delicate wench.

SEBASTIAN
  Ay, and a subtle, as he most learnedly delivered.

ADRIAN
  The air breathes upon us here most sweetly.   40

SEBASTIAN
  As if it had lungs, and rotten ones.

44: **save**: except for

46: **lush**: soft, tender (not necessarily luxuriant)

48: **eye**: shade, tinge; as with Antonio's "tawny," mocks Gonzalo's proclivity to state the obvious

51: **rarity**: exceptional thing

52: **vouched rarities**: wonders sworn to be true

56: **pockets...lies?**: Ariel had earlier attested to Gonzalo's claim, so Antonio's disagreement further suggests the differences in perception the island seems to induce. Kean (1857) had the other courtiers curiously examine their own garments after Gonzalo's observation, as if noticing this fact for the first time.

ANTONIO
Or as 'twere perfumed by a fen.

GONZALO
Here is everything advantageous to life.

ANTONIO
True, save means to live.

SEBASTIAN
Of that there's none, or little.   45

GONZALO
How lush and lusty the grass looks! How green!

ANTONIO
The ground indeed is tawny.

SEBASTIAN
With an eye of green in't.

ANTONIO
He misses not much.

SEBASTIAN
No, he doth but mistake the truth totally.   50

GONZALO
But the rarity of it is—which is indeed almost beyond credit—

SEBASTIAN
As many vouched rarities are.

GONZALO
That our garments, being, as they were, drenched in the sea, hold
notwithstanding their freshness and gloss, being rather new-dyed
than stained with salt water.   55

ANTONIO
If but one of his pockets could speak, would it not say he lies?

64: widow Dido: Dido, Queen of Carthage in the antiquity of Virgil's *Aeneid*, was the widow of Sychaeus, and later abandoned by her lover Aeneas; Aeneas's wife Creusa died in the fall of Troy. Antonio's objection here is complex: he may be decrying Gonzalo's bad tact for saying "widow" in the context of Claribel's marriage (thus Sebastian's "what if he had said widower"); or, more likely, he disputes "widow" as a valid epithet for someone merely forsaken by her lover—and thus, as does Sebastian, forgetting the pre-history behind Virgil's epic episode. (The mention of Dido, and the ensuing debate about Tunis and Carthage, were often cut from nineteenth century productions)

68: study of: reflect on

70: Tunis...Carthage: the ancient North African city of Carthage was destroyed in 698 A.D., whereupon the nearby city of Tunis took its place as the commercial center of the region; Gonzalo's claim depends less on geographical precision than on the ambiguous relation of past to present that this and other such moments in the play register

71: miraculous harp: according to legend, Amphion's harp raised the walls of Thebes

72: houses too: i.e., Gonzalo has not only raised the walls (of Carthage), but built the whole city

SEBASTIAN
    Ay, or very falsely pocket up his report.

GONZALO
    Methinks our garments are now as fresh as when we put them on
    first in Afric, at the marriage of the King's fair daughter Claribel
    to the King of Tunis.   60

SEBASTIAN
    'Twas a sweet marriage, and we prosper well in our return.

ADRIAN
    Tunis was never graced before with such a paragon to their
    queen.

GONZALO
    Not since widow Dido's time.

ANTONIO
    Widow? A pox o' that! How came that "widow" in? Widow Dido!   65

SEBASTIAN
    What if he had said "widower Aeneas" too? Good lord, how you
    take it!

ADRIAN
    "Widow Dido" said you? You make me study of that. She was of
    Carthage, not of Tunis.

GONZALO
    This Tunis, sir, was Carthage.   70

ANTONIO
    His word is more than the miraculous harp.

SEBASTIAN
    He hath raised the wall, and houses too.

ANTONIO
    What impossible matter will he make easy next?

76: "And, sowing the kernels of it in the sea, bring forth more islands": Christopher Walken as Antonio and Tom Atkins as Alonso in the 1974 Mitzi E. Newhouse production directed by Edward Berkeley

Photo: George Joseph

77: **I**: editors have traditionally emended the Folio to read "Ay" (the Jacobean spelling was interchangeable), perhaps Gonzalo's feeble attempt to play along with Antonio; but this does not accord with Antonio's subsequent line, and it seems more consistent to imagine Gonzalo trying to begin a new sentence and once again being rudely interrupted

78: **in good time**: sarcastic: at long last (he resumes talking)

83: **Bate...Dido**: 1) except for the widow Dido, or 2) i.e., please do not mention Dido again

85: **doublet**: a close-fitting jacket

86: **in a sort**: i.e., somewhat

87: **sort...fished for**: 1) Gonzalo's qualification (like his doublet) is fishy, and 2) with a pun on "sort" as in drawing lots

SEBASTIAN
I think he will carry this island home in his pocket, and give it his
son for an apple.   75

ANTONIO
And, sowing the kernels of it in the sea, bring forth more islands.

GONZALO
I—

ANTONIO
Why, in good time.—

GONZALO
[*To ALONSO*] Sir, we were talking that our garments seem now as
fresh as when we were at Tunis at the marriage of your daughter,   80
who is now queen.

ANTONIO
And the rarest that e'er came there.

SEBASTIAN
Bate, I beseech you, widow Dido.

ANTONIO
O, widow Dido? Ay, widow Dido!

GONZALO
Is not, sir, my doublet as fresh as the first day I wore it? I mean,   85
in a sort—

ANTONIO
That sort was well fished for—

GONZALO
When I wore it at your daughter's marriage.

ALONSO
You cram these words into mine ears against

90: **stomach...sense**: temper of my perception

92: **rate**: estimation

103: **o'er...bowed**: the land projected out over its ("his") eroded base, as in a coastal cliff

106: **thank yourself**: have yourself to thank

108: **loose**: a standard Jacobean spelling for "lose," but occasionally used with the connotation—especially significant here—of "to release or set free," as with a prisoner or an animal; in nineteenth century America, predictably, the entire line referring to Claribel's African husband was cut by both Burton (1854) and Daly (1897)

113–114: **weighed...bow**: a double construction: Claribel both pondered over, and herself hung in the balance between, her hatred of the match and her obedience to her father

The stomach of my sense. Would I had never   90
Married my daughter there! For coming thence
My son is lost; and, in my rate, she too,
Who is so far from Italy removed
I ne'er again shall see her. O thou mine heir
Of Naples and of Milan, what strange fish   95
Hath made his meal on thee?

FRANCISCO
                        Sir, he may live.
I saw him beat the surges under him
And ride upon their backs; he trod the water,
Whose enmity he flung aside, and breasted
The surge most swoll'n that met him; his bold head   100
'Bove the contentious waves he kept, and oared
Himself with his good arms in lusty stroke
To th' shore, that o'er his wave-worn basis bowed,
As stooping to relieve him. I not doubt
He came alive to land.

ALONSO
                        No, no, he's gone.   105

SEBASTIAN
Sir, you may thank yourself for this great loss,
That would not bless our Europe with your daughter,
But rather loose her to an African,
Where she, at least, is banished from your eye,
Who hath cause to wet the grief on't.

ALONSO
                        Prithee, peace.   110

SEBASTIAN
You were kneeled to and importuned otherwise
By all of us, and the fair soul herself
Weighed, between loathness and obedience, at
Which end o' th' beam should bow; we have lost your son,
I fear, forever. Milan and Naples have   115

117: **bring**: return (Sebastian assumes, as do the others, that the whole fleet has been lost)

118: "So is the dear'st o' th' loss": Paul Greenwood as Alonso and the Ensemble in the 1993 Royal Shakespeare Company production directed by Sam Mendes
Photo: Donald Cooper

121: **time**: an appropriate time

122: **Very well**: (1) so be it (2) well said (sarcastic)

123: **chirurgeonly**: like a surgeon (Antonio may be extending Sebastian's mockery of Gonzalo, or defending Sebastian's harsh words as medicinal)

125: **foul...foul**: Sebastian and Antonio perhaps intend some further pun here on "fowl," since they earlier referred to Gonzalo as "old cock"

126: **plantation**: the right to colonize (Antonio and Sebastian mistake it as planting)

127: **docks...mallows**: like nettles, thick weeds inimical to agriculture; but also antidotes to nettle-stings, and hence perhaps complementary

More widows in them of this business' making
Than we bring men to comfort them.
The fault's your own.

ALONSO

                So is the dear'st o' th' loss.

GONZALO

My Lord Sebastian,
The truth you speak doth lack some gentleness,   120
And time to speak it in. You rub the sore
When you should bring the plaster.

SEBASTIAN

                Very well.

ANTONIO

And most chirurgeonly.

GONZALO

[*To ALONSO*] It is foul weather in us all, good sir,
When you are cloudy.

SEBASTIAN

          Foul weather?

ANTONIO

              Very foul.   125

GONZALO

Had I plantation of this isle, my lord—

ANTONIO

He's sow't with nettle-seed.

SEBASTIAN

           Or docks, or mallows.

GONZALO

And were the king on't, what would I do?

130–146: Scene: **I' th' commonwealth...innocent people**: (Gonzalo's speech closely follows a passage from Montaigne's essay "Of the Cannibals," translated by John Florio in 1603. Its stage treatment has reflected current ideology: in the nineteenth century it was habitually cut by British productions and retained by American ones; after World War II the pattern briefly reversed. In Brook (1990), which began 2.1 with island spirits building sandcastles before the courtiers' arrival, Gonzalo absent-mindedly knocked them down as he spoke)

130: **by contraries**: contrary to custom

131: **traffic**: trade

133: **Letters**: literature, higher learning

134: **use of service**: institutionalized servitude; **succession**: inheritance

135: **Bourne...land**: laws for property disputes, i.e., limits, boundaries; **tilth**: tillage, crops

138: **innocent and pure**: Gonzalo's amendment counters the proverb "idleness begets lust"

140: **latter end**: 1) of Gonzalo's speech or 2) of the compound word "commonwealth"

141: **in common**: communally, equally

143: **engine**: weapon, warlike device

145: **foison**: plenty

150: **Golden Age**: in classical mythology, the reign of the Roman god Saturn, who presided over a period of idyllic peace and prosperity before the introduction of civilization and strife; Saturn was deposed by his son Jove

SEBASTIAN
  'Scape being drunk, for want of wine.

GONZALO
  I' th' commonwealth I would by contraries   130
  Execute all things. For no kind of traffic
  Would I admit; no name of magistrate;
  Letters should not be known; riches, poverty,
  And use of service, none; contract, succession,
  Bourne, bound of land, tilth, vineyard, none;   135
  No use of metal, corn, or wine, or oil;
  No occupation, all men idle, all;
  And women, too, but innocent and pure;
  No sovereignty.

SEBASTIAN
                  Yet he would be king on't.

ANTONIO
  The latter end of his commonwealth forgets the beginning.   140

GONZALO
  All things in common nature should produce
  Without sweat or endeavor; treason, felony,
  Sword, knife, pike, gun, or need of any engine
  Would I not have; but nature should bring forth
  Of its own kind, all foison, all abundance   145
  To feed my innocent people.

SEBASTIAN
  No marrying 'mong his subjects?

ANTONIO
  None, man, all idle—whores and knaves.

GONZALO
  I would with such perfection govern, sir,
  T'excel the Golden Age.   150

150: **'Save**: God save

154: **minister occasion**: provide opportunity

155: **sensible**: sensitive; volatile

161: **An**: if; **flat-long**: blow struck with the flat of the sword, i.e., ineffectively

164: Stage Direction: **_Enter ARIEL...music_**: The instrument may be a lyre as before, but varies with the style of each production. Ariel, presumably no longer dressed as a water-nymph, plays throughout the ensuing dialogue until Alonso is asleep; only Antonio and Sebastian are immune to the spell, and some stagings account for this—as well as suggest that it fulfills Prospero's ploy to demonstrate Antonio's evil—by having Ariel target specific courtiers; Burton's (1854) female Ariel touched each one with her harp during pauses in the music, while Strehler's (1978) "shot" sleep at them from a pipe. Others, meanwhile, dispense with the music; Brook's (1990) rubbed his victims' eyes.

165: **a-batfowling**: 1) hunting birds at night with sticks, here using the moon like a lantern, 2) slang term for scamming a simpleton

SEBASTIAN

    'Save his majesty!   150

ANTONIO
 Long live Gonzalo!

GONZALO
 And—do you mark me, sir?

ALONSO
 Prithee no more. Thou dost talk nothing to me.

GONZALO
 I do well believe your Highness, and did it to minister occasion to
 these gentlemen, who are of such sensible and nimble lungs that 155
 they always use to laugh at nothing.

ANTONIO
 'Twas you we laughed at.

GONZALO
 Who, in this kind of merry fooling, am nothing to you. So you may
 continue, and laugh at nothing still.

ANTONIO
 What a blow was there given!   160

SEBASTIAN
 An it had not fall'n flat-long.

GONZALO
 You are gentlemen of brave mettle; you would lift the moon out
 of her sphere if she would continue in it five weeks without
 changing.
       Enter ARIEL [invisible] playing solemn music

SEBASTIAN
 We would so, and then go a-batfowling.   165

167: **adventure...weakly**: risk my judgment 1) through such weak behavior, and 2) on so feeble an object

168: **heavy**: tired

169: **hear us**: i.e., hear us laughing while you sleep

173: **omit**: neglect

178: "What a strange drowsiness possesses them!": Liev Schreiber as Sebastian in the 1995 Joseph Papp Public Theater production directed by George C. Wolfe
Photo: Michal Daniel

ANTONIO
 Nay, good my lord, be not angry.

GONZALO
 No, I warrant you, I will not adventure my discretion so weakly.
 Will you laugh me asleep? For I am very heavy.

ANTONIO
 Go sleep, and hear us.
                    [All sleep except ALONSO, SEBASTIAN and ANTONIO]

ALONSO
 What, all so soon asleep? I wish mine eyes   170
 Would, with themselves, shut up my thoughts. I find
 They are inclined to do so.

SEBASTIAN
                         Please you, sir,
 Do not omit the heavy offer of it.
 It seldom visits sorrow; when it doth,
 It is a comforter.

ANTONIO
                         We two, my lord,   175
 Will guard your person while you take your rest,
 And watch your safety.

ALONSO
                    Thank you. Wondrous heavy.
                              [ALONSO sleeps. Exit ARIEL.]

SEBASTIAN
 What a strange drowsiness possesses them!

ANTONIO
 It is the quality o' th' climate.

SEBASTIAN
                         Why

186: **speaks**: speaks to, calls to

187–188: Scene: **My strong...head**: Strehler (1978) had Alonso's crown slip off his head when he nodded off, and Antonio fix his gaze on it—though it is unlikely (but in itself significant) that Alonso would still be wearing it after the shipwreck. Strehler also played the conspiracy as a seduction, with Antonio standing very close to Sebastian, touching him and holding him.

188: **waking**: awake (a rhetorical question, but here with an added meaning)

195: **wink'st**: shut your eyes

200: **trebles thee o'er**: increases your value three times over

Doth it not then our eyelids sink? I find   180
Not myself disposed to sleep.

ANTONIO
                                 Nor I; my spirits are nimble.
They fell together all, as by consent
They dropped, as by a thunderstroke. What might,
Worthy Sebastian, O what might?—No more.
And yet methinks I see it in thy face,   185
What thou shouldst be. Th' occasion speaks thee, and
My strong imagination sees a crown
Dropping upon thy head.

SEBASTIAN
                                What? Art thou waking?

ANTONIO
Do you not hear me speak?

SEBASTIAN
                                I do, and surely
It is a sleepy language, and thou speak'st   190
Out of thy sleep. What is it thou didst say?
This is a strange repose, to be asleep
With eyes wide open—standing, speaking, moving—
And yet so fast asleep.

ANTONIO
                                Noble Sebastian,
Thou let'st thy fortune sleep—die, rather; wink'st   195
Whiles thou art waking.

SEBASTIAN
                                Thou dost snore distinctly;
There's meaning in thy snores.

ANTONIO
I am more serious than my custom. You
Must be so too, if heed me; which to do
Trebles thee o'er.   200

200: **standing water**: at slack tide; hence, waiting to be moved (though Sebastian contradicts this two lines later)

202: **hereditary sloth**: 1) natural laziness, or 2) complacency imposed by birth, i.e., by being Alonso's younger brother and not expecting to succeed to the throne

203: **cherish**: enrich; the sense is, "the more you mock it the more you desire it"

205: **invest**: clothe

209: **A matter**: something significant

210: **throes...yield**: pains you to produce (referring to Antonio's prolonged preamble)

211–215: **this lord...to persuade**: i.e., Gonzalo

211: **remembrance**: memory

212–213: **as little...earthed**: equally forgotten when buried

214–215: **only / Professes**: functions only (i.e., Gonzalo can do nothing but persuade)

SEBASTIAN

                Well. I am standing water.   200

ANTONIO

I'll teach you how to flow.

SEBASTIAN

                  Do so—to ebb

Hereditary sloth instructs me.

ANTONIO

             O!

If you but knew how you the purpose cherish
Whiles thus you mock it, how in stripping it
You more invest it! Ebbing men, indeed—   205
Most often—do so near the bottom run
By their own fear or sloth.

SEBASTIAN

                Prithee say on.

The setting of thine eye and cheek proclaim
A matter from thee; and a birth, indeed,
Which throes thee much to yield.

ANTONIO

                Thus, sir: 210

Although this lord of weak remembrance, this
Who shall be of as little memory
When he is earthed, hath here almost persuaded—
For he's a spirit of persuasion, only
Professes to persuade—the King his son's alive,   215
'Tis as impossible that he's undrowned
As he that sleeps here swims.

SEBASTIAN

                I have no hope

That he's undrowned.

221–222: Ambition...discovery there: Antonio's syntax is fittingly excited and confused, but the sense is probably "ambition itself cannot glimpse anything further than what you hope for" (i.e., a crown)

226: Ten...life: hyperbole: 1) further than a man could ever swim, or 2) in the middle of nowhere (one league = three miles)

227: note: communication; **post**: courier

228: man...slow: (because the moon takes 28 days to complete its transit, and the sun only takes one)

228–229: till new-born...razorable: until a new-born grows to be an adolescent (i.e., it would take half a generation for Claribel to learn of this)

229: that from whom: i.e., on our return from whom

230: cast: cast up, but also related to the theatrical metaphor Antonio proceeds to develop

233: discharge: power to perform

236: cubit: an ancient linear unit of measurement based on the length of the forearm, from elbow to the tip of the middle finger, usually from 17 to 21 inches (43 to 53 centimeters)

238: measure us: traverse us ("us" refers to the cubits, who are imagined to be speaking)

ANTONIO

O, out of that hope
What great hope have you! No hope that way is
Another way so high a hope that even   220
Ambition cannot pierce a wink beyond,
But doubt discovery there. Will you grant with me
That Ferdinand is drowned?

SEBASTIAN

He's gone.

ANTONIO

Then tell me,
Who's the next heir of Naples?

SEBASTIAN

Claribel.

ANTONIO

She that is Queen of Tunis; she that dwells   225
Ten leagues beyond man's life; she that from Naples
Can have no note—unless the sun were post,
The man i' th' moon's too slow—till new-born chins
Are rough and razorable; she that from whom
We all were sea-swallowed, though some cast again,   230
And by that destiny to perform an act
Whereof what's past is prologue, what to come
In yours and my discharge.

SEBASTIAN

What stuff if this? How say you?
'Tis true my brother's daughter's Queen of Tunis;
So is she heir of Naples; 'twixt which regions   235
There is some space.

ANTONIO

A space whose every cubit
Seems to cry out, "How shall that Claribel
Measure us back to Naples? Keep in Tunis,

240: **them**: the other courtiers; **no worse**: i.e., no different

242: **prate**: prattle

245: **chough**: jackdaw, a crow often taught to speak like a parrot; related to slang "chuff," a crude or boorish person (Antonio's point is that a royal court is easily replaceable)

248–249: **content / Tender**: i.e., is your will inclined to look favorably on

252: **feater**: more elegantly

253: **fellows...men**: equals...servants

255: **kibe**: chilblain (an ulcerated inflammation, here of the foot)

258–259: **candied...molest**: i.e., could have been frozen and melted before they interfered with me

And let Sebastian wake." Say this were death
That now hath seized them, why, they were no worse   240
Than now they are. There be that can rule Naples
As well as he that sleeps, lords that can prate
As amply and unnecessarily
As this Gonzalo; I myself could make
A chough of as deep chat. O, that you bore   245
The mind that I do—what a sleep were this
For your advancement! Do you understand me?

SEBASTIAN
    Methinks I do.

ANTONIO
                    And how does your content
    Tender your own good fortune?

SEBASTIAN
                              I remember
    You did supplant your brother Prospero.

ANTONIO
                                        True.   250
    And look how well my garments sit upon me,
    Much feater than before. My brother's servants
    Were then my fellows, now they are my men.

SEBASTIAN
    But for your conscience—

ANTONIO
    Ay, sir, where lies that? If 'twere a kibe,   255
    'Twould put me to my slipper; but I feel not
    This deity in my bosom. Twenty consciences
    That stand 'twixt me and Milan, candied be they,
    And melt ere they molest! Here lies your brother,
    No better than the earth he lies upon,   260
    If he were that which now he's like—that's dead—
    Whom I with this obedient steel, three inches of it,

264: **To...put**: might put (Gonzalo) to eternal sleep

268–269: **tell...the hour**: chime along with whatever business we deem fit; i.e., become yes-men

272: **the tribute...payest**: i.e., Antonio had become Alonso's vassal in order to usurp Prospero; Sebastian offers to enlarge him

275: Stage Direction: *[They draw]*: They may draw their swords here, or after their conference (e.g., at Antonio's "Then let us both be sudden"); the choice depends on how much last-second hesitation (or stupidity) Sebastian projects.

275: Scene: **but one word**: Occasionally productions cut Sebastian's delay, having Ariel enter at this moment and freeze them with a charm; they remain poised to strike while Ariel delivers his alarm to Gonzalo, so that they can be discovered in that pose when he wakes. In some cases Ariel's entrance is transposed just before this line, with some gesture that explains Sebastian's delay as itself the effect of a charm.

275: Stage Direction: *music and song*: may imply either that he plays an instrument, or is accompanied by musicians (possibly house musicians or even onstage spirits)

276-277: "My master through his art foresees the danger / That you, his friend, are in, and sends me forth": Aunjanue Ellis as Ariel in the 1995 Joseph Papp Public Theater production directed by George C. Wolfe

Photo: Michal Daniel

276–278: Scene: **My master...living**: Ariel speaks to Gonzalo, but since Gonzalo later recalls the speech—or perhaps only the music—as merely "a humming," Ariel serves as a chorus here, narrating for the benefit of the audience.

278: **them**: i.e., Alonso and Gonzalo

280: **conspiracy**: (rhymed with "lie")

281: **time**: moment, opportunity

ACT 2 : SCENE 1 [LINES 263-285

Can lay to bed forever; whiles you, doing thus,
To the perpetual wink for aye might put
This ancient morsel, this Sir Prudence, who   265
Should not upbraid our course. For all the rest,
They'll take suggestion as a cat laps milk;
They'll tell the clock to any business that
We say befits the hour.

SEBASTIAN
                        Thy case, dear friend,
Shall be my precedent. As thou got'st Milan,   270
I'll come by Naples. Draw thy sword. One stroke
Shall free thee from the tribute which thou payest,
And I the king shall love thee.

ANTONIO
                        Draw together—
And when I rear my hand, do you the like,
To fall it on Gonzalo.
                                              [They draw]

SEBASTIAN
                        O—but one word.   275
                                        [They talk apart]
                Enter ARIEL [invisible] with music and song

ARIEL
My master through his art foresees the danger
That you, his friend, are in, and sends me forth—
For else his project dies—to keep them living.
            (*Sings in GONZALO's ear*)
            While you here do snoring lie,
            Open-eyed conspiracy   280
                His time doth take;
            If of life you keep a care,
            Shake off slumber, and beware:
                Awake, awake!

ANTONIO
Then let us both be sudden.   285

287: **Why...drawn?**: probably asked of Sebastian and Antonio, but possibly of Gonzalo, who may, after shaking the king, leap to his feet and draw his sword against them; thus it is Gonzalo who answers, with his own question to Antonio and Sebastian

288: **ghastly**: ghostly, fearful (could refer either to Antonio and Sebastian or to Gonzalo)

295: **Heard you this**: Though the courtiers' reaction to Sebastian and Antonio's story is left up to interpretation, Antonio's repetition of Sebastian's "lions" may invite momentary skepticism in Alonso's voice.

300: **verily**: true

GONZALO

[*Waking*] Now, good angels   285
Preserve the king!

ALONSO

[*Waking*] Why, how now—ho, awake! Why are you drawn?
Wherefore this ghastly looking?

GONZALO

What's the matter?

SEBASTIAN

Whiles we stood here securing your repose,
Even now, we heard a hollow burst of bellowing,   290
Like bulls—or rather lions. Did't not wake you?
It struck mine ear most terribly.

ALONSO

I heard nothing.

ANTONIO

O, 'twas a din to fright a monster's ear,
To make an earthquake—sure it was the roar
Of a whole herd of lions.

ALONSO

Heard you this, Gonzalo?   295

GONZALO

Upon mine honor, sir, I heard a humming,
And that a strange one too, which did awake me.
I shaked you, sir, and cried; as mine eyes opened,
I saw their weapons drawn. There was a noise,
That's verily. 'Tis best we stand upon our guard,   300
Or that we quit this place. Let's draw our weapons.

ALONSO

Lead off this ground, and let's make further search
For my poor son.

304: **sure i' th'**: surely somewhere on

305: "Prospero my lord shall know what I have done": Daniel Breaker as Ariel in the 2005 Shakespeare Theatre Company production directed by Kate Whoriskey
Photo: Richard Termine

306: Stage Direction: *Exeunt*: (Ariel probably exits in a different direction)

GONZALO

        Heavens keep him from these beasts!
For he is sure i' th' island.

ALONSO

        Lead away.

ARIEL

Prospero my lord shall know what I have done.   305
So, King, go safely on to seek thy son.

Exeunt

0: Location: another part of the island

0: Stage Direction: *a burden of wood*: The size of Caliban's load can vary to indicate the severity of his oppression; it may suggest a comparison, or contrast, with Ferdinand's in 3.1. Strehler's (1978) Caliban dragged a tree trunk behind him, but most carry planks or logs. (some productions run 2.1 and 2.2 continuously)

2: **flats**: swamps
3: **by inchmeal**: inch by inch

3: Stage Direction: *A noise of thunder*: The First Folio prints this as part of the opening stage direction, but it seems more likely here, since Caliban interprets it as a threatening response to his curse.

5: **urchin-shows**: apparitions of hedgehog-shaped goblins (compare 1.2.328-330)
6: **firebrand**: torch; Caliban's simile for a will-o'-the-wisp, a mischievous nocturnal light that lured wanderers astray in forests
7: **unless he bid 'em**: (Caliban thinks the spirits, but not Prospero, have heard him curse.)
9: **mow**: make grotesque faces
13: **wound with**: entwined by

14: Stage Direction/Speech Prefix: *TRINCULO*: related to Italian *trincare*, to drink heavily, and *trincone*, drunkard; he would likely have been dressed in fool's motley, and most productions retain this clown flavor

18: **bear off**: keep off
20: **bombard**: 1) cannon, or 2) leather jug, (hence "shed his liquor")

23: Scene: **What have we here**: Macready in 1838 began the tradition of having Trinculo stumble backwards over Caliban as he retreats from the thunder.

25: **Poor John**: dried, salted fish
25–30: **Were I... dead Indian**: Native Americans were put on commercial display in Europe, and promptly died from disease; nineteenth century British stagings often cut this passage.

Enter CALIBAN, with a burden of wood

CALIBAN
All the infections that the sun sucks up
From bogs, fens, flats, on Prosper fall, and make him
By inchmeal a disease!

A noise of thunder heard

His spirits hear me,
And yet I needs must curse. But they'll nor pinch,
Fright me with urchin-shows, pitch me i' th' mire,   5
Nor lead me like a firebrand in the dark
Out of my way, unless he bid 'em. But
For every trifle are they set upon me,
Sometime like apes that mow and chatter at me,
And after bite me; then like hedgehogs, which   10
Lie tumbling in my barefoot way, and mount
Their pricks at my footfall; sometime am I
All wound with adders, who with cloven tongues
Do hiss me into madness—

Enter TRINCULO

Lo, now, lo!
Here comes a spirit of his, and to torment me   15
For bringing wood in slowly. I'll fall flat.
Perchance he will not mind me.

[Lies down and covers himself with his cloak]

TRINCULO
Here's neither bush nor shrub to bear off any weather at all, and
another storm brewing—I hear it sing i' th' wind. Yond same
black cloud, yond huge one, looks like a foul bombard that would   20
shed his liquor; if it should thunder as it did before, I know not
where to hide my head. Yond same cloud cannot choose but fall
by pailfuls. What have we here—a man or a fish? Dead or alive?
A fish; he smells like a fish, a very ancient and fish-like smell; a
kind of not-of-the-newest Poor John. A strange fish! Were I in   25

26: **painted**: i.e., painted on a sign, to attract spectators (as at a fair-booth)
28: **make a man**: 1) be considered a man, 2) make a man's fortune
29: **doit**: coin of minimal value

31: Scene: **Warm, o' my troth**: On or before this line, Trinculo peers under the cloak and feels Caliban; where on his body is unclear.

31–32: **let loose...no longer**: from the proverb "a fool's bolt [i.e., opinion] is soon shot"
32–33: **lately suffered by a thunderbolt**: recently perished from lightning strike (This idea forms Trinculo's theory of how Caliban can be both dead and still "warm".)
35: **gaberdine**: cloak, or the coarse cloth of which it is made

37: Stage Direction: *[Crawls...cloak]*: Trinculo's climbing under the cloak with Caliban evidently produces enough agitation for Caliban throughout Stephano's speech to culminate in a cry of pain; that Caliban thinks him one of Prospero's spirits suggests that he perceives it as violent tickling, but the cause is indeterminate, and it has spawned a rich tradition of comic stage business. Most productions attribute it to Trinculo's revulsion at Caliban's smell; Mendes (1993) went so far as to have Trinculo sniff his crotch and wince before submerging. The sexual connotation of two men gyrating under a sheet is not farfetched, however, and the rest of the scene—the play as a whole, in fact—is rife with innuendos of sodomy.

42: **swabber**: seaman who cleans the decks
46: **tang**: sting
48: **tar; pitch**: water-repellent adhesives used on ships; **She loved not the savor of tar nor of pitch**: i.e., Kate did not fancy sailors
49: **a tailor**: a man lacking virility; **scratch...itch**: have sex with

England now, as once I was, and had but this fish painted, not a
holiday-fool there but would give a piece of silver. There would
this monster make a man: any strange beast there makes a man.
When they will not give a doit to relieve a lame beggar, they will
lay out ten to see a dead Indian. Legged like a man, and his fins   30
like arms! Warm, o' my troth! I do now let loose my opinion, hold
it no longer: this is no fish, but an islander, that hath lately suffered by a thunderbolt.

[Thunder]

Alas, the storm is come again! My best way is to creep under his
gaberdine; there is no other shelter hereabout. Misery acquaints a   35
man with strange bedfellows. I will here shroud till the dregs of
the storm be past.

[Crawls under CALIBAN's cloak]
Enter STEPHANO, singing [and carrying a bottle]

STEPHANO
    I shall no more to sea, to sea,
    Here shall I die ashore—
This is a very scurvy tune to sing at a man's funeral. Well, here's   40
my comfort.

Drinks

    (*Sings*)
    The master, the swabber, the boatswain, and I,
        The gunner, and his mate,
    Loved Moll, Meg, and Marian, and Margery,
        But none of us cared for Kate.   45
        For she had a tongue with a tang,
        Would cry to a sailor, "go hang!"
    She loved not the savor of tar nor of pitch,
    Yet a tailor might scratch her where'er she did itch.
        Then to sea, boys, and let her go hang!   50
This is a scurvy tune too. But here's my comfort.

Drinks

CALIBAN
Do not torment me! O!

54: **men of Ind**: inhabitants of the West Indies; complementary of "savages"

55: Scene: **four legs**: Trinculo and Caliban have contorted themselves into a crab-like position, with the head of each apparently nestled between the protruding legs of the other.

56–57: **as proper...ground**: Stephano adapts the expression from two legs to four
61: **ague**: shivering fever, convulsions
62: **recover**: 1) restore to health, 2) take possession of
64: **neat's-leather**: cowhide
69: **will not take too much**: i.e., there will be no such thing as too much; **pay...hath him**: i.e., reward handsomely he who has his keeping
71: **anon**: soon
74: **cat**: alluding to the proverb "liquor that would make a cat speak"
74–75: **shake your shaking**: chase away your tremors

76: "You cannot tell who's your friend; open your chaps again": Barry Stanton as Stephano, Robert Glenister as Caliban, and Adrian Schiller as Trinculo in the 1998 Royal Shakespeare Company production directed by Adrian Noble
Photo: Donald Cooper

76: **cannot...friend**: do not know what is good for you; do not know when someone is doing you a favor (Caliban manifests a dislike for his first mouthful; alternately, he refuses the bottle on Stephano's first attempt, and drinks only after "chaps." Productions sometimes begin the force-feeding at the first instance of "open your mouth," with Caliban's initial resistance here—he may bite Stephano—prompting the therapeutic reassurances); **chaps**: lips (usually emended to "chops," (i.e., jaws), but the Folio's reading is perfectly consistent with the sense, and adds an ironic resonance with Stephano's "friend")

STEPHANO

What's the matter? Have we devils here? Do you put tricks upon's with savages and men of Ind, ha? I have not scaped drowning to be afeard now of your four legs; for it hath been said,   55 "as proper a man as ever went on four legs cannot make him give ground"—and it shall be said so again, while Stephano breathes at nostrils.

CALIBAN

The spirit torments me! O!

STEPHANO

This is some monster of the isle, with four legs, who hath got, as   60 I take it, an ague. Where the devil should he learn our language? I will give him some relief, if it be but for that. If I can recover him, and keep him tame, and get to Naples with him, he's a present for any emperor that ever trod on neat's-leather.

CALIBAN

Do not torment me, prithee! I'll bring my wood home faster.   65

STEPHANO

He's in his fit now, and does not talk after the wisest. He shall taste of my bottle. If he have never drunk wine afore, it will go near to remove his fit. If I can recover him, and keep him tame, I will not take too much for him; he shall pay for him that hath him, and that soundly.   70

CALIBAN

Thou dost me yet but little hurt; thou wilt anon, I know it by thy trembling. Now Prosper works upon thee.

STEPHANO

Come on your ways. Open your mouth. Here is that which will give language to you, cat. Open your mouth. This will shake your shaking, I can tell you, and that soundly.   75

[Gives CALIBAN a drink]

You cannot tell who's your friend; open your chaps again.

[Gives CALIBAN a drink]

78: "I should know that voice!": nineteenth Century engraving by G. Greatbach from a daguerreotype by Mayall

Courtesy of Mary Evans Picture Library

79, 80: Scene: **forward, backward**: Since Stephano has until now been facing Caliban, an arachnoid rotation of the actors may be implied, or Stephano himself may move to the other end. However, Stephano's "Amen!" also implies that he first feeds more liquor to Caliban before proceeding to Trinculo, whom he calls the "other mouth," so "forward" and "backward" registers a moral value rather than a spatial one.

81–82: **If...ague**: i.e., if it takes all the wine in my bottle, I will cure him

85: **call me**: i.e., by my name

86: **spoon**: alluding to the proverb, "he who eats with the devil must have a long spoon"

89: **lesser**: shorter (Robert Armin, Shakespeare's clown actor, was reputedly dwarfish; thus, a theatrical inside-joke)

90: Stage Direction: *[Pulls him out...]*: Stephano's subsequent reference to Caliban as "mooncalf" implies that Caliban rises at this point as well, becoming discernible as a separate creature

91: **siege**: excretion, excrement

92: **mooncalf**: monstrosity (from the malign astrological influence of the moon at birth); **vent**: defecate

94: **hope...not drowned**: (Trinculo's incredulity seems to require him to touch Stephano, to reassure himself that he is not a ghost)

98: **turn me about**: spin me around

98: Scene: **do not...not constant**: Trinculo's jubilant embraces—possibly a celebratory dance with him—are making the drunken Stephano sick. In performance, Stephano may actually vomit, as did Donellan's, in this case into Trinculo's trousers; Miller (1970) had Caliban desperately trying to join their dance, and imitating their salutatory gestures, in an uncomprehending attempt to gain acceptance.

TRINCULO

I should know that voice! It should be—but he is drowned, and
these are devils. O, defend me!

STEPHANO

Four legs and two voices—a most delicate monster! His forward
voice now is to speak well of his friend; his backward voice is to   80
utter foul speeches and to detract. If all the wine in my bottle will
recover him, I will help his ague. Come!

[Gives CALIBAN a drink]

Amen! I will pour some in thy other mouth.

TRINCULO

Stephano?

STEPHANO

Doth thy other mouth call me? Mercy, mercy! This is a devil, and   85
no monster. I will leave him; I have no long spoon.

TRINCULO

Stephano! If thou beest Stephano, touch me, and speak to me; for
I am Trinculo—be not afeard—thy good friend Trinculo.

STEPHANO

If thou beest Trinculo, come forth: I'll pull thee by the lesser legs.
If any be Trinculo's legs, these are they.   90

[Pulls him out from under CALIBAN's cloak]

Thou art very Trinculo indeed! How cam'st thou to be the siege
of this mooncalf? Can he vent Trinculos?

TRINCULO

I took him to be killed with a thunder-stroke. But art thou not
drowned, Stephano? I hope now thou art not drowned. Is the
storm overblown? I hid me under the dead mooncalf's gaberdine   95
for fear of the storm. And art thou living, Stephano? O Stephano,
two Neapolitans 'scaped!

STEPHANO

Prithee do not turn me about; my stomach is not constant.

99: "These be fine things, an if they be not sprites": Illustration by Arthur Rackham, ca. 1926, published by Heinemann
Courtesy of Mary Evans Picture Library

99: **an if**: if

101: **kneel**: (Caliban does not necessarily kneel, though some servile posture is intended)

103: **sack**: generic term for sweet white Spanish wine

108: Scene: **Here**: May refer to Trinculo, but if Caliban, a terse, perfunctory reply that illustrates—better than simply ignoring him—how indifferent to him Stephano has suddenly become; he may absent-mindedly proffer him the bottle here, or just as absent-mindedly retract it before Caliban has a chance to drink, so that it can immediately be given to Trinculo.

111: **kiss the book**: solemnize your oath (with the bottle as a bible)

112: **made like a goose**: i.e., wobbling to and fro (from drink)

CALIBAN
> [*Aside*] These be fine things, an if they be not sprites.
> That's a brave god, and bears celestial liquor.   100
> I will kneel to him.

STEPHANO
> How didst thou 'scape? How cam'st thou hither? Swear by this
> bottle how thou cam'st hither—I escaped upon a butt of sack
> which the sailors heaved o'erboard—by this bottle, which I made
> of the bark of a tree with mine own hands since I was cast ashore.   105

CALIBAN
> I'll swear upon that bottle, to be thy true subject, for the liquor is
> not earthly.

STEPHANO
> Here. [*To TRINCULO*] Swear then how thou escap'st.

TRINCULO
> Swum ashore, man, like a duck. I can swim like a duck, I'll be
> sworn.   110

STEPHANO
> Here, kiss the book.
>
> > *[Gives TRINCULO a drink]*
> Though thou canst swim like a duck, thou art made like a goose.

TRINCULO
> O Stephano, hast any more of this?

STEPHANO
> The whole butt, man. My cellar is in a rock by the seaside, where
> my wine is hid. [*To CALIBAN*] How now, mooncalf? How does   115
> thine ague?

CALIBAN
> Hast thou not dropped from heaven?

118–121: man i' th' moon...bush: In folklore, the man in the moon was banished there either for stealing a bundle of kindling or for gathering it on the sabbath; hence his "bush." (The source of his "dog" is more obscure.)

119: when time was: once upon a time

121: mistress: (presumably Miranda, not Sycorax)

124: this good light: i.e., the sun; **shallow:** 1) tractable, harmless, 2) easily drunk

126: Well drawn: a hearty draft (presumably Caliban drinks throughout Trinculo's remarks); **in good sooth:** truly

127: "I'll show thee every fertile inch o' th' island": Big G, Demond, and Sammie perform in the 2005 documentary Shakespeare Behind Bars by Philomath Films
Courtesy of Philomath Films; Photo: Hank Rogerson

128–131: Scene: kiss thy foot...kiss thy foot: Caliban repeats this vow, so possibly he does not perform it the first time; Stephano's "down and swear" after the second suggests he does so here, but "swear" has also meant "drink," so he may merely be giving him the bottle again.

129: When's: when his (Trinculo's speculation about the true object of Caliban's loyalty explains why he calls him "perfidious")

STEPHANO

Out o' th' moon, I do assure thee. I was the man i' th' moon,
when time was.

CALIBAN

I have seen thee in her, and I do adore thee.   120
My mistress showed me thee, and thy dog, and thy bush.

STEPHANO

Come, swear to that. Kiss the book. I will furnish it anon with
new contents. Swear.

[CALIBAN drinks]

TRINCULO

By this good light, this is a very shallow monster. I afeard of him?
A very weak monster! The man i' th' moon? A most poor, credu-   125
lous monster! Well drawn, monster, in good sooth.

CALIBAN

I'll show thee every fertile inch o' th' island;
And I will kiss thy foot. I prithee be my god.

TRINCULO

By this light, a most perfidious and drunken monster. When's
god's asleep he'll rob his bottle.   130

CALIBAN

I'll kiss thy foot. I'll swear myself thy subject.

STEPHANO

Come on then. Down and swear.

TRINCULO

I shall laugh myself to death at this puppy-headed monster. A
most scurvy monster! I could find in my heart to beat him—

STEPHANO

Come, kiss.   135

136: "But that the poor monster's in drink. An abominable monster!": Alec Clunes as Caliban, Patrick Wymark as Stephano, and Clive Revill as Trinculo in the 1957 Royal Shakespeare Company production directed by Peter Brook

Courtesy of Angus McBean, © Royal Shakespeare Company

143: **crabs:** Though crabapples are more consistent with Caliban's predominantly woodland catalogue, their proverbial sourness suggests he may mean shellfish.

144: **pig-nuts:** sweet tubers, earthnuts

145: **jay's nest:** Since everything else Caliban mentions is food, he may mean eggs; but jays were also prized for their plumage, and their nests tend to be hard to find.

146: **marmoset:** a small monkey (considered edible)

147: **filberts:** hazelnuts

148: **scamels:** obscure: either a crustacean or a small shorebird (perhaps a misprint of seamels, i.e., seagulls), but possibly a breed of South American fish recorded in travel literature

150: **inherit:** take possession

151: Scene: **bear my bottle:** Stephano styles the bottle his royal standard; whom he designates his squire is less certain. Calling Trinculo by name in the preceding and following sentences can argue both for and against Trinculo, and Caliban seems the likelier holder of this trivial office; nevertheless, the indeterminacy allows for more comic stage business, and an opportunity to establish Caliban and Trinculo's rivalry as they bicker over the bottle.

152: **fill him:** 1) Caliban, or 2) the bottle

156: **firing:** firewood

TRINCULO
But that the poor monster's in drink. An abominable monster!

CALIBAN
I'll show thee the best springs; I'll pluck thee berries;
I'll fish for thee, and get thee wood enough.
A plague upon the tyrant that I serve!
I'll bear him no more sticks, but follow thee,   140
Thou wondrous man.

TRINCULO
A most ridiculous monster, to make a wonder of a poor drunkard!

CALIBAN
I prithee let me bring thee where crabs grow;
And I with my long nails will dig thee pig-nuts,
Show thee a jay's nest, and instruct thee how   145
To snare the nimble marmoset; I'll bring thee
To clust'ring filberts, and sometimes I'll get thee
Young scamels from the rock. Wilt thou go with me?

STEPHANO
I prithee now, lead the way without any more talking. Trinculo,
the king and all our company else being drowned, we will inherit 150
here. [To CALIBAN] Here, bear my bottle. Fellow Trinculo, we'll
fill him by and by again.

CALIBAN
        (Sings drunkenly)
        Farewell, master, farewell, farewell!

TRINCULO
A howling monster; a drunken monster!

CALIBAN
        [Sings]
        No more dams I'll make for fish,   155
            Nor fetch in firing
            At requiring,

158: **trenchering**: trenchers, wooden plates

161: **get a new man**: addressed to Prospero, or perhaps more directly to the burden of wood

162: Scene: **Freedom...freedom!**: In performance Stephano and Trinculo often join in on this line, as all three take hands and dance in a hectic ring; the loss of irony in keeping the line only Caliban's is perhaps made up for by the other two's mindless appropriation of it.

162: **high-day**: holiday

Nor scrape trenchering, nor wash dish.
   'Ban, 'Ban,
    Ca—Caliban   160
  Has a new master—get a new man!
Freedom, high-day! High-day, freedom! Freedom, high-day, freedom!

STEPHANO
  O brave monster! Lead the way.

                                                Exeunt

[The Tempest

Act 3

0: Stage Direction: ***bearing a log***: This opening direction offers a potential parallel or contrast with Caliban's burden in 2.2, which can shape our response to their respective servitudes. Bogdanov's (BBC, 1997) production deliberately superposed the intensity of their labor, having a shackled, sweaty and overtasked Ferdinand work continuously throughout the speech; Daniels's (RSC, 1982) production showed Ferdinand comparatively idle, taking a break.

1–2: **their labor...sets off**: either 1) "their labor adds luster to the pleasure we take in them," or more probably, 2) "the pleasure we take in them mitigates the labor they require"

3: **most poor**: exceedingly poor

6: **quickens**: brings to life

11: **sore injunction**: harsh command (with a pun on "sore" meaning "weary")

12–13: **such baseness...executor**: i.e., such a base office was never performed by one so noble

13: **forget**: to do my work (by virtue of pausing to reflect; however industrious Ferdinand has been until now, he has evidently paused)

15: **busilest**: A famous textual crux: the Folio enigmatically reads "busie lest," and editors sometimes emend to "busy least," but Ferdinand means his thoughts of Miranda *increase* in proportion to his work, so "busilest" is the best solution that has been proposed.

15-17: "Alas, now pray you / Work not so hard. I would the lightning had / Burnt up those logs that you are enjoined to pile!": "Scene with Miranda and Ferdinand", painting ca. 1782 by Angelica Kauffmann

Angelica Kauffmann (1741-1807)

15: Stage Direction: ***Enter...and Prospero [hidden]***: What position Prospero takes to signify his concealment is unclear; in some productions he is invisible, and exploits it to stand close by, while in others he more conventionally eavesdrops. Burton's Prospero entered only after Miranda, looking over her shoulder, was satisfied of their privacy; others delay it still further.

19: **weep**: exude resin

21: **He's safe**: i.e., you are/we are safe from him

Act 3, Scene 1]

Enter FERDINAND (bearing a log)

FERDINAND
    There be some sports are painful, and their labor
    Delight in them sets off; some kinds of baseness
    Are nobly undergone, and most poor matters
    Point to rich ends. This my mean task
    Would be as heavy to me, as odious, but   5
    The mistress which I serve quickens what's dead,
    And makes my labors pleasures. O, she is
    Ten times more gentle than her father's crabbed,
    And he's composed of harshness. I must remove
    Some thousands of these logs, and pile them up,   10
    Upon a sore injunction. My sweet mistress
    Weeps when she sees me work, and says such baseness
    Had never like executor. I forget,
    But these sweet thoughts do even refresh my labors,
    Most busilest when I do it.
                    Enter MIRANDA and PROSPERO [hidden]

MIRANDA
                        Alas, now pray you   15
    Work not so hard. I would the lightning had
    Burnt up those logs that you are enjoined to pile!
    Pray set it down, and rest you. When this burns,
    'Twill weep for having wearied you. My father
    Is hard at study; pray now, rest yourself,   20
    He's safe for these three hours.

FERDINAND
                        O most dear mistress,
    The sun will set before I shall discharge
    What I must strive to do.

MIRANDA
                        If you'll sit down,

24: Scene: **give me that**: Depending on Ferdinand's level of exertion, Miranda either asks for the log he is carrying or asks leave to pick one up.

28: **lazy**: Ferdinand means this as an exaggeration, whether ironic or not

32: **worm**: i.e., Miranda; any small creature, whether a term of endearment (as here) or of contempt. Also usually the source of infection in the "love-as-flower" poetic metaphor

33: **visitation**: 1) charitable visit to the sick or needy, or 2) outbreak of plague, following from "infected"

35: **by at night**: Ferdinand has not yet spent a night on the island, so his praise—like much of what follows—is steeped in poetic convention

38-40: "Admired Miranda– / Indeed the top of admiration, worth / What's dearest to the world!": Samantha Soule as Miranda and Duane Boutté as Ferdinand in the 2005 Shakespeare Theatre Company production directed by Kate Whoriskey
Photo: Richard Termine

38: **hest**: behest, injunction; **Admired Miranda**: "Admired" is a pun on the Latin meaning of "Miranda" (to be admired)

41: **best regard**: highest approval

43: **diligent**: attentive; **several**: various

I'll bear your logs the while. Pray give me that.
I'll carry it to the pile.

FERDINAND
                      No, precious creature;   25
I had rather crack my sinews, break my back,
Than you should such dishonor undergo
While I sit lazy by.

MIRANDA
                 It would become me
As well as it does you; and I should do it
With much more ease, for my good will is to it   30
And yours it is against.

PROSPERO
[*Aside*] Poor worm, thou art infected!
This visitation shows it.

MIRANDA
               You look wearily.

FERDINAND
No, noble mistress, 'tis fresh morning with me
When you are by at night. I do beseech you—   35
Chiefly that I might set it in my prayers—
What is your name?

MIRANDA
             Miranda.—O my father,
I have broke your hest to say so!

FERDINAND
              Admired Miranda—
Indeed the top of admiration, worth
What's dearest to the world! Full many a lady   40
I have eyed with best regard, and many a time
Th' harmony of their tongues hath into bondage
Brought my too diligent ear; for several virtues

45: **with...soul**: so wholeheartedly

46: **owed**: possessed

47: **put it to the foil**: marred it; or, from the fencing metaphor of "quarreled," rivaled it

51–53: **nor have I...father**: (compare with her claim at 1.2.448-450)

53–54: **How...skilless**: i.e., I am ignorant of what people look like elsewhere

54: **modesty**: virginity

55: **dower**: dowry

58: **to like of**: 1) with which to compare, and 2) to desire

60: **condition**: social station

tracks 11-13

60–97:
Jamie Glover as Ferdinand, Jennifer Ehle as Miranda, Bob Peck as Prospero
Benedict Cumberbatch as Ferdinand, Emilia Fox as Miranda, Ian McKellen
as Prospero

62: **would not**: wish it were not

64: **flesh-fly**: fly that lays its eggs in rotting flesh; **blow**: (here) breed, corrupt, rot

65-68: "The very instant that I saw you did / My heart fly to your service, there resides / To make me slave to it, and for your sake / Am I this patient log-man": Kamar De Los Reyes as Ferdinand and Carrie Preston as Miranda in the 1995 Joseph Papp Public Theater production directed by George C. Wolfe
Photo: Michal Daniel

70: **kind event**: favorable outcome

Have I liked several women, never any
With so full soul but some defect in her   45
Did quarrel with the noblest grace she owed,
And put it to the foil. But you, O you,
So perfect and so peerless, are created
Of every creature's best.

MIRANDA
                              I do not know
One of my sex, no woman's face remember,   50
Save, from my glass, mine own; nor have I seen
More that I may call men than you, good friend,
And my dear father. How features are abroad
I am skilless of, but by my modesty,
The jewel in my dower, I would not wish   55
Any companion in the world but you—
Nor can imagination form a shape
Besides yourself to like of. But I prattle
Something too wildly, and my father's precepts
I therein do forget.

FERDINAND
                              I am, in my condition,   60
A prince, Miranda, I do think a king—
I would not so!—and would no more endure
This wooden slavery than to suffer
The flesh-fly blow my mouth. Hear my soul speak.
The very instant that I saw you did   65
My heart fly to your service, there resides
To make me slave to it, and for your sake
Am I this patient log-man.

MIRANDA
                              Do you love me?

FERDINAND
O heaven, O earth, bear witness to this sound,
And crown what I profess with kind event   70
If I speak true; if hollowly, invert

60–97:
Jamie Glover as Ferdinand, Jennifer Ehle as Miranda, Bob Peck as Prospero
Benedict Cumberbatch as Ferdinand, Emilia Fox as Miranda, Ian McKellen
as Prospero

72: **boded me**: destined for me
76: **affections**: i.e., Ferdinand and Miranda's love for one another

77: "Wherefore weep you?": Sheridan Fitzgerald as Miranda and Alan Rickman as Ferdinand in the 1978 Royal Shakespeare Company production directed by Clifford Williams
Photo: Donald Cooper

78–82: Scene: **dare not...cunning**: Miranda's self-cancelling "offer" is overtly sexual; she goes on to renounce her coquettishness ("bashful cunning") and to propose marriage instead. Tree's Ferdinand was visibly taken aback by her forwardness; most Prosperos react frowningly.
80: **die**: (with additional sense of sexual climax; in Renaissance slang, "to die" meant to achieve orgasm); **want**: 1) lack, go without, 2) obtain (as in above meaning)
81–82: **seeks...shows**: i.e., like a poorly concealed pregnancy
85: **maid**: virgin, but here with connotations of servitude as well; **fellow**: spouse, equal
88: Scene: **thus humble**: (the demonstrative may be a cue for Ferdinand to kneel; some physical gesture seems warranted to solemnize their betrothal)
90: **e'er**: i.e., ever was

What best is boded me to mischief. I,
Beyond all limit of what else i' th' world,
Do love, prize, honor you.

MIRANDA
                      I am a fool
To weep at what I am glad of.

PROSPERO
                  [*Aside*] Fair encounter   75
Of two most rare affections! Heavens rain grace
On that which breeds between 'em!

FERDINAND
                      Wherefore weep you?

MIRANDA
At mine unworthiness, that dare not offer
What I desire to give, and much less take
What I shall die to want. But this is trifling—   80
And all the more it seeks to hide itself,
The bigger bulk it shows. Hence, bashful cunning,
And prompt me, plain and holy innocence!
I am your wife, if you will marry me;
If not, I'll die your maid. To be your fellow   85
You may deny me, but I'll be your servant
Whether you will or no.

FERDINAND
                My mistress, dearest,
And I thus humble ever.

MIRANDA
                My husband then?

FERDINAND
Ay, with a heart as willing
As bondage e'er of freedom. Here's my hand.   90

tracks 11-13

60–97:
Jamie Glover as Ferdinand, Jennifer Ehle as Miranda, Bob Peck as Prospero
Benedict Cumberbatch as Ferdinand, Emilia Fox as Miranda, Ian McKellen
as Prospero

91: Scene: **my heart in't:** (may cue Miranda not only to take Ferdinand's hand but to kiss it; she often kisses him on the cheek at "I am your wife" as well)

92: **half an hour hence:** Since Miranda believes Prospero is "hard at study" for the next three hours, there is no reason for her to depart, nor for "half an hour" to be their next interval; but Ferdinand must resume his work, and theatrically the scene must end; **thousand thousand:** a million, i.e., a million times over

93-94: "So glad of this as they I cannot be, / Who are surprised withal; but my rejoicing / At nothing can be more": Patrick Stewart as Prospero in the 1995 Joseph Papp Public Theater production directed by George C. Wolfe
Photo: Michal Daniel

94: **withal:** with all of this

97: **appertaining:** pertinent

MIRANDA

And mine, with my heart in't. And now farewell
Till half an hour hence.

FERDINAND

A thousand thousand.
Exit [FERDINAND and MIRANDA separately]

PROSPERO

So glad of this as they I cannot be,
Who are surprised withal; but my rejoicing
At nothing can be more. I'll to my book,   95
For yet ere suppertime I must perform
Much business appertaining.

Exit

0: Stage Direction: ***Enter...and Trinculo***: Since the characters are staggering drunk, an entrance allows for sufficient comic stage business, but some productions find it more revealing to discover them instead: Alexander's (1994) Stephano lounged on a "throne" made of empty bottle-crates; Tree's (1904) Caliban sat by himself, gazing at his reflection in a pool, while the other two sang offstage; Bridges-Adams's (1919) curtain parted to reveal all three sprawled on the ground.

1-2: "Tell not me! When the butt is out we will drink water, not before. / Therefore bear up and board 'em. Servant-monster, drink to me": Sammie as Trinculo and Demond as Stephano in the 2005 documentary Shakespeare Behind Bars by Philomath Films

Courtesy of Philomath Films; Photo: Hank Rogerson

1: **butt is out**: cask of wine is empty
2: **bear...'em**: drink up; the naval command to pull abreast of and storm an enemy ship
5: **brained**: 1) (un)intelligent, 2) inebriated
6: **set**: fixed catatonically (which Trinculo jokingly mistakes as "placed")
12: **five and thirty leagues**: i.e., more than a hundred miles, an obviously absurd claim (hence followed by "off and on")
13: **standard**: standard-bearer
14: **standard**: 1) (someone) capable of standing up, and 2) (someone) capable of standing his/her ground; **he's no standard**: i.e., 1) he is not capable of standing up, or 2) he is not capable of standing his ground
15: **run**: 1) flee the enemy, but also 2) urinate (prompting the secondary sense of Trinculo's retort)
16: **go**: walk, and also 2) urinate

Act 3, Scene 2]

Enter CALIBAN, STEPHANO, and TRINCULO

STEPHANO
Tell not me! When the butt is out we will drink water, not before.
Therefore bear up and board 'em. Servant-monster, drink to me.

TRINCULO
Servant-monster? The folly of this island! They say there's but
five upon this isle; we are three of them. If th' other two be
brained like us, the state totters.   5

STEPHANO
Drink, servant-monster, when I bid thee; thy eyes are almost set
in thy head.

TRINCULO
Where should they be set else? He were a brave monster indeed if
they were set in his tail.

STEPHANO
My man-monster hath drowned his tongue in sack. For my part,   10
the sea cannot drown me. I swam, ere I could recover the shore,
five and thirty leagues, off and on. By this light, thou shalt be my
lieutenant-monster, or my standard.

TRINCULO
Your lieutenant, if you list; he's no standard.

STEPHANO
We'll not run, Monsieur Monster.   15

TRINCULO
Nor go neither; but you'll lie like dogs, and yet say nothing neither.

STEPHANO
Mooncalf, speak once in thy life, if thou beest a good mooncalf.

19: **him**: i.e., Trinculo

20: **in case**: fit, ready (either a boast of strength or of drunkenness, and hence valor)

25: **natural**: here, fool, idiot; (Trinculo's pun is that monsters are by definition un-natural)

26: Scene: **Bite him to death**: Caliban's exhortation suggests Stephano approaches Trinculo at this point, for what Caliban expects to be physical discipline; many productions emphasize a threat of real physical violence here, and the comic knock-about between Caliban and Trinculo leading up to it has a tendency to become genuinely hostile.

28: **tree**: i.e., for hanging

32: Stage Direction: ***invisible***: The audience has already "seen" Ariel being invisible twice by now, but both Prospero's instructions and Ariel's music helped to establish this; here those cues are absent, but the use of "a robe for to go invisibell," such as the prop owned by the Lord Admiral's Men in the 1590s, may have been common stage practice.

35: Scene: **Thou liest**: Only Alexander's (1994) Ariel spoke these interjections earnestly, as if intent on decrying Caliban in his own person; their effect, however, clearly implies that Ariel is ventriloquizing Trinculo's voice. Most often he stands directly behind him, some Ariels manipulate Trinculo's hands to point and gesture.

CALIBAN
How does thy honor? Let me lick thy shoe.
I'll not serve him, he is not valiant.

TRINCULO
Thou liest, most ignorant monster. I am in case to jostle a con-   20
stable. Why, thou debauched fish thou, was there ever man a
coward that hath drunk so much sack as I today? Wilt thou tell a
monstrous lie, being but half a fish and half a monster?

CALIBAN
Lo, how he mocks me! Wilt thou let him, my lord?

TRINCULO
"Lord," quoth he? That a monster should be such a natural!   25

CALIBAN
Lo, lo, again! Bite him to death, I prithee.

STEPHANO
Trinculo, keep a good tongue in your head. If you prove a muti-
neer, the next tree! The poor monster's my subject, and he shall
not suffer indignity.

CALIBAN
I thank my noble lord. Wilt thou be pleased   30
To hearken once again to the suit I made to thee?

STEPHANO
Marry, will I. Kneel, and repeat it. I will stand, and so shall Trinculo.
                                        Enter ARIEL invisible

CALIBAN
As I told thee before, I am subject to a tyrant,
A sorcerer, that by his cunning hath
Cheated me of the island.

ARIEL
                    Thou liest.   35

46: this thing: possibly Trinculo, whose valor Caliban continues to impugn, but possibly self-referential

48: "Thou shalt be lord of it, and I'll serve thee": Teagle F. Bougere as Caliban, Bill Irwin as Trinculo, and John Pankow as Stephano in the 1995 Joseph Papp Public Theater production directed by George C. Wolfe
Photo: Michal Daniel

49: compassed: accomplished

50: party: person

CALIBAN
[*To TRINCULO*] Thou liest, thou jesting monkey thou!
I would my valiant master would destroy thee!
I do not lie.

STEPHANO
Trinculo, if you trouble him any more in's tale, by this hand, I will
supplant some of your teeth.   40

TRINCULO
Why, I said nothing.

STEPHANO
Mum, then, and no more.—Proceed.

CALIBAN
I say by sorcery he got this isle;
From me he got it. If thy greatness will
Revenge it on him—for I know thou dar'st,   45
But this thing dare not—

STEPHANO
That's most certain.

CALIBAN
Thou shalt be lord of it, and I'll serve thee.

STEPHANO
How now shall this be compassed? Canst thou bring me to the
party?   50

CALIBAN
Yea, yea, my lord. I'll yield him thee asleep,
Where thou mayst knock a nail into his head.

ARIEL
Thou liest, thou canst not.

54: **pied ninny**: i.e., Trinculo's parti-colored costume; **patch**: clown

58: **quick freshes**: life-giving, i.e., freshwater, springs; see 1.2.340

60: **by this hand**: a common oath, but in this context may imply that Stephano has already physically reprimanded him

61: **stockfish**: dried cod, prepared by beating

62: Scene: **farther off**: Trinculo cannot get very far, since he is about to be beaten by Stephano three lines later; Stephano may forcibly restrain him at "Didst thou not say he lied?"

65: Stage Direction: *[Beats TRINCULO]*: Stephano's "Take thou that!" makes plain that he proceeds to abuse Trinculo, and stage realizations have ranged from a single blow to a prolonged beating, as well as from conventionally slapstick to potentially life-threatening; Donnellan's (1988) Stephano held a knife to his face.

66: **give me the lie**: call me a liar

68: **murrain**: disease (of livestock)

73–74: **Beat...too**: Since Stephano goes on instructing Trinculo without apparent interruption, this may be an aside—and, unless a production has already had Caliban strike Trinculo himself, this remark offers a dark insight into Caliban's psychology.

CALIBAN
What a pied ninny's this! Thou scurvy patch!
I do beseech thy greatness, give him blows,   55
And take his bottle from him. When that's gone,
He shall drink naught but brine, for I'll not show him
Where the quick freshes are.

STEPHANO
Trinculo, run into no further danger! Interrupt the monster one
word further, and by this hand, I'll turn my mercy out o' doors,   60
and make a stockfish of thee.

TRINCULO
Why, what did I? I did nothing! I'll go farther off.

STEPHANO
Didst thou not say he lied?

ARIEL
Thou liest.

STEPHANO
Do I so? Take thou that!   65
                                          [Beats TRINCULO]
As you like this, give me the lie another time.

TRINCULO
I did not give the lie! Out o' your wits, and hearing too? A pox o'
your bottle! This can sack and drinking do. A murrain on your
monster, and the devil take your fingers!

CALIBAN
Ha, ha, ha!   70

STEPHANO
Now, forward with your tale. [To TRINCULO] Prithee stand further off.

CALIBAN
Beat him enough. After a little time
I'll beat him too.

75: **Stand farther**: (presumably, farther than Trinculo has already removed himself)

tracks 14–16

76–105:
Ben Onwukwe as Caliban, John Hodgkinson as Stephano, Ian Talbot
as Trinculo, and Scott Handy as Ariel
Wayne Best as Caliban, Peter Donaldson as Stephano, Stephen Ouimette
as Trinculo, and Michael Therriault as Ariel

76–77: **'tis a custom...sleep**: Caliban may not be wrong; however, the play takes place during one afternoon, and the mention of a habit is puzzling.

78–79: **or...or**: either...or

79: **paunch**: stab in the gut

80: **wesand**: windpipe

82: **sot**: fool

85: **utensils**: furnishings, but possibly implements of magic

89: **nonpareil**: incomparable (French)

93: **brave**: comely

94: **become**: suit, enhance

97: **save our graces!**: Stephano prematurely salutes himself

98: **plot**: 1) strategy, conspiracy, or 2) outline of a play

100: Scene: **Give me thy hand**: This line can either extend Stephano's cruelty or suggest genuine reconciliation; Hytner's (1988) Stephano squeezed Trinculo's fingers until he yelped in pain, while Purcarete's (1995) Trinculo refused Stephano's hand until he offered his apology.

STEPHANO
    [*To TRINCULO*] Stand farther. [*To CALIBAN*] Come, proceed.   75

CALIBAN
    Why, as I told thee, 'tis a custom with him
    I' th' afternoon to sleep. There thou mayst brain him,
    Having first seized his books: or with a log
    Batter his skull, or paunch him with a stake,
    Or cut his wesand with thy knife. Remember   80
    First to possess his books; for without them
    He's but a sot, as I am, nor hath not
    One spirit to command—they all do hate him
    As rootedly as I. Burn but his books.
    He has brave utensils, for so he calls them,   85
    Which when he has a house, he'll deck withal.
    And that most deeply to consider is
    The beauty of his daughter. He himself
    Calls her a nonpareil. I never saw a woman
    But only Sycorax my dam, and she;   90
    But she as far surpasseth Sycorax
    As great'st does least.

STEPHANO
    Is it so brave a lass?

CALIBAN
    Ay, lord; she will become thy bed, I warrant,
    And bring thee forth brave brood.   95

STEPHANO
    Monster, I will kill this man. His daughter and I will be king and
    queen—save our graces!—and Trinculo and thyself shall be
    viceroys. Dost thou like the plot, Trinculo?

TRINCULO
    Excellent.

STEPHANO
    Give me thy hand. I am sorry I beat thee; but while thou liv'st,   100
    keep a good tongue in thy head.

76–105:
Ben Onwukwe as Caliban, John Hodgkinson as Stephano, Ian Talbot
as Trinculo, and Scott Handy as Ariel
Wayne Best as Caliban, Peter Donaldson as Stephano, Stephen Ouimette
as Trinculo, and Michael Therriault as Ariel

107: **jocund**: whimsical, jocular; **troll the catch**: sing the round
108: **whilere**: just now, a while ago
109: **any reason**: anything reasonable

110: Stage Direction: ***Sings***: The Folio gives the direction in singular, but that does not mean Trinculo ignores Stephano's request. They may both sing, and usually do; Caliban may join in as well, and the song is often expanded into a round.

111: **cout**: obscure, but cannot be a Folio misprint for "scout," to which it is often corrected; to be consistent with the rest of the song, probably a word implying derision
112: **scout**: mock
114: **not the tune**: Caliban either has not participated in the song until now, or Stephano and Trinculo corrupt it, introducing some variation that displeases him; Daniel's (1982) Stephano lost the tune, and Trinculo began an operatic solo.

114: Stage Direction: ***Ariel plays***: The stage directions upon Ariel's entrance (3.2.32) omit the instruments; if he did not enter with them anyway, he may have simply been handed them at the stage door during the scene itself. Some modern productions do not handle the music representationally; the music is understood to emanate from Ariel, though he plays no instruments; ***tabor and pipe***: traditional English instrument combination for rustic, solo performance, consisting of a small drum slung on the hip and a pipe played with the non-drumstick hand (modern productions have substituted a tambourine, trumpet, song or whistling)

116: **the picture of Nobody**: i.e., by an invisible person; "Nobody" was a popular folk-figure, depicted with long arms and legs but no torso (i.e., no body), prominent on shop-signs and featured in an early seventeenth century play called *Nobody and Somebody*
117-118: **If thou beest a man...take't as thou list**:(backwards: it is the devil who must be commanded to show himself); **take't as thou list**: do as you please

CALIBAN
> Within this half hour will he be asleep.
> Wilt thou destroy him then?

STEPHANO
> Ay, on mine honor.

ARIEL
> [*Aside*] This will I tell my master.   105

CALIBAN
> Thou mak'st me merry. I am full of pleasure;
> Let us be jocund. Will you troll the catch
> You taught me but whilere?

STEPHANO
> At thy request, monster, I will do reason, any reason. Come on,
> Trinculo, let us sing.   110
> > (*Sings*)
> > Flout 'em and cout 'em
> > And scout 'em and flout 'em!
> > > Thought is free.

CALIBAN
> That's not the tune.

> > > *ARIEL plays the tune on a tabor and pipe*

STEPHANO
> What is this same?   115

TRINCULO
> This is the tune of our catch, played by the picture of Nobody.

STEPHANO
> If thou beest a man, show thyself in thy likeness. If thou beest a
> devil, take't as thou list.

TRINCULO
> O, forgive me my sins!

120: Scene: **Mercy upon us!**: Stephano's bravado suddenly deserts him; he may fall to his knees, as Trinculo probably does at "O forgive me my sins!"

121: "Art thou afeared?": Robert Glenister as Caliban in the 1998 Royal Shakespeare Company production directed by Adrian Noble
Photo: Donald Cooper

135: **by and by**: soon enough

136: Scene: **sound...away**: Presumably Ariel moves toward the door, if this is not already his cue to exit; Tree's Ariel flew around the stage, leading Stephano and Trinculo like a will-o-the-wisp, while Caliban danced and sang in the same spot.

138: **lays it on**: 1) beats his drum; 2) plays with gusto

STEPHANO
   He that dies pays all debts. I defy thee. Mercy upon us!   120

CALIBAN
   Art thou afeard?

STEPHANO
   No, monster, not I.

CALIBAN
   Be not afeard. The isle is full of noises,
   Sounds and sweet airs, that give delight and hurt not.
   Sometimes a thousand twangling instruments   125
   Will hum about mine ears; and sometime voices,
   That if I then had waked after long sleep,
   Will make me sleep again; and then, in dreaming,
   The clouds methought would open, and show riches
   Ready to drop on me, that when I waked   130
   I cried to dream again.

STEPHANO
   This will prove a brave kingdom to me, where I shall have my
   music for nothing.

CALIBAN
   When Prospero is destroyed.

STEPHANO
   That shall be by and by. I remember the story.   135

TRINCULO
   The sound is going away. Let's follow it, and after do our work.

STEPHANO
   Lead, monster, we'll follow. I would I could see this taborer; he
   lays it on.

TRINCULO
   [*To CALIBAN*] Wilt come? I'll follow Stephano.
                                                        Exeunt

1: **By'r lakin**: by our ladykin (i.e., the Virgin Mary)

2: **aches**: ache

3: **forthrights and meanders**: straight ways and winding paths

5: **attached**: seized (a legalism)

8: **my flatterer**: i.e., Gonzalo

10: **frustrate**: vain

14: **throughly**: thoroughly

15: **now**: now that; **travail**: labor, trial; also a seventeenth century spelling of "travel"

17: Stage Direction: ***on the top***: technical term for the uppermost level of the Jacobean stage, above the spectators' galleries—possibly a music room—giving Prospero a god-like view over the rest of the scene, and from which invisibility was probably implicit; adjacent, probably, to a playing area called the "heavens." (Naturalistic scenery might require Prospero to stand atop a high promontory.)

Act 3, Scene 3]

Enter ALONSO, SEBASTIAN, ANTONIO,
GONZALO, ADRIAN, FRANCISCO

GONZALO
    By'r lakin, I can go no further, sir,
    My old bones aches. Here's a maze trod indeed
    Through forthrights and meanders! By your patience,
    I needs must rest me.

ALONSO
                  Old lord, I cannot blame thee,
    Who am myself attached with weariness   5
    To th' dulling of my spirits. Sit down and rest.
    Even here I will put off my hope, and keep it
    No longer for my flatterer. He is drowned
    Whom thus we stray to find, and the sea mocks
    Our frustrate search on land. Well, let him go.   10

ANTONIO
    [*Aside to SEBASTIAN*] I am right glad that he's so out of hope.
    Do not for one repulse forgo the purpose
    That you resolved t' effect.

SEBASTIAN
              [*Aside to ANTONIO*] The next advantage
    Will we take throughly.

ANTONIO
             [*Aside to SEBASTIAN*] Let it be tonight;
    For, now they are oppressed with travail, they   15
    Will not nor cannot use such vigilance
    As when they are fresh.

SEBASTIAN
          [*Aside to ANTONIO*] I say tonight. No more.
    Solemn and strange music, and PROSPERO on the top (invisible)

19: Stage Direction: *several strange shapes*: other island spirits, presumably members of Ariel's "quality," who serve Prospero in tormenting Caliban and who later assist in the staging of the masque. Their realization has ranged from the bucolic and mytho-logical, as in Kean's ballet of twelve naiads (nymphs), twenty-four dryads (tree spirits), and twelve satyrs (half-men, half-goats), to grotesque and horrifying; Hall's 1974 production had deformed miscreants with extra or missing or mutilated limbs. Multicultural resonances are possible as well—they have been depicted as Native Americans or as Caribbean voodoo dolls—but these depend on the aims of the particular production; *bringing in a banquet*: Originally, a trick table rose out of the stage and was set by the "shapes" with food and drink; *inviting*: Alonso later calls this motion "dumb discourse," and most stage interpretations have restricted the shapes to pantomime.

20: **kind keepers**: good guardian angels

21: **living drollery**: 1) a puppet show come to life, or 2) a comic play occurring in real life

23: **phoenix**: a mythical bird, thought to be unique, and to nest in a single tree in Arabia; its method of reproduction was to consume itself in flame and be reborn from its own ashes

25: **what...credit**: lack credibility, i.e., anything else considered unbelievable

30: **for certes**: for certain

ALONSO
What harmony is this? My good friends, hark!

GONZALO
Marvelous sweet music!

> *Enter several strange shapes, bringing in a banquet;*
> *and dance about it with gentle actions of salutations;*
> *and inviting the King, etc., to eat, they depart.*

ALONSO
Give us kind keepers, heavens! What were these?   20

SEBASTIAN
A living drollery! Now I will believe
That there are unicorns; that in Arabia
There is one tree, the phoenix' throne, one phoenix
At this hour reigning there.

ANTONIO
                    I'll believe both;
And what does else want credit, come to me,   25
And I'll be sworn 'tis true. Travelers ne'er did lie,
Though fools at home condemn 'em.

GONZALO
                    If in Naples
I should report this now—would they believe me
If I should say I saw such islanders?
For certes these are people of the island,   30
Who though they are of monstrous shape, yet note
Their manners are more gentle, kind, than of
Our human generation you shall find
Many—nay, almost any.

PROSPERO
                    [*Aside*] Honest lord,
Thou hast said well; for some of you there present   35
Are worse than devils.

36: **cannot...muse**: cannot marvel enough at

37: **such sound**: (the music, since the spirit-shapes themselves were silent)

39: **Praise in departing**: proverbial: save your praise until the end (as with a play)

40-43: "No matter, since / They have left their viands behind, for we have stom-achs. / Will't please you taste of what is here?": Liev Schreiber as Sebastian in the 1995 Joseph Papp Public Theater production directed by George C. Wolfe
Photo: Michal Daniel

42: Scene: **please you taste**: (Sebastian may at this point begin eating. Gonzalo seems willing to join him, but might not do so because he has a speech to deliver; Ariel's denunciation of the "three men of sin" at the table may also require him to remain separate)

44: **mountaineers**: mountain dwellers (Gonzalo may be recalling reports of a goitrous tribe of men supposedly discovered in the Swiss Alps)

45: **Dewlapped**: with a flap of skin or bulge of tissue under the chin

46–47: **men...breasts**: i.e., the anthropophagi (another traveler's legend, alluded to in *Othello* 1.3.158)

48: **putter-out of five-for-one**: i.e., traveler. To recoup his expenses, the traveler could deposit a sum with a broker in London, which would be repaid fivefold ("five-for-one") if he returned safely with proof he had reached his destination, but the deposit would be forfeited if he failed to do so or died.

49: **stand to**: fall to it, commence

50: **Although**: i.e., if it be

52: Stage Direction: *harpy*: a terrifying mythological creature with a woman's face and breasts, but with the wings, body and talons of a bird of prey (thus requiring Ariel to descend from the heavens, flying); the scene is similar to an incident in Book III of Virgil's *Aeneid*; *quaint device*: ingenious mechanism. The stage direction has never been explained, but may have involved a stagehand hidden under the skirts of the table who removed a false top, causing the dishes to drop down through the middle. Some productions conflate this effect with Ariel's entrance: Williams's 1963 table overturned to reveal Ariel, while Mendes's (1993) Ariel erupted from the center of it.

53: **three men of sin**: i.e., Alonso, Antonio and Sebastian

ALONSO

I cannot too much muse
Such shapes, such gesture, and such sound—expressing,
Although they want the use of a tongue, a kind
Of excellent dumb discourse.

PROSPERO

[*Aside*] Praise in departing.

FRANCISCO
They vanished strangely.

SEBASTIAN

No matter, since   40
They have left their viands behind, for we have stomachs.
Will't please you taste of what is here?

ALONSO

Not I.

GONZALO
Faith, sir, you need not fear. When we were boys,
Who would believe that there were mountaineers
Dewlapped like bulls, whose throats had hanging at 'em   45
Wallets of flesh? Or that there were such men
Whose heads stood in their breasts? Which now we find
Each putter-out of five-for-one will bring us
Good warrant of.

ALONSO

I will stand to, and feed;
Although my last, no matter, since I feel   50
The best is past. Brother, my lord the duke,
Stand to and do as we.
        Thunder and lightning. Enter ARIEL, (like a harpy), claps his wings
                upon the table, and with a quaint device the banquet vanishes.

ARIEL
You are three men of sin, whom destiny,

tracks17-19

53–82:
Adrian Lester as Ariel
Scott Handy as Ariel

54: **to instrument**: as its instrument
59: **with suchlike valor**: i.e., with the desperate courage of an insane person

60–65: Scene: **You fools...plume:** (the lords may actually attempt to attack Ariel, or Ariel may simply be reacting to their intention to do so; Benthall's lords, in his 1951 production, rushed at him but were charmed)

61–64: **elements...waters:** earth and fire (from which swords are made) are powerless against air and water
64: **still-closing**: ever-enclosing; **still-closing waters**: water merely parts around objects in its path
65: **dowl**: feather fiber
66: **like**: likewise
67: **massy**: heavy
67: Scene: **too massy for your strengths**: Thacker's lords here found they could not lift their weapons, and fell.
71: **requit it**: avenged the deed
77: **ling'ring perdition**: 1) slow, inexorable ruin, or 2) living death
79: **whose wraths**: i.e., those of the powers; **guard you from**: prevent
81: **is nothing**: demands nothing else; **heart's sorrow**: contrition, repentance
82: **clear**: guiltless

82: Stage Direction: *vanishes*: The original Ariel would merely have ascended rapidly back to the heavens; *mocks and mows*: contemptuous gestures and grimaces

83: Scene/Stage Direction: [*Aside*]: Prospero addresses Ariel at the start of this speech, but Ariel probably remains absent; most productions show the lords transfixed ("knit up") during and after the dance of the shapes that follows Ariel's exit, to convey that they cannot hear Prospero.

84: **devouring**: rapturous (a pun, since Ariel abruptly removed the banquet)
85: **bated**: omitted

That hath to instrument this lower world
And what is in't, the never-surfeited sea   55
Hath caused to belch up you, and on this island
Where man doth not inhabit—you 'mongst men
Being most unfit to live—I have made you mad,
And even with suchlike valor men hang and drown
Their proper selves.
              [ALONSO, SEBASTIAN and ANTONIO draw their swords]
                    You fools! I and my fellows   60
Are ministers of fate. The elements
Of whom your swords are tempered may as well
Wound the loud winds, or with bemocked-at stabs
Kill the still-closing waters, as diminish
One dowl that's in my plume. My fellow ministers   65
Are like invulnerable. If you could hurt,
Your swords are now too massy for your strengths,
And will not be uplifted. But remember—
For that's my business to you—that you three
From Milan did supplant good Prospero,   70
Exposed unto the sea, which hath requit it,
Him and his innocent child; for which foul deed
The powers—delaying, not forgetting—have
Incensed the seas and shores, yea all the creatures,
Against your peace. Thee of thy son,   75
Alonso, they have bereft, and do pronounce by me
Ling'ring perdition, worse than any death
Can be at once, shall step by step attend
You and your ways; whose wraths to guard you from,
Which here, in this most desolate isle, else falls   80
Upon your heads, is nothing but heart's sorrow,
And a clear life ensuing.
              He vanishes in thunder. Then (to soft music)
         enter the shapes again, and dance (with mocks and mows),
                    and carrying out the table. [They depart]

PROSPERO
    [*Aside*] Bravely the figure of this harpy hast thou
Performed, my Ariel; a grace it had, devouring.
Of my instruction hast thou nothing bated   85

86: **so**: likewise

86–87: **good...strange**: natural performance and wonderful obedience

88: **several kinds**: various roles

94–95: **why...stare**: why are you staring amazedly (only Alonso, Antonio and Sebastian could hear Ariel's speech)

96: **billows**: clouds; **it**: i.e., my sin

99: **bass**: 1) proclaim deeply, 2) supply the bass part for the revelation of my guilt, or 3) with a play on "utter the baseness of"

100: **Therefore**: for that

102–103: Scene: **But one fiend...*Exeunt***: Now able to move, Sebastian may stab with his sword at the empty air, as may Antonio. Despite their threats, however, their sudden exit suggests they run away rather than chase the spirits, although both readings work.

103: **o'er**: one after another (Sebastian complains that they were outnumbered)

107: **of suppler joints**: stronger, more composed

In what thou hadst to say; so, with good life
And observation strange, my meaner ministers
Their several kinds have done. My high charms work,
And these, mine enemies, are all knit up
In their distractions. They now are in my pow'r;   90
And in these fits I leave them, while I visit
Young Ferdinand, whom they suppose is drowned,
And his and mine loved darling.

                                             [Exit, above]

GONZALO
I' th' name of something holy, sir, why stand you
In this strange stare?

ALONSO
                    O, it is monstrous, monstrous!   95
Methought the billows spoke and told me of it,
The winds did sing it to me, and the thunder,
That deep and dreadful organ-pipe, pronounced
The name of Prosper: it did bass my trespass.
Therefore my son i' th' ooze is bedded; and   100
I'll seek him deeper than e'er plummet sounded,
And with him there lie mudded.

                                                        Exit

SEBASTIAN
                    But one fiend at a time,
I'll fight their legions o'er!

ANTONIO
                    I'll be thy second.
                    Exeunt [SEBASTIAN and ANTONIO]

GONZALO
All three of them are desperate. Their great guilt,
Like poison given to work a great time after,   105
Now 'gins to bite the spirits. I do beseech you
That are of suppler joints, follow them swiftly,

108: **ecstasy**: delirium

111: Stage Direction: ***Exeunt omnes***: Latin for "they go out"

1783 Engraving by J. Heath
Courtesy of Mary Evans Picture Library

And hinder them from what this ecstasy
May now provoke them to.

ADRIAN
Follow, I pray you.   110
                                                          Exeunt omnes

[The Tempest

Act 4

0: Stage Direction: **Enter**: The exact configuration in which they enter is significant, but unspecified by the Folio; Prospero's "I have given you" would seem to imply that Miranda enters linked to Ferdinand, but Prospero proceeds to give her away several more times thereafter, and this compulsive redundancy has been used to emphasize his conflict. Some productions treat this scene as an actual wedding, with Miranda in a bridal gown, others as a betrothal.

tracks 20-22

1–32:
William Hutt as Prospero and Paul Miller as Ferdinand
Ian McKellen as Prospero and Benedict Cumberbatch as Ferdinand

1: **austerely**: severely; **punished**: recalling, despite his subsequent confession of "trials of thy love," Prospero's fabricated charges of treason from 1.2

3: **third**: Editors since the eighteenth century have emended this to "thread," but Prospero uses a similar formula at the end of the play ("every third thought"); most likely "a vital part," since Miranda represents a third of his family—thus forming only the second time he alludes, however indirectly, to his wife.

7: **strangely**: wonderfully

11: **halt**: limp

12: **against**: i.e., over the word of

14: **worthily purchased**: deservedly or excellently won (with mercantile overtones)

16: **sanctimonious**: sanctifying

18: **aspersion**: shower, here of blessing or fertility

19: **grow**: prosper, breed

23: **Hymen**: classical god of marriage; **Hymen's lamps**: wedding torches (a figure of speech); clear flames predicted a happy union, smoke a troubled one

Act 4 Scene 1]

PROSPERO
    If I have too austerely punished you,
    Your compensation makes amends; for I
    Have given you here a third of mine own life,
    Or that for which I live—who once again
    I tender to thy hand. All thy vexations   5
    Were but trials of thy love, and thou
    Hast strangely stood the test. Here, afore heaven,
    I ratify this my rich gift. O Ferdinand,
    Do not smile at me that I boast of her,
    For thou shalt find she will outstrip all praise   10
    And make it halt behind her.

FERDINAND
                    I do believe it
    Against an oracle.

PROSPERO
    Then as my gift, and thine own acquisition
    Worthily purchased, take my daughter. But
    If thou dost break her virgin-knot before   15
    All sanctimonious ceremonies may
    With full and holy right be ministered,
    No sweet aspersion shall the heavens let fall
    To make this contract grow; but barren hate,
    Sour-eyed disdain, and discord shall bestrew   20
    The union of your bed with weeds so loathly
    That you shall hate it both. Therefore take heed,
    As Hymen's lamps shall light you.

FERDINAND
                  As I hope
    For quiet days, fair issue, and long life,

1–32:
William Hutt as Prospero and Paul Miller as Ferdinand
Ian McKellen as Prospero and Benedict Cumberbatch as Ferdinand

26: **opportune**: (accented on second syllable)

27: **worser genius can**: bad angel can make

29: **edge**: passion, sexual anticipation

30–31: **or Phoebus'...below**: either the sun-god's horses have stalled, or night is pre-vented from rising (Ferdinand imagines their wedding day as feeling interminable)

33: **What**: now then

37: **rabble**: i.e., the lesser spirits

39: **quick motion**: lifelike action

39–42: **I must bestow...from me**: Holding a masque for a betrothal rather than a wedding is apparently Shakespeare's invention, since it is without precedent in Jacobean court culture.

41: **vanity**: indulgence, trifle

42: **Presently**: immediately

43: **with a twink**: in the blink of an eye

44–48: Scene: **Before you can...No?**: Ariel's speech is sometimes handled as a song, with music, but his final line has been given special poignancy: Barton's (1970) music stopped here; Macready's (1838) Ariel turned around to ask it; Mendes's (1993) emphasized "me"; Williams's (1963) converted the rhetorical "no?" into an answer of his own question; many productions make this a moment of physical contact between them.

47: **mop and mow**: grimaces (compare with the "mocks and mows" of their earlier dance in 3.3.82SD)

With such love as 'tis now, the murkiest den,   25
The most opportune place, the strong'st suggestion
Our worser genius can, shall never melt
Mine honor into lust, to take away
The edge of that day's celebration
When I shall think or Phoebus' steeds are foundered,   30
Or night kept chained below.

PROSPERO
                              Fairly spoke.
Sit then and talk with her, she is thine own.
What, Ariel! My industrious servant Ariel!

                                                    Enter ARIEL

ARIEL
What would my potent master? Here I am.

PROSPERO
Thou and thy meaner fellows your last service   35
Did worthily perform; and I must use you
In such another trick. Go bring the rabble
O'er whom I give thee pow'r here to this place.
Incite them to quick motion, for I must
Bestow upon the eyes of this young couple   40
Some vanity of mine art. It is my promise,
And they expect it from me.

ARIEL
                              Presently?

PROSPERO
Ay, with a twink.

ARIEL
              Before you can say "come," and "go,"
              And breathe twice, and cry "so, so,"   45
              Each one, tripping on his toe,
              Will be here with mop and mow.
              Do you love me, master? No?

50: **conceive**: imagine, understand
51: **true**: i.e., to your vow

51: Scene: **Look thou be true!**: Prospero may have caught the lovers in a suggestive embrace—or sharing a perfectly innocent exchange—or may be returning obsessively to the theme without provocation; depending on his previous moment with Ariel, potentially ironic.

55: **white...heart**: i.e., the chastity of my beloved, or of my love for her
56: **liver**: according to Renaissance physiology, the seat of the passions
57–58: **corollary...want**: one too many rather than lack one
58: **pertly**: briskly

58: Stage Direction: *soft music*: Prospero's masque has varied enormously: productions from the eighteenth and nineteenth century elaborated its fantasy; in the twentieth century it was used to make meta-theatrical, ethnic or parodic statements. In Strehler's (1978) and Purcarete's (1995), the audience could not see it.

59: Stage Direction: *IRIS*: goddess of the rainbow, and female messenger to the other gods; played by a spirit

60: **Ceres**: Juno's sister, goddess of earth and patroness of agriculture, especially grains; her daughter Proserpine was abducted by Pluto, god of the underworld, and allowed to rejoin her mother for half the year, causing Ceres to create spring and fall to mark her transits; **leas**: meadows, wild fields
61: **vetches**: vicia, a legume
63: **stover**: leaves and stalks left for winter forage
64: **pionèd and twillèd**: trenched by the current and fenced with tangled branches; often emended to "peonied and lilied," but unlikely, since "spongy April" here washes them away rather than grows them, and flowers are not "chaste"
66: **broom groves**: clumps of shrubs; broom was often associated with casting love-spells
68: **poll-clipped**: pollarded, i.e., pruned
69: **sea-marge**: seashore
70: **queen o' th' sky**: i.e., Juno, wife of Jupiter (i.e., Jove) and queen of the Roman gods

PROSPERO
    Dearly, my delicate Ariel. Do not approach
    Till thou dost hear me call.

ARIEL
                        Well; I conceive.   50
                                                            Exit

PROSPERO
    [*To FERDINAND*] Look thou be true! Do not give dalliance
    Too much the rein; the strongest oaths are straw
    To th' fire i' th' blood. Be more abstemious,
    Or else good night your vow.

FERDINAND
                        I warrant you, sir,
    The white cold virgin snow upon my heart   55
    Abates the ardor of my liver.

PROSPERO
                    Well.
    Now come, my Ariel. Bring a corollary
    Rather than want a spirit. Appear, and pertly!
                                                    Soft music
    [*To FERDINAND and MIRANDA*] No tongue! All eyes! Be silent!
                                                    Enter IRIS

IRIS
    Ceres, most bounteous lady, thy rich leas   60
    Of wheat, rye, barley, vetches, oats, and pease;
    Thy turfy mountains, where live nibbling sheep,
    And flat meads thatched with stover, them to keep;
    Thy banks with pionèd and twillèd brims,
    Which spongy April at thy hest betrims   65
    To make cold nymphs chaste crowns; and thy broom groves,
    Whose shadow the dismissèd bachelor loves,
    Being lass-lorn; thy poll-clipped vineyard,
    And thy sea-marge sterile and rocky-hard,
    Where thou thyself dost air. The queen o' th' sky, 70

71: **wat'ry arch**: rainbow

72: **leave these**: i.e., all the haunts of Ceres just catalogued

74: **peacocks**: Juno's sacred birds, as doves were to Venus; here, of the peacocks draw her chariot; **amain**: at full speed

74: Stage Direction: *[Juno's chariot...stage]*: The Folio has *Juno descends* here, but this is too early; *descends* could serve merely to indicate the appearance of a deity floating overhead, i.e., descended from heaven.

81: **bosky**: bushy; **unshrubbed down**: plains

83: **short-grassed green**: manicured lawn (either implying that Prospero keeps the grounds around his cell distinct from the overgrowth of the island, or a self-conscious reference to the conditions of the Jacobean stage itself); see "In Production" essay

84-86: "A contract of true love to celebrate, / And some donation freely to estate / On the blessed lovers": Franchelle Stewart Dorn as Iris, Felicia Wilson as Juno, and Beverly Cosham as Ceres in the 1997 Shakespeare Theatre Company production directed by Garland Wright

Photo: Carol Rosegg

85: **estate**: bestow

86: **heavenly bow**: i.e., Iris

87: **her son**: Cupid, traditionally depicted as a blind or blindfolded boy

89: **Dis**: Pluto (from the Greek, "wealth," because the underworld contained vast riches)

88–89: **plot...got**: Cupid's arrow made Pluto (Dis) fall in love with Proserpine; according to Ovid, Venus was trying to extend her power into the underworld

90: **scandaled**: infamous

92: **her deity**: playful variation on "her majesty"

93: **Paphos**: in Cyprus, center of Venus's cult

96: **bed-right**: i.e., consummation

Whose wat'ry arch and messenger am I,
Bids thee leave these, and with her sovereign grace,
Here on this grass plot, in this very place,
To come and sport. Her peacocks fly amain.
                    [JUNO's chariot appears suspended over the stage]
Approach, rich Ceres, her to entertain.   75
                    Enter CERES [played by ARIEL]

CERES
    Hail, many-colored messenger, that ne'er
    Dost disobey the wife of Jupiter;
    Who, with thy saffron wings, upon my flow'rs
    Diffusest honey-drops, refreshing show'rs,
    And with each end of thy blue bow dost crown   80
    My bosky acres and my unshrubbed down,
    Rich scarf to my proud earth. Why hath thy queen
    Summoned me hither to this short-grassed green?

IRIS
    A contract of true love to celebrate,
    And some donation freely to estate   85
    On the blessed lovers.

CERES
                    Tell me, heavenly bow,
    If Venus or her son, as thou dost know,
    Do now attend the queen? Since they did plot
    The means that dusky Dis my daughter got,
    Her and her blind boy's scandaled company   90
    I have forsworn.

IRIS
                    Of her society
    Be not afraid. I met her deity
    Cutting the clouds toward Paphos, and her son
    Dove-drawn with her. Here thought they to have done
    Some wanton charm upon this man and maid,   95
    Whose vows are that no bed-right shall be paid
    Till Hymen's torches be lighted—but in vain.

Set Design from the 1951 Royal Shakespeare Company production directed by
Michael Benthall

Courtesy of Angus McBean, © Royal Shakespeare Company

98: Mars's...again: i.e., Venus, the sluttish mistress of Mars, has returned whence she
came (Venus's husband, Vulcan, once discovered her in bed with Mars, god of war)
99: waspish-headed: angry and inclined to sting (with his arrows)
100: play with sparrows: sparrows symbolized lechery, and so are fit playmates for
Cupid
101: boy...out: cease being a god, and become a boy outright
102: gait: bearing, carriage, procession (probably does not imply that Juno walks on
the stage)
103: Go with me: 1) enter my chariot, 2) join me (in singing)

105: Stage Direction: *They sing*: i.e., as a duet, not in unison. If Ceres has entered
Juno's chariot, the chariot may at this point rise and hover as they deliver their
benedictions.

108: still: always
110: foison: abundance
111: garners: granaries
114–115: Spring...harvest!: may spring begin for you as early as possible, at the end of
autumn; (Ceres' blessing cancels the effects of Proserpine's rape, namely barren
winter)
119: charmingly: 1) musically, 2) bewitchingly

Mars's hot minion is returned again;
Her waspish-headed son has broke his arrows,
Swears he will shoot no more, but play with sparrows   100
And be a boy right out.

CERES

                         Highest queen of state,
Great Juno comes; I know her by her gait.
                         [JUNO's chariot descends to the stage]

JUNO

[*To CERES*] How does my bounteous sister? Go with me
To bless this twain, that they may prosperous be,
And honored in their issue.   105
                                                            They sing

JUNO

     [*Sings*]
     In honor, riches, marriage-blessing,
     Long continuance, and increasing,
     Heavenly joys be still upon you!
     Juno sings her blessings on you.

[CERES]

     [*Sings*]
     Earth's increase, foison plenty,   110
     Barns and garners never empty,
     Vines with clust'ring bunches growing,
     Plants with goodly burden bowing;
     Spring come to you at the farthest,
     In the very end of harvest!   115
     Scarcity and want shall shun you;
     Ceres' blessing so is on you.

FERDINAND

This is a most majestic vision, and
Harmonious charmingly. May I be bold
To think these spirits?   120

123: wondered: wonderful; wife: a notorious textual crux: the Folio's "wiſe" had long been thought to be "wise," but the crossbar on the "f" had simply broken off during production—yielding a slightly less obsequious, more forthright Ferdinand)

124: Stage Direction: *on employment*: on a task (to summon the nymphs and the reapers; the exchange need not involve Juno and Ceres' speaking to Iris in turn, but perhaps merely pointing to her)

124: **Sweet**: i.e., 1) all right (an intensive), or 2) Ferdinand (a common term of male intimacy)

128: **windring**: a blend of "winding" and "wand'ring"

129: **sedged crowns**: garlands made of sedge, a river plant; **ever-harmless**: innocent

132: **temperate**: chaste (nymphs served Diana, the huntress-goddess of virginity)

133: Stage Direction: *certain NYMPHS*: Many nineteenth century productions introduced glade or grotto scenery here to show the nymphs emerging from the water, often accompanied by tritons.

137: **encounter**: join, pair up with

138: **country footing**: rustic dancing

138: Stage Direction: *properly habited*: suitably attired; *a graceful dance*: This bare direction leaves out the rationale for the dance; Tree imposed an elaborate narrative of courtship between the reapers and the nymphs, at one point involving (somewhat inappropriately, given the themes of the masque) Cupid shooting arrows at the latter. Ferdinand and Miranda sometimes join in, and Hall's 1974 version had the dance terminate the instant they entered. Juno's chariot hovered above the stage; *starts...vanish*: refers to the action immediately following the direction; the words Prospero "speaks" are his ensuing aside and dismissal of the spirits; *strange...noise*: i.e., musical harmony dissolves into discord; *heavily*: abruptly

139-140: "I had forgot that foul conspiracy / Of the beast Caliban and his confederates / Against my life": Ted van Griethuysen as Prospero in the 1997 Shakespeare Theatre Company production directed by Garland Wright

Photo: Carol Rosegg

PROSPERO
                    Spirits, which by mine art   120
I have from their confines called to enact
My present fancies.

FERDINAND
                Let me live here ever.
So rare a wondered father, and a wife
Makes this place paradise.
         JUNO and CERES whisper, and send IRIS on employment

PROSPERO
              Sweet now, silence!
Juno and Ceres whisper seriously.   125
There's something else to do. Hush, and be mute,
Or else our spell is marred.

IRIS
You nymphs, called Naiads, of the windring brooks,
With your sedged crowns and ever-harmless looks,
Leave your crisp channels, and on this green land   130
Answer your summons, Juno does command.
Come, temperate nymphs, and help to celebrate
A contract of true love. Be not too late.
                     Enter certain NYMPHS
You sunburned sicklemen, of August weary,
Come hither from the furrow, and be merry.   135
Make holiday: your rye-straw hats put on,
And these fresh nymphs encounter every one
In country footing.
       Enter certain REAPERS, (properly habited); they join
    with the NYMPHS in a graceful dance, towards the end whereof
        PROSPERO starts suddenly and speaks, after which,
    to a strange hollow and confused noise, they heavily vanish.

PROSPERO
[*Aside*] I had forgot that foul conspiracy
Of the beast Caliban and his confederates   140
Against my life: the minute of their plot

142: **avoid**: begone, disappear

142: Stage Direction: ***chariot ascends***: probably with Juno in it, if not Ceres as well, since it must exit the way it came and is no less magical a departure than that of the other spirits; but it may have been difficult to achieve this effect with the alacrity Prospero's command requires

tracks 23-26

146–163:
Donald Wolfit as Prospero
William Hutt as Prospero
Ian McKellen as Prospero

146: **movèd sort**: distressed state

148: **revels**: 1) entertainment, celebration, 2) the dance at the end of the masque in particular

149: **foretold you**: told you before

151: **baseless fabric**: structure without foundation or purpose

154: **it inherit**: possess it

156: **rack**: wisp (e.g., of cloud or mist)

157: **on**: of

164: **with a thought**: as swiftly as I think of you (i.e., instantly); **I thank thee**: Editors sometimes use Prospero's singular "thee," rather than the plural "you," to argue that he addresses Ariel; but the imminence of Caliban's plot makes it unlikely he would here thank (an as-yet absent) Ariel for the masque, and its belatedness, if addressed to either Ferdinand or Miranda, is consistent with his distraction.

Is almost come. [*To the spirits*] Well done, avoid! No more.

                [JUNO's chariot ascends. Exeunt spirits.]

FERDINAND

    This is strange. Your father's in some passion
    That works him strongly.

MIRANDA

                Never till this day
    Saw I him touched with anger, so distempered.   145

PROSPERO

    You do look, my son, in a movèd sort,
    As if you were dismayed. Be cheerful, sir;
    Our revels now are ended. These our actors,
    As I foretold you, were all spirits, and
    Are melted into air, into thin air;   150
    And, like the baseless fabric of this vision,
    The cloud-capped towers, the gorgeous palaces,
    The solemn temples, the great globe itself,
    Yea, all which it inherit, shall dissolve,
    And, like this insubstantial pageant faded,   155
    Leave not a rack behind. We are such stuff
    As dreams are made on, and our little life
    Is rounded with a sleep. Sir, I am vexed.
    Bear with my weakness, my old brain is troubled;
    Be not disturbed with my infirmity.   160
    If you be pleased, retire into my cell
    And there repose. A turn or two I'll walk
    To still my beating mind.

FERDINAND and MIRANDA

            We wish your peace.
               Exit [FERDINAND and MIRANDA]

PROSPERO

    [*To ARIEL*] Come, with a thought! [*To FERDINAND and MIRANDA*]
      I thank thee.—Ariel, come!
                    Enter ARIEL

Costume rendering for Ariel by Deborah M. Dryden from the 2007 Oregon Shakespeare Festival production directed by Libby Appel

Courtesy of Oregon Shakespeare Festival

167: **presented Ceres**: most likely "acted the part of," and the reason editors usually assign Ceres to Ariel, but possibly "introduced," making Ariel Iris, though the actor playing Ariel (a singer) would probably not have been given a non-singing part in the masque

170: **varlets**: 1) thugs, 2)slaves

174: **bending**: aiming

176: **unbacked**: unbroken, untamed

177: **Advanced**: raised

178: **As**: as if

182: **mantled**: covered with scum

184: **o'erstunk their feet**: a confusing insult. Since Stephano, Trinculo and Caliban are in it "up to th' chins," Ariel simply means that the pool smelled even worse than their feet.

186: **trumpery**: literally, 1) alluring surfaces, 2) worthless trickery (e.g., the shiny costumes, the "glistering apparel," with which Ariel returns)

187: **stale**: bait

ARIEL
Thy thoughts I cleave to. What's thy pleasure?

PROSPERO
                                        Spirit,   165
We must prepare to meet with Caliban.

ARIEL
Ay, my commander. When I presentèd Ceres
I thought to have told thee of it, but I feared
Lest I might anger thee.

PROSPERO
Say again, where didst thou leave these varlets?   170

ARIEL
I told you, sir, they were red-hot with drinking,
So full of valor that they smote the air
For breathing in their faces, beat the ground
For kissing of their feet; yet always bending
Towards their project. Then I beat my tabor,   175
At which like unbacked colts they pricked their ears,
Advanced their eyelids, lifted up their noses
As they smelt music; so I charm'd their ears
That, calf-like, they my lowing followed through
Toothed briars, sharp furze, pricking gorse, and thorns   180
Which entered their frail shins. At last I left them
I' th' filthy mantled pool beyond your cell,
There dancing up to th' chins, that the foul lake
O'er stunk their feet.

PROSPERO
                    This was well done, my bird.
Thy shape invisible retain thou still.   185
The trumpery in my house, go bring it hither
For stale to catch these thieves.

ARIEL
I go, I go.
                                                    Exit

THE TEMPEST [216

Philip Goodwin as Prospero and Michael Rudko as Alonso in the 2005 Shakespeare
Theatre Company production directed by Kate Whoriskey
Photo: Richard Termine

193: **cankers**: festers, rots

194: **line**: linden or lime tree, though modern productions, such as Benthall's (1951)
and Brook's (1990), have interpreted this as "clothesline"

197: **fairy**: i.e., Ariel

198: **played the jack with**: made a fool of (i.e., knave, as in cards)

199: **smell all**: smell all like

202: **look you**: i.e., watch out

206: **hoodwink this mischance**: eclipse or negate our bad luck (to hoodwink was to
cover the eyes with a cloth—compare "pull the wool over"; Caliban's prediction
proves ironic)

PROSPERO
A devil, a born devil, on whose nature
Nurture can never stick; on whom my pains,   190
Humanely taken all, all lost, quite lost.
And as with age his body uglier grows,
So his mind cankers. I will plague them all,
Even to roaring.
                        Enter ARIEL, laden with glistering apparel, etc.
                Come, hang them on this line.
                        [PROSPERO and ARIEL remain, invisible.]
                Enter CALIBAN, STEPHANO, and TRINCULO, all wet.

CALIBAN
Pray you tread softly, that the blind mole may not   195
Hear a footfall. We now are near his cell.

STEPHANO
Monster, your fairy—which you say is a harmless fairy—has done
little better than played the jack with us.

TRINCULO
Monster, I do smell all horse-piss, at which my nose is in great
indignation.   200

STEPHANO
So is mine. Do you hear monster? If I should take a displeasure
against you, look you—

TRINCULO
Thou wert but a lost monster.

CALIBAN
Good my lord, give me thy favor still.
Be patient, for the prize I'll bring thee to   205
Shall hoodwink this mischance. Therefore speak softly;
All's hushed as midnight yet.

TRINCULO
Ay, but to lose our bottles in the pool—

214: "Prithee, my King, be quiet": Chad Coleman as Caliban in the 1997 Shakespeare Theatre Company production directed by Garland Wright
Photo: Carol Rosegg

211: **more...wetting**: 1) more valuable to me than sustenance, 2) more troublesome to me than my being made wet
213: **fetch off**: 1) recover, 2) finish drinking; **o'er-ears**: submerged (here, Stephano may attempt to leave)
218: **For aye**: as well

220: Scene: **O...worthy Stephano!**: Trinculo invokes a popular song called "King Stephen was a worthy peer," a ballad about costly clothing; also alluded to in *Othello* 2.3.75-82. Trinculo may only now notice the clothes, or notice them during Caliban and Stephano's exchange; Stephano, knife drawn, is often approaching Prospero's cell when Trinculo diverts him.

222: **trash**: reminiscent of Prospero's earlier, surprisingly related usage at 1.2.82
223: **We know...frippery**: i.e., we know trash, and this is not it; **frippery**: second-hand clothing shop

223: Stage Direction: *[Puts on a robe]*: The clothes are presumably Prospero's old robes of state; Strehler (1978) made them those of Alonso's court, rescued from the supposedly wrecked ship, stressing the parallels between past and present conspirators.

226: Scene: **Thy grace shall have it**: Trinculo often concedes the garment reluctantly.

STEPHANO

There is not only disgrace and dishonor in that, monster, but an
infinite loss.   210

TRINCULO

That's more to me than my wetting; yet this is your harmless
fairy, monster!

STEPHANO

I will fetch off my bottle, though I be o'er-ears for my labor.

CALIBAN

Prithee, my King, be quiet. Seest thou here,
This is the mouth o' th' cell. No noise, and enter.   215
Do that good mischief which may make this island
Thine own forever, and I, thy Caliban,
For aye thy foot-licker.

STEPHANO

                        Give me thy hand.
I do begin to have bloody thoughts.

TRINCULO

O King Stephano, O peer, O worthy Stephano! Look what a   220
wardrobe is here for thee!

CALIBAN

Let it alone, thou fool! It is but trash.

TRINCULO

O ho, monster! We know what belongs to a frippery.
                                                [Puts on a robe]
O King Stephano!

STEPHANO

Put off that gown, Trinculo; by this hand, I'll have that gown.   225

TRINCULO

Thy grace shall have it.

227: **dropsy**: disease of excessive water accumulation in bodily tissue; used figuratively for any insatiable thirst; **this fool**: probably Trinculo, but possibly, Stephano

228: **luggage**: i.e., dead weight, junk

232: **Mistress Line**: Stephano addresses the lime tree as a woman (a necessary pretense for what follows)

233: **Now...line**: literally, "off the tree," but precipitates a dense network of obscene jokes; "under the line" could mean below a woman's waist, or past the equator, the torrid zone associated with carnality, sexually transmitted disease (e.g., syphilis) or any number of tropical fevers likewise resulting in hair loss

235: **Do, do**: go on (either stealing or punning); **by line and level**: according to the rules (with pun on "line"); **an't like**: if it please

238: **pass of pate**: thrust of wit

240: **lime**: birdlime, a sticky substance (hence appropriate for thievery); another pun on the type of tree

243: **barnacles**: either crustaceans or geese (then believed to be related animals)

244: **villainous**: vilely

245: **lay to**: apply

CALIBAN

The dropsy drown this fool! What do you mean
To dote thus on such luggage? Let't alone,
And do the murder first! If he awake,
From toe to crown he'll fill our skins with pinches,   230
Make us strange stuff.

STEPHANO

Be you quiet, monster. Mistress Line, is not this my jerkin?
                                        [Takes it down from the tree]
Now is the jerkin under the line; now, jerkin, you are like to lose
your hair, and prove a bald jerkin.

TRINCULO

Do, do! We steal by line and level, an't like your grace.   235

STEPHANO

I thank thee for that jest; here's a garment for it.
                            [Takes down a garment and gives it to him]
Wit shall not go unrewarded while I am king of this country!
"Steal by line and level" is an excellent pass of pate. There's
another garment for it.
                        [Takes down another garment and gives it to him]

TRINCULO

Monster, come put some lime upon your fingers, and away with   240
the rest.

CALIBAN

I will have none on't—we shall lose our time,
And all be turned to barnacles, or to apes
With foreheads villainous low.

STEPHANO

Monster, lay to your fingers. Help to bear this away, where my   245
hogshead of wine is, or I'll turn you out of my kingdom. Go to,
carry this—

TRINCULO

And this.

249: Stage Direction: *A noise of hunters*: may refer to Prospero and Ariel's subsequent calls, or to less articulate cries from offstage

249: Stage Direction: *Enter...hunting them about*: Tree's (1904) scene took place entirely inside Prospero's cell, which abruptly turned a dreadful color, with Stephano, Trinculo and Caliban being met by monsters at every direction they tried to escape; Macready (1838) and Burton (1854) used imps with dog heads, while Kean (1857) summoned apes, dogs, cyclopses, fire-fiends and serpents. Hall's (1974) dogs were bears, and Daniels' (1982) dog-skeletons; Wolfe's (1995) were shadow-puppets projected on a sheet-screen, while Benthall's (1951) shapes did not enter at all, but emerged from the rocky background in which they had been camouflaged and present all along.

252: "Fury, Fury! There, Tyrant, there! Hark, hark!": Patrick Stewart as Prospero in the 1995 Joseph Papp Public Theater production directed by George C. Wolfe
Photo: Michal Daniel

250–252: **Mountain**; **Silver**; **Tyrant**: Prospero and Ariel name the phantasmagoric dogs

253: **their**: i.e., Caliban's, Stephano's and Trinculo's

254: **dry**: resulting from a deficiency of humors or vital bodily fluids

256: **pard or cat o' mountain**: leopard or catamount (i.e., spotted animals); **roar**: presumably demanding offstage screams from Stephano, Trinculo and Caliban

257: **soundly**: 1) thoroughly, or 2) a play on Ariel's remark, i.e., loudly

261: Stage Direction: *Exeunt*: Prospero and Ariel both reappear for the opening of Act 5, taken by some as evidence for a cut scene, by others for an intentional act division; it most likely implies that an intermission—or perhaps an interlude—separated the acts in performance. If, as is suspected, the Folio text derives from a script prepared for production at the Blackfriars, the need to tend the candles that provided house lights for the indoor theater would have required an intermission between every act, probably filled with musical entertainment, but many modern stagings run this scene directly into the next.

STEPHANO
Ay, and this.

[They load CALIBAN with the remaining garments.]
A noise of hunters heard. Enter divers spirits
in shape of dogs and hounds, hunting them about,
PROSPERO and ARIEL setting them on.

PROSPERO
Hey, Mountain, hey!   250

ARIEL
Silver! There it goes, Silver!

PROSPERO
Fury, Fury! There, Tyrant, there! Hark, hark!
                    [CALIBAN, STEPHANO and TRINCULO are driven off]
Go charge my goblins that they grind their joints
With dry convulsions, shorten up their sinews
With agèd cramps, and more pinch-spotted make them   255
Than pard or cat o' mountain.

ARIEL
                    Hark, they roar!

PROSPERO
Let them be hunted soundly. At this hour
Lies at my mercy all mine enemies.
Shortly shall all my labors end, and thou
Shalt have the air at freedom. For a little,   260
Follow, and do me service.
                                                                    Exeunt

[The Tempest

Act 5

1: "Now does my project gather to a head": Vanessa Redgrave as Prospero and Geraldine Alexander as Ariel in the 2000 production at Shakespeare's Globe directed by Lenka Udovicki
Photo: Donald Cooper

2: **crack**: fail

2–3: **time...carriage**: walks upright (or moves quickly) because its carriage (i.e., the remaining hours of the day) is light; i.e., it is late

3: **How's the day?**: What time is it?

4: **sixth hour**: i.e., past prime (six o'clock in the afternoon; see 1.2.241)

10: **line-grove**: grove of lime trees; **weather-fends**: shields from the weather

11: **till your release**: until you release them

17: **eaves of reeds**: thatched roofs

Act 5, Scene 1]

PROSPERO
Now does my project gather to a head.
My charms crack not, my spirits obey, and time
Goes upright with his carriage. How's the day?

ARIEL
On the sixth hour, at which time, my lord,
You said our work should cease.

PROSPERO
                    I did say so   5
When first I raised the tempest. Say, my spirit,
How fares the king and's followers?

ARIEL
                      Confined together
In the same fashion as you gave in charge,
Just as you left them—all prisoners, sir,
In the line-grove which weather-fends your cell;   10
They cannot budge till your release. The king,
His brother, and yours, abide all three distracted,
And the remainder mourning over them
Brim full of sorrow and dismay; but chiefly
Him that you termed, sir, the good old Lord Gonzalo,   15
His tears runs down his beard like winter's drops
From eaves of reeds. Your charm so strongly works 'em
That if you now beheld them, your affections
Would become tender.

PROSPERO
                 Dost thou think so, spirit?

ARIEL
Mine would, sir, were I human.   20

20: Scene: **And mine shall**: Prospero's answer here ambiguously suggests either a confirmation or a persuasion, leaving open the possibility that he had not initially intended forgiveness; many contemporary productions prefer the latter reading, and this is potentially a key moment in performance as a result.

23-24: "One of their kind, that relish all as sharply / Passion as they, be kindlier moved than thou art?": Patrick Stewart as Prospero in the 1995 Joseph Papp Public Theater production directed by George C. Wolfe
Photo: Michal Daniel

23–24: **that relish...as they**: who experience suffering just as acutely as they do
25: **quick**: core, vital essence of one's being
33–50: **Ye elves...potent art**: The syntax of this apostrophe pivots on "by whose aid," at which point Prospero's catalogue shifts from descriptions of the spirits to a list of the feats he has achieved through them (and ends without a main verb); it closely parallels one of Medea's speeches from Ovid's *Metamorphoses*.
36: **demi-puppets**: little dolls
37: **green sour ringlets**: fairy rings (circular patches of sour grass caused by toad-stools, but thought to be the tracks of fairy-dances)
39: **midnight mushrumps**: mushrooms that grow overnight; **that**: i.e., you who
40: **curfew**: 1) the evening bell, rung at 9 p.m., or 2) the hour when spirits begin to roam
41: **masters**: agents or instruments (of magic); "weak" not just because Prospero can control them, but because they require Prospero's control to focus their power
45: **rifted**: split
46: **spurs**: roots
50: **rough**: brute
51: **required**: requested

PROSPERO

                       And mine shall.   20
Hast thou—which art but air—a touch, a feeling
Of their afflictions, and shall not myself,
One of their kind, that relish all as sharply
Passion as they, be kindlier moved than thou art?
Though with their high wrongs I am struck to th' quick,   25
Yet with my nobler reason 'gainst my fury
Do I take part. The rarer action is
In virtue than in vengeance. They being penitent,
The sole drift of my purpose doth extend
Not a frown further. Go, release them, Ariel;   30
My charms I'll break, their senses I'll restore,
And they shall be themselves.

ARIEL

                    I'll fetch them, sir.

                                             Exit

PROSPERO

Ye elves of hills, brooks, standing lakes, and groves,
And ye that on the sands with printless foot
Do chase the ebbing Neptune, and do fly him   35
When he comes back; you demi-puppets that
By moonshine do the green sour ringlets make,
Whereof the ewe not bites; and you whose pastime
Is to make midnight mushrumps, that rejoice
To hear the solemn curfew, by whose aid—   40
Weak masters though ye be—I have bedimmed
The noontide sun, called forth the mutinous winds,
And 'twixt the green sea and the azured vault
Set roaring war; to the dread rattling thunder
Have I given fire, and rifted Jove's stout oak   45
With his own bolt; the strong-based promontory
Have I made shake, and by the spurs plucked up
The pine and cedar; graves at my command
Have waked their sleepers, oped, and let 'em forth
By my so potent art. But this rough magic   50
I here abjure; and when I have required

53: **their senses that**: the senses of those whom

54: Scene: **break my staff**: Hall's 1988 production had Prospero actually do so here, though the language suggests it is only a promise.

57: Stage Direction: **_before_**: at the fore (i.e., leading the others in); **_a frantic gesture...like manner_**: Presumably Alonso, Antonio and Sebastian manifest their special harrowing in some way; Hall's (1974) Alonso tried to stab himself, only to be prevented by Gonzalo; Mendes's (1993) "men of sin" were filthier than anyone else; **_circle...had made_**: (during the preceding speech) At precisely what point is unclear, but he may be slowly tracing it with his staff throughout; many productions have him do it only during his renunciation. Ninagawa (1992) shined a wide spotlight instead; **_stand charmed_**: They cannot see or hear Prospero until he reveals himself at line 106; most courtiers freeze, but the courtiers in Ninagawa's production shuffled listlessly around the ring until named.

59: **unsettled fancy**: disturbed imagination

59–60: **cure thy brains...thy skull**: referring to Alonso, the leader of the party; as leader, he would be nearest to Prospero, as the following phrase ("There stand") implies

63: **sociable**: sympathetic; **show**: sight

64: **Fall**: let fall

65: **as the morning...so**: a metaphor for their awakening (yet it is still evening on the island)

66: **their rising senses**: Most productions show each character's trance gradually beginning to lift at the mention of their names; Antonio's, however, is never spoken.

70–71: **pay...Home**: repay your favors fully

76: **nature**: kinship; **whom**: often emended to "who," but if not a Folio misprint, a potentially useful insight into Prospero's confusion (or Shakespeare's) at this emotionally heightened moment

79–82: **Their understanding...muddy**: the captives' returning reason is like the sea gradually washing away the mud of low tide; as with "the charm dissolves apace," this phrase is as much performative (since Prospero is actively causing it to happen) as declarative.

82: **Not one of them**: i.e., there is not one of them

Some heavenly music—which even now I do—
To work mine end upon their senses that
This airy charm is for, I'll break my staff,
Bury it certain fathoms in the earth,   55
And deeper than did ever plummet sound
I'll drown my book.

> *Solemn music. Here enters ARIEL before; then ALONSO,*
> *with a frantic gesture, attended by GONZALO, SEBASTIAN; and*
> *ANTONIO, in like manner, attended by ADRIAN and*
> *FRANCISCO. They all enter the circle*
> *which PROSPERO had made, and there stand charmed,*
> *which, PROSPERO observing, speaks.*

A solemn air, and the best comforter
To an unsettled fancy, cure thy brains,
Now useless, boiled within thy skull! There stand,   60
For you are spell-stopped.
Holy Gonzalo, honorable man,
Mine eyes, ev'n sociable to the show of thine,
Fall fellowly drops. The charm dissolves apace,
And as the morning steals upon the night,   65
Melting the darkness, so their rising senses
Begin to chase the ignorant fumes that mantle
Their clearer reason. O good Gonzalo,
My true preserver, and a loyal sir
To him that follow'st, I will pay thy graces   70
Home both in word and deed. Most cruelly
Didst thou, Alonso, use me and my daughter.
Thy brother was a furtherer in the act;
Thou art pinched for't now, Sebastian. Flesh and blood,
You, brother mine, that entertained ambition,   75
Expelled remorse and nature; whom, with Sebastian—
Whose inward pinches therefore are most strong—
Would here have killed your king: I do forgive thee,
Unnatural though thou art. Their understanding
Begins to swell, and the approaching tide   80
Will shortly fill the reasonable shore,
That now lies foul and muddy. Not one of them

Sketch of *The Tempest* in 1845 by Kenny Meadows
© Shakespeare Birthplace Trust

84: **hat and rapier**: standard accessories of aristocratic dress
85: **discase**: disrobe
86: **sometime Milan**: i.e., when I was Duke of Milan
92: **After**: i.e., in pursuit of, as with migratory birds
96: Scene: **So, so, so**: The First Folio is silent about what Prospero's idle mutterings might mean; he may be stroking Ariel farewell, or fastidiously adjusting the attire Ariel has helped him don.
97: **To**: i.e., go to
100: **Being awake**: having been woken (by Ariel)
102: **drink the air**: i.e., devour the space between

106-134:

William Hutt as Prospero, Eric Donkin as Alonso, Brian Tree as Gonzalo
Donald Wolfit as Prospero, Richard Warner as Alonso, George Merritt as Gonzalo
Ian McKellen as Prospero, Roger Hammond as Alonso, David Burke as Gonzalo

tracks 27-30

That yet looks on me, or would know me. Ariel,
Fetch me the hat and rapier in my cell.

                    [Exit ARIEL and return immediately]
I will discase me, and myself present   85
As I was sometime Milan. Quickly, spirit!
Thou shalt ere long be free.

                  ARIEL sings, and helps to attire him

ARIEL
      Where the bee sucks, there suck I;
        In a cowslip's bell I lie;
      There I couch when owls do cry;   90
        On the bat's back I do fly
        After summer merrily.
      Merrily, merrily shall I live now,
      Under the blossom that hangs on the bough.

PROSPERO
Why, that's my dainty Ariel! I shall miss   95
Thee, but yet thou shalt have freedom. So, so, so.
To the king's ship, invisible as thou art;
There shalt thou find the mariners asleep
Under the hatches. The master and the boatswain
Being awake, enforce them to this place—   100
And presently, I prithee.

ARIEL
I drink the air before me, and return
Or ere your pulse twice beat.

                        Exit

GONZALO
All torment, trouble, wonder, and amazement
Inhabits here. Some heavenly power guide us   105
Out of this fearful country!

PROSPERO
               Behold, sir king,
The wrongèd Duke of Milan, Prospero.

tracks 27-30

106-134:
William Hutt as Prospero, Eric Donkin as Alonso, Brian Tree as Gonzalo
Donald Wolfit as Prospero, Richard Warner as Alonso, George Merritt
as Gonzalo
Ian McKellen as Prospero, Roger Hammond as Alonso, David Burke as Gonzalo

111: **Whe'er**: whether

112: **enchanted trifle**: trick of sorcery; **abuse**: deceive, mistreat

113: **have been**: i.e., thus abused

116: **crave**: need, entail

117: **story**: explanation

124: **subtleties**: 1) illusions, or 2) sugary dessert pastries, playing on "taste"

126–129: Scene: **But you...no tales**: Productions sometimes have Prospero deliver these lines in the full hearing of the other courtiers, making his promise not to expose their treachery quite Machiavellian in its contradiction; but Sebastian's accusatory response of witchcraft need not be a public denial of a public charge, and can simply be a private expression of fear.

126: **brace**: pair

127: **pluck**: lower, bring down

128: **justify**: prove

For more assurance that a living prince
Does now speak to thee, I embrace thy body,
And to thee, and thy company, I bid   110
A hearty welcome.

[Embraces ALONSO]

ALONSO
                        Whe'er thou beest he or no,
Or some enchanted trifle to abuse me,
As late I have been, I not know. Thy pulse
Beats as of flesh and blood; and, since I saw thee,
Th' affliction of my mind amends, with which,   115
I fear, a madness held me. This must crave—
An if this be at all—a most strange story.
Thy dukedom I resign, and do entreat
Thou pardon me my wrongs. But how should Prospero
Be living, and be here?

PROSPERO
                        [To GONZALO] First, noble friend,   120
Let me embrace thine age, whose honor cannot
Be measured or confined.

[Embraces GONZALO]

GONZALO
                        Whether this be,
Or be not, I'll not swear.

PROSPERO
                        You do yet taste
Some subtleties o' th' isle, that will not let you
Believe things certain. Welcome, my friends all.   125
[Aside to SEBASTIAN and ANTONIO] But you, my brace of lords,
        were I so minded,
I here could pluck his Highness' frown upon you,
And justify you traitors. At this time
I will tell no tales.

tracks 27-30

106-134:
William Hutt as Prospero, Eric Donkin as Alonso, Brian Tree as Gonzalo
Donald Wolfit as Prospero, Richard Warner as Alonso, George Merritt
as Gonzalo
Ian McKellen as Prospero, Roger Hammond as Alonso, David Burke as Gonzalo

129: Scene: **No**: Much depends on the force and direction of this statement; the actor and director must decide if Prospero is merely reiterating his vow of silence publicly, or privately rebutting Sebastian's scoff—in which case his tone may reflect anything from flared anger to casual dismissal. Nevertheless, he goes on to address Antonio openly.

130-134: Scene: **For you...must restore**: The text leaves uncertain not only Prospero's body language toward Antonio, and hence the sincerity of his forgiveness—Brook's 1990 Prospero embraced him coolly, Hytner's (1988) wept, and gave him a kiss so forced it seemed to turn his stomach—but also, more importantly, Antonio's silent response. Some Antonios, like Macready's (1838) and Donnellan's (1988), knelt in genuine humility and repentance, while Alexander's (1994) and Thacker's (1995) were more reluctant to surrender their title. Mendes's (1993) and Tipton's (1991) turned their backs, suggesting aloofness and even defiance.

139: **woe**: sorry

142: **of**: by

143: **her sovereign aid**: her (i.e., Patience's) help (here Patience is equated with the Virgin Mary metaphorically)

145: **late**: recent

145–146: **supportable...loss**: to make the grievous loss bearable (inverted syntax)

146: **have I means much weaker**: weaker because I lack the female compassion of a daughter (or simply another child), which Alonso still has in Claribel, and also because I lack courtiers

SEBASTIAN
>   [*Aside*] The devil speaks in him!

PROSPERO
>   No.
> [*To ANTONIO*] For you, most wicked sir, whom to call brother   130
> Would even infect my mouth, I do forgive
> Thy rankest fault—all of them—and require
> My dukedom of thee, which perforce I know
> Thou must restore.

ALONSO
>   If thou beest Prospero,
> Give us particulars of thy preservation;   135
> How thou hast met us here, who three hours since
> Were wrecked upon this shore, where I have lost—
> How sharp the point of this remembrance is!—
> My dear son Ferdinand.

PROSPERO
>   I am woe for't, sir.

ALONSO
> Irreparable is the loss, and patience   140
> Says it is past her cure.

PROSPERO
>   I rather think
> You have not sought her help, of whose soft grace
> For the like loss I have her sovereign aid,
> And rest myself content.

ALONSO
>   You the like loss?

PROSPERO
> As great to me as late; and supportable   145
> To make the dear loss, have I means much weaker
> Than you may call to comfort you; for I
> Have lost my daughter.

154: **admire**: wonder, stare in amazement (and, considering Prospero's sudden shift in subject, another pun on Miranda's name)
156: **do offices**: perform the function
157: **natural breath**: i.e., actually being spoken, rather than occurring in a dream (the clause is an extension of "scarce think")
160: **strangely**: wonderfully
163: **day by day**: i.e., to be told over many days
164: **relation**: story

165–167: Scene: **Welcome...look in**: Prospero here gestures at the mouth of his cell, inviting Alonso and his retinue to inspect it; for the original staging, however, this is a diversion so the actor can move to the discovery place unnoticed and reveal Ferdinand and Miranda.

171: Stage Direction: *discovers*: uncovers, discloses, probably by drawing aside a curtain to an area of the stage called the discovery place, located between the two stage doors (one door served as the courtiers' entrance, and the other as Prospero's cell, into which he has just invited them to look). Eighteenth and nineteenth century productions, with more realistic staging, actually opened the entrance to the cell to reveal them; in the twentieth century, Strehler's (1978) Prospero spread his robe and, when he stepped aside, Ferdinand and Miranda were behind it, while Brook's 1990 lovers physically entered, unseen, during Prospero's preceding speech; *playing at chess*: In Donnellan's 1988 production, Ferdinand was shown cheating by surreptitiously moving pieces. Hytner's (1988) lovers burst from Prospero's cell in a shower of chess pieces, which Miranda had flung at Ferdinand; they chased each other around the stage, with Ferdinand hugging the board for safety. Other productions have taken more literally the metaphor of chess play and sexual dalliance.

174: **wrangle**: contend; given Miranda's dismissal of Ferdinand's protest, however, the word also implies dishonest manipulation (paralleling the "kingdoms" of the chess match with the real-world territorial stakes of the play)

ALONSO

A daughter?
O heavens, that they were living both in Naples,
The king and queen there! That they were,   150
Myself I wish were mudded in that oozy bed
Where my son lies. When did you lose your daughter?

PROSPERO

In this last tempest. I perceive these lords
In this encounter do so much admire
That they devour their reason, and scarce think   155
Their eyes do offices of truth, their words
Are natural breath. But howsoe'er you have
Been jostled from your senses, know for certain
That I am Prospero, and that very duke
Which was thrust forth of Milan, who most strangely   160
Upon this shore, where you were wrecked, was landed
To be the lord on't. No more yet of this,
For 'tis a chronicle of day by day,
Not a relation for a breakfast, nor
Befitting this first meeting. Welcome, sir;   165
This cell's my court. Here have I few attendants,
And subjects none abroad. Pray you look in.
My dukedom since you have given me again,
I will requite you with as good a thing,
At least bring forth a wonder to content ye   170
As much as me my dukedom.

Here PROSPERO discovers FERDINAND
and MIRANDA playing at chess

MIRANDA
Sweet lord, you play me false.

FERDINAND

No, my dearest love,
I would not for the world.

MIRANDA
Yes, for a score of kingdoms you should wrangle,
And I would call it fair play.   175

176: **vision**: illusion

177: Scene: **A most high miracle**: often delivered as a sarcastic aside, depending on Sebastian's characterization as unregenerate, since Ferdinand's survival crushes his hopes

181–184: Scene: **O wonder...in't**: Generally treated as addressed to the whole stage, but even more ironic if to Antonio and Sebastian in particular; Barton had her kneel to her uncle, creating a disturbing parallel with Caliban's first sight of Stephano.

184: Scene: **'Tis...thee**: An index of Prospero's reconciliation: the line has been spoken variously with tender bemusement or with guarded pessimism, accompanied by a sudden protective move toward his daughter.

186: **eld'st**: longest

187-188: **Is she the goddess...thus together**: perhaps an instinctive superstitious assumption, since Alonso does not know Prospero was responsible. Compared to Ferdinand's first response to Miranda at 1.2.425-426, this is decidedly odd, since whereas Ferdinand's evidence was the beautiful song of a sea-nymph, Alonso may think he has already seen this goddess in the form of Ariel's harpy.

ALONSO

                              If this prove   175
    A vision of the island, one dear son
    Shall I twice lose.

SEBASTIAN

                    A most high miracle!

                              [FERDINAND comes forward]

FERDINAND
    Though the seas threaten, they are merciful—
    I have cursed them without cause.

                              [Kneels before ALONSO]

ALONSO

                         Now all the blessings
    Of a glad father compass thee about!   180
    Arise, and say how thou cam'st here.

                              [FERDINAND rises]

MIRANDA

                         O wonder!
    How many goodly creatures are there here!
    How beauteous mankind is! O brave new world,
    That has such people in't!

PROSPERO

                    'Tis new to thee.

ALONSO
    What is this maid with whom thou wast at play?   185
    Your eld'st acquaintance cannot be three hours.
    Is she the goddess that hath severed us
    And brought us thus together?

FERDINAND

                         Sir, she is mortal;
    But by immortal providence, she's mine.
    I chose her when I could not ask my father   190

196: **I am hers**: i.e., I am, therefore, likewise her second father

199: **remembrances**: reminiscences, reunions

200: **heaviness**: grief; guilt

201: **ere this**: before now

203: **you**: (ambiguous; either the gods or the young couple; if the former, however, Gonzalo reinforces Alonso's naively supernatural theory of events); **chalked...way**: charted the true course, as with a chalk line

205: **Milan...Milan**: i.e., the Duke (expelled) from the dukedom; **that**: so that; **issue**: i.e., Prospero's (male) descendents, Miranda's future children with Ferdinand

213: **When...own**: i.e., when we had lost our senses (with, however, other thematic resonances)

For his advice, nor thought I had one. She
Is daughter to this famous Duke of Milan,
Of whom so often I have heard renown,
But never saw before; of whom I have
Received a second life; and second father   195
This lady makes him to me.

ALONSO
                      I am hers.
But O, how oddly will it sound that I
Must ask my child forgiveness!

PROSPERO
                      There, sir, stop.
Let us not burden our remembrances with
A heaviness that's gone.

GONZALO
                      I have inly wept,   200
Or should have spoke ere this. Look down, you gods,
And on this couple drop a blessèd crown;
For it is you that have chalked forth the way
Which brought us hither.

ALONSO
                      I say amen, Gonzalo.

GONZALO
Was Milan thrust from Milan that his issue   205
Should become kings of Naples? O, rejoice
Beyond a common joy, and set it down
With gold on lasting pillars! In one voyage
Did Claribel her husband find at Tunis,
And Ferdinand her brother found a wife   210
Where he himself was lost; Prospero his dukedom
In a poor isle; and all of us, ourselves,
When no man was his own.

ALONSO [To FERDINAND and MIRANDA]
                      Give me your hands.

214: **still**: forever

215: Stage Direction: ***Enter Ariel...following***: Precisely how Ariel leads the Master and Boatswain is difficult to convey; Strehler's (1978) Ariel held the Boatswain's hand unbeknownst to him. This portion of the scene is often cut in performance, its necessary information about the state of the ship reapportioned elsewhere—thus solving, at least, the bizarre problem of the Master's presence onstage with no lines to speak; ***amazedly***: in a stupefied trance

218: **blasphemy**: inveterate blasphemer, blasphemy personified (although it was Sebastian who had accused the Boatswain of cursing)

219: **swear'st grace o'erboard**: drives God's grace from the ship by swearing

220: **Hast...news?**: Since Gonzalo's interrogatives shift from pointed taunts to more basic inquiry, he may pause between them to register the Boatswain's total speech-lessness.

223: **three glasses since**: three hours ago; **gave out**: declared

224: **yare**: trim, seaworthy

225: **all this service**: Ariel thus accounts for why it has taken him considerably longer to return than "ere your pulse twice beat" (5.1.103)

226: **tricksy**: playful; resourceful

232: **several**: various

235: **straightway at liberty**: instantly set free

236: **trim**: garments

236–237: **freshly...ship**: i.e., saw our ship as fresh and unharmed as we were

Let grief and sorrow still embrace his heart
That doth not wish you joy.

GONZALO

Be it so—amen! 215
Enter ARIEL, with the MASTER and
BOATSWAIN, amazedly following

O, look, sir, look sir, here is more of us!
I prophesied if a gallows were on land
This fellow could not drown. [*To BOATSWAIN*] Now, blasphemy,
That swear'st grace o'er-board, not an oath on shore?
Hast thou no mouth by land? What is the news? 220

BOATSWAIN

The best news is, that we have safely found
Our king, and company; the next, our ship,
Which but three glasses since we gave out split,
Is tight and yare and bravely rigged as when
We first put out to sea.

ARIEL

[*Aside to PROSPERO*] Sir, all this service 225
Have I done since I went.

PROSPERO

[*Aside to ARIEL*] My tricksy spirit!

ALONSO

These are not natural events. They strengthen
From strange to stranger. Say, how came you hither?

BOATSWAIN

If I did think, sir, I were well awake,
I'd strive to tell you. We were dead of sleep, 230
And—how we know not—all clapped under hatches,
Where but even now, with strange and several noises
Of roaring, shrieking, howling, jingling chains,
And more diversity of sounds, all horrible,
We were awaked, straightway at liberty, 235
Where we, in all our trim, freshly beheld

236–237: **freshly...ship**: i.e., saw our ship as fresh and unharmed as we were

238: **Cap'ring to eye**: dancing for joy to see; **On a trice**: in an instant

239: **them**: i.e., the rest of the mariners

240: **moping**: 1) dazed, sluggish; dreaming, 2) grimacing (compare "mop and mow" 4.1.47)

244: **conduct**: conductor, director

245-247: "Sir, my liege, / Do not infest your mind with beating on / The strangeness of this business": Sam Waterston in the 1974 Mitzi E. Newhouse production directed by Edward Berkeley

Photo: George Joseph

247: **picked leisure**: moments of leisure time that we will find

248: **Which...single**: which will soon be continuous or uninterrupted (often broken as "which shall be shortly, single I'll resolve you"—i.e., privately; but the Folio phrasing is coherent as a modifier of "leisure," since both monarchs will soon retire from their civic duties); **resolve you**: i.e., resolve your questions with answers

249: **probable**: plausible; **every**: every one of

255: Stage Direction: ***Enter Ariel...stolen apparel***: Both "drives" and Prospero's "untie the spell" suggest that Stephano, Trinculo and Caliban still believe they are being chased by hounds. Though the frippery scene already suggested it, many productions make their "stolen apparel" explicitly royal garb; Hytner (1988) had both Stephano and Trinculo wearing crowns, which, since Prospero also wore one, both affirmed his legitimacy and called it into question.

256–257: **Every...himself**: The drunken Stephano gets his mercenary advice backwards; compare a similar reversal at 3.2.131-132.

257: **Coragio**: courage (Italian); **bully**: term of endearment and solidarity

258: **If...head**: i.e., if I trust the report of my eyes

Our royal, good, and gallant ship, our Master
Cap'ring to eye her. On a trice, so please you,
Even in a dream, were we divided from them,
And were brought moping hither.

ARIEL [*Aside to PROSPERO*]
                                    Was't well done?   240

PROSPERO [*Aside to ARIEL*]
Bravely, my diligence. Thou shalt be free.

ALONSO
This is as strange a maze as e'er men trod,
And there is in this business more than nature
Was ever conduct of. Some oracle
Must rectify our knowledge.

PROSPERO
                            Sir, my liege,   245
Do not infest your mind with beating on
The strangeness of this business. At picked leisure—
Which shall be shortly single—I'll resolve you,
Which to you shall seem probable, of every
These happened accidents; till when, be cheerful   250
And think of each thing well. [*Aside to ARIEL*] Come hither, spirit.
Set Caliban and his companions free;
Untie the spell.
                                         [*Exit ARIEL*]
        [*To ALONSO*] How fares my gracious sir?
There are yet missing of your company
Some few odd lads that you remember not.   255
                Enter ARIEL, driving in CALIBAN, STEPHANO
                and TRINCULO, in their stolen apparel

STEPHANO
Every man shift for all the rest, and let no man take care for himself—for all is but fortune. Coragio, bully monster, coragio!

TRINCULO
If these be true spies which I wear in my head, here's a goodly sight.

259–261: **O...me**: Caliban may kneel and grovel before Prospero here, but his lines can be read ambiguously as both a formal supplication and as a cynical aside to the audience.

259: **Setebos**: Sycorax's (and by extension Caliban's) god; see 1.2.375

260: **fine**: resplendent, regal

261: **chastise**: if merely "reprove," Caliban's fear seems oddly mild given the gravity of his situation; but the word is also linked to sexual deprivation, suggesting "castrate"

263: **Will money buy 'em?**: Are they for sale?

265: **badges**: liveries; heraldic devices worn as identification by servants of aristocratic households (may refer either to their underlying clothes or to their stolen ones)

266: **true**: honest

269: **deal...power**: direct the moon's influence 1) beyond its natural range of operation, or 2) beyond her (Sycorax's) immediate physical presence

273: **own**: claim yours

273–274: Scene: **this thing...mine**: Prospero's words are rich with significance but are vague in their intention; in performance he may do anything from strike Caliban to stroke him lovingly, depending on the humanity a production confers on both. It is next to impossible that he is admitting biological paternity, though Donellan's 1988 staging attempted this interpretation.

277: **reeling-ripe**: so drunk as to be on the verge of reeling (i.e., dancing or toppling over)

278: **gilded**: glazed over (perhaps also alluding to the coat of scum they retain from the pond, thus setting up Trinculo's pun on "pickle")

279: **pickle**: 1) predicament, 2) preserving liquor

CALIBAN

O Setebos, these be brave spirits indeed!
How fine my master is! I am afraid   260
He will chastise me.

SEBASTIAN

          Ha, ha!
What things are these, my Lord Antonio?
Will money buy 'em?

ANTONIO

             Very like. One of them
Is a plain fish and no doubt marketable.

PROSPERO

Mark but the badges of these men, my lords,   265
Then say if they be true. This misshapen knave,
His mother was a witch, and one so strong
That could control the moon, make flows and ebbs,
And deal in her command without her power.
These three have robbed me, and this demi-devil—   270
For he's a bastard one—had plotted with them
To take my life. Two of these fellows you
Must know and own; this thing of darkness I
Acknowledge mine.

CALIBAN

           I shall be pinched to death.

ALONSO

Is not this Stephano, my drunken butler?   275

SEBASTIAN

He is drunk now. Where had he wine?

ALONSO

And Trinculo is reeling-ripe. Where should they
Find this grand liquor that hath gilded 'em?
How cam'st thou in this pickle?

280: **pickle:** bath of preservatives
281: **fly-blowing:** i.e., corruption or decomposition
282: Scene: **Why...Stephano?:** Sebastian at this point lays a hand on Stephano—usually a slap on the back or a tap on the shoulder; his response at least implies an attempt at physical contact
284: **sirrah:** a contemptuous, belittling form of address
285: **sore:** 1) sorry, incompetent, 2) pained
287: **manners:** 1) courtesy, 2) morality
288: **As:** if
290: **trim:** fix up (with connotations either of "prepare" or "restore")

293-294: "Was I to take this drunkard for a god, / And worship this dull fool!": James Earl Jones as Caliban in the 1962 Delacorte Theater production directed by Gerald Freedman
Photo: George Joseph

291–294: Scene: **Ay, that I will...dull fool!:** As with his previous remark, Caliban's repentance may be genuine, grudging or altogether feigned; in many productions he indicates Stephano in the last two lines by kicking him, which still preserves the uncertainty of his remorse.
296: Stage Direction: *[Exeunt...Trinculo]:* The Folio prescribes no exit though most editors insert a collective one only after Sebastian's line, but this has real interpretive implications. Since Prospero's "go to" seems aimed at Caliban, and Alonso can command only Stephano and Trinculo (who are the only ones wearing the garments he tells them to "bestow"), Caliban ought to exit two lines earlier; but Prospero has also told him to escort his companions. If he lingers, is it defiance? If he obeys, is a departure also defiance, since Prospero's orders are themselves contradictory? Most productions avoid the problem of multiple exits—i.e., Prospero dismisses all three—but Strehler (1978) and Mendes (1993) each had Caliban leave via the trapdoor, as if willfully crawling back into his cave, while the other two went to the cell.

TRINCULO
I have been in such a pickle since I saw you last that I fear me will   280
never out of my bones. I shall not fear fly-blowing.

SEBASTIAN
Why, how now, Stephano?

STEPHANO
O, touch me not! I am not Stephano, but a cramp.

PROSPERO
You'd be king o' the isle, sirrah?

STEPHANO
I should have been a sore one then.   285

ALONSO
[*Indicating CALIBAN*] This is as strange a thing as e'er I looked on.

PROSPERO
He is as disproportioned in his manners
As in his shape. Go, sirrah, to my cell;
Take with you your companions. As you look
To have my pardon, trim it handsomely.   290

CALIBAN
Ay, that I will; and I'll be wise hereafter,
And seek for grace. What a thrice-double ass
Was I to take this drunkard for a god,
And worship this dull fool!

PROSPERO
                         Go to, away.

ALONSO
Hence, and bestow your luggage where you found it.   295

SEBASTIAN
Or stole it, rather.
                    [Exeunt CALIBAN, STEPHANO and TRINCULO]

297–313: Scene: **Sir, I invite...far off**: Prospero may begin gesturing the courtiers into his cell.

299: **waste**: spend, consume (not pejorative)
302: **accidents**: events
306: **solemnizèd**: accented on the second and fourth syllables
310: **take...strangely**: grip the listener wonderfully; **deliver**: 1) relate, 2) redeem
312: **sail**: i.e., voyage; **that**: that it

313: Scene: **My Ariel**: Prospero's valediction may or may not be an aside, potentially leaving the others mystified, since until now no one has been aware of Ariel; many productions move "*Exeunt omnes*" to before this, making Prospero's "draw near" directed at the audience.

315: Stage Direction: *[Exit ARIEL]*: Ariel's exit may occur with or after the others', or he may deserve his own; it has been variously realized as joyful, sad or angry. In nineteenth century productions, he often sang and took flight; Wright's Prospero followed his course with his eyes. Retallach's 1983 Ariel collapsed, his assumed body releasing his spirit, while freedom for Strehler's 1978 Ariel meant a *loss* of (theatrical) flight—Prospero unhooked him from his wires, and he ran out jubilantly into the audience. Mendes's 1993 Ariel, by contrast, spat in Prospero's face.

315: **draw near**: come in (to the cell; addressed to all, but Bridges-Adams's 1934 production cleared the stage except for Antonio, and Prospero spoke the line to him)

315: Stage Direction: *[Manet PROSPERO]*: Since Prospero's epilogue is not just that of an actor in a play but of a character in—and attempting to prolong—a fiction, rather than disrupt that fiction by exiting, he would probably remain onstage after motioning the other characters off.

PROSPERO

    Sir, I invite your highness and your train
    To my poor cell, where you shall take your rest
    For this one night, which part of it I'll waste
    With such discourse as I not doubt shall make it   300
    Go quick away—the story of my life,
    And the particular accidents gone by
    Since I came to this isle. And in the morn
    I'll bring you to your ship, and so to Naples,
    Where I have hope to see the nuptial   305
    Of these our dear-belov'd solemnizèd;
    And thence retire me to my Milan, where
    Every third thought shall be my grave.

ALONSO

                        I long
    To hear the story of thy life, which must
    Take the ear strangely.

PROSPERO

                  I'll deliver all,   310
    And promise you calm seas, auspicious gales,
    And sail so expeditious that shall catch
    Your royal fleet far off.—My Ariel, chick,
    That is thy charge. Then to the elements
    Be free, and fare thou well.

                      [Exit ARIEL]

        Please you draw near.   315
            Exeunt omnes. [Manet PROSPERO]

1–20:
Donald Wolfit as Prospero
William Hutt as Prospero
Ian McKellen as Prospero

0: Scene: *Epilogue*: Meant to be continuous with the preceding scene, but some-times given a different setting; Brook's 1957 Prospero, like Kean's (1857), stood on the deck of the departing ship. The epilogue is unusual in that Prospero addresses the audience in character rather than calling attention to himself as an actor; some pro-ductions, however, elaborate on the conventional humility of his appeal by having him remove his hat (or crown), take off his costume, and kneel. Many Prosperos, such as Burton's (1854), Daniels' (1982), Ninagawa's (1992), and Mendes's (1993), break their staff and/or discard their book (if they have not already done so in Act 5), but the text nowhere prescribes this act.

9: **bands**: bonds
10 **help...hands**: applause, the traditional request of epilogues; sudden, loud noises, like clapping, were thought to break spells
11–12: **Gentle...fill**: i.e., my sails can only be filled by your gentle breath (or kind opinion of the performance)

16: Scene: **prayer**: Putting his hands together forms the iconic gesture of prayer. Since Prospero's metaphor has shifted from release to a more violent ("assaults / Mercy") intercession with God, and since necromancy was a sin punishable by eternal damnation, it is unclear whether his plea here goes beyond mere applause.
18: **frees**: i.e., frees from
20: Stage Direction/Scene: *Exit*: Theatrical productions have often resisted treating Prospero' exit as the end of the play, and used it as the prelude to a final coda or tableau. Kean's (1857) for instance, had the ship sail off into the distance, while Coghill's (1949) Prospero appeared at the stern, to throw his book into the sea. Directors since the nineteenth century have also returned to the island and its abandoned inhabitants: Tree's (1904) production came back after a blackout to the sounds of an invisible Ariel, high above, singing "Where the bee sucks," with Caliban stretched across a rock watching the ship sail away (see introduction). Contempo-rary stagings have turned the same device to even more ironic effect: Barton's and Ciulei's (1981) Calibans crept on during Prospero's epilogue, stole the fragments of his staff, and slunk away; Miller's 1970 Ariel entered afterward, pieced the staff back together, and held it aloft.

Epilogue]

Spoken by PROSPERO

Now my charms are all o'erthrown,
And what strength I have's mine own,
Which is most faint. Now 'tis true
I must be here confined by you,
Or sent to Naples. Let me not,   5
Since I have my dukedom got
And pardoned the deceiver, dwell
In this bare island by your spell;
But release me from my bands
With the help of your good hands.   10
Gentle breath of yours my sails
Must fill, or else my project fails,
Which was to please. Now I want
Spirits to enforce, art to enchant;
And my ending is despair   15
Unless I be relieved by prayer,
Which pierces so that it assaults
Mercy itself, and frees all faults.
As you from crimes would pardoned be,
Let your indulgence set me free.   20

Exit

A Voice Coach's Perspective on Speaking Shakespeare

KEEPING SHAKESPEARE PRACTICAL

Andrew Wade

Introduction to Speaking Shakespeare: Sir Derek Jacobi
Speaking Shakespeare: Andrew Wade with John Tufts

Why, you might be wondering, is it so important to keep Shakespeare practical? What do I mean by practical? Why is this the way to discover how to speak the text and understand it?

Plays themselves are not simply literary events—they demand interpreters in the deepest sense of the word, and the language of Shakespeare requires, therefore, not a vocal demonstration of writing techniques but an imaginative response to that writing. The key word here is imagination. The task of the voice coach is to offer relevant choices to the actor so that the actor's imagination is titillated, excited by the language, which he or she can then share with an audience, playing on that audience's imagination. Take the word "IF"—it is only composed of two letters when written, but if you say it aloud and listen to what it implies, then your reaction, the way the word plays through you, can change the perception of meaning. "Ifffffffff"… you might hear and feel it implying "possibilities," "choices," "questioning," "trying to work something out." The saying of this word provokes active investigation of thought. What an apt word to launch a play: "If music be the food of love, play on" (Act 1, Scene 1 in *Twelfth Night, or What You Will*). How this word engages the listener and immediately sets up an involvement is about more than audibility. How we verbalize sounds has a direct link to meaning and understanding. In the words of Touchstone in *As You Like It*, "Much virtue in if."

I was working with a company in Vancouver on *Macbeth,* and at the end of the first week's rehearsal—after having explored our voices and opening out different pieces of text to hear the possibilities of the rhythm, feeling how the meter affects the thinking and feeling, looking at structure and form— one of the actors admitted he was also a writer of soap operas and that I had completely changed his way of writing. Specifically, in saying a line like, "The multitudinous seas incarnadine / Making the green one red" he heard the complexity of meaning revealed in the use of polysyllabic words becom- ing monosyllabic, layered upon the words' individual dictionary definitions. The writer was reminded that merely reproducing the speech of everyday life was nowhere near as powerful and effective as language that is shaped.

Do you think soap operas would benefit from rhyming couplets? Somehow this is difficult to imagine! But, the writer's comments set me thinking. As I am constantly trying to find ways of exploring the acting process, of opening out actors' connection with language that isn't their own, I thought it would be a good idea to involve writers and actors in some practical work on language. After talking to Cicely Berry (Voice Director, the Royal Shakespeare Company) and Colin Chambers (the then RSC Production Adviser), we put together a group of writers and actors who were interested in taking part. It was a fasci- nating experience all round, and it broke down barriers and misconceptions.

The actors discovered, for instance, that a writer is not coming from a very different place as they are in their creative search; that an idea or an image may result from a struggle to define a gut feeling and not from some crafted, well-formed idea in the head. The physical connection of language to the body was reaffirmed. After working with a group on Yeats' poem *Easter 1916*, Ann Devlin changed the title of the play she was writing for the Royal Shakespeare Company to *After Easter*. She had experienced the poem read aloud by a circle of participants, each voice becoming a realization of the shape of the writing. Thus it made a much fuller impact on her and caused her thinking to shift. Such practical exchanges, through language work and voice, feed and stimulate my work to go beyond making sure the actors' voices are technically sound.

It is, of course, no different when we work on a Shakespeare play. A similar connection with the language is crucial. Playing Shakespeare, in many ways, is crafted instinct. The task is thus to find the best way to tap into someone's imagination. As Peter Brook put it, "People forget that a text is dumb. To make it speak, one must create a communication machine. A living network, like a nervous system, must be made if a text which comes from far away is to touch the sensibility of the present."

This journey is never to be taken for granted. It is the process that every text must undergo every time it is staged. There is no definitive rehearsal that would solve problems or indicate ways of staging a given play. Again, this is where creative, practical work on voice can help forge new meaning by offering areas of exploration and challenge. The central idea behind my work comes back to posing the question, "How does meaning change by speaking out aloud?" It would be unwise to jump hastily to the end process for, as Peter Brook says, "Shakespeare's words are records of the words that he wanted spoken, words issuing from people's mouths, with pitch, pause and rhythm and gesture as part of their meaning. A word does not start as a word—it is the end product which begins as an impulse, stimulated by attitude and behavior which dictates the need for expression" (1).

PRACTICALLY SPEAKING

Something happens when we vocalize, when we isolate sounds, when we start to speak words aloud, when we put them to the test of our physicality, of our anatomy. We expose ourselves in a way that makes taking the language back more difficult. Our body begins a debate with itself, becomes alive with the vibrations of sound produced in the mouth or rooted deep in the muscles that aim at defining sound. In fact, the spoken words bring into play all the senses, before sense and another level of meaning are reached.

"How do I know what I think, until I see what I say," Oscar Wilde once said. A concrete illustration of this phrase was reported to me when I was leading a workshop recently. A grandmother said the work we had done that day reminded her of what her six-year-old grandson had said to his mother while they were driving through Wales: "Look, mummy, sheep! Sheep! Sheep!" "You don't have to keep telling us," the mother replied, but the boy said, "How do I know they're there, if I don't tell you?!"

Therefore, when we speak of ideas, of sense, we slightly take for granted those physical processes which affect and change their meaning. We tend to separate something that is an organic whole. In doing so, we become blind to the fact that it is precisely this physical connection to the words that enables the actors to make the language theirs.

The struggle for meaning is not just impressionistic theater mystique; it is an indispensable aspect of the rehearsal process and carries on during the life of every production. In this struggle, practical work on Shakespeare is vital and may help spark creativity and shed some light on the way meaning is born into language. After a performance of *More Words*, a show devised and directed by Cicely Berry and myself, Katie Mitchell (a former artistic director of The Other Place in Stratford-upon-Avon) gave me an essay by Ted Hughes that echoes with the piece. In it, Ted Hughes compares the writing of a poem—the coming into existence of words—to the capture of a wild animal. You will notice that in the following passage Hughes talks of "spirit" or "living parts" but never of "thought" or "sense." With great care and precaution, he advises, "It is better to call [the poem] an assembly of living parts moved by a single spirit. The living parts are the words, the images, the rhythms. The spirit is the life which inhabits them when they all work together. It is impossible to say which comes first, parts or spirit."

This is also true of life in words, as many are connected directly to one or several of our senses. Here Hughes talks revealingly of "the five senses," of "word," "action," and "muscle," all things which a practical approach to language is more likely to allow one to perceive and do justice to.

Words that live are those which we hear, like "click" or "chuckle," or which we see, like "freckled" or "veined," or which we taste, like "vinegar" or "sugar," or touch, like "prickle" or "oily," or smell, like "tar" or "onion," words which belong to one of the five senses. Or words that act and seem to use their muscles, like "flick" or "balance" (2).

In this way, practically working on Shakespeare to arrive at understanding lends itself rather well, I think, to what Adrian Noble (former artistic director of the RSC) calls "a theater of poetry," a form of art that, rooted deeply in its classical origins, would seek to awaken the imagination of its audiences through love and respect for words while satisfying our eternal craving for myths and twice-told tales.

This can only be achieved at some cost. There is indeed a difficult battle to fight and hopefully to win: "the battle of the word to survive." This phrase was coined by Michael Redgrave at the beginning of the 1950s, a period when theater began to be deeply influenced by more physical forms, such as mime (3). Although the context is obviously different, the fight today is of the same nature.

LISTENING TO SHAKESPEARE

Because of the influence of television, our way of speaking as well as listening has changed. It is crucial to be aware of this. We can get fairly close to the way *Henry V* or *Hamlet* was staged in Shakespeare's time; we can try also to reconstruct the way English was spoken. But somehow, all these fall short of the real and most important goal: the Elizabethan ear. How did one "hear" a Shakespeare play? This is hardest to know. My personal view is that we will probably never know for sure. We are, even when we hear a Shakespeare play or a recording from the past, bound irrevocably to modernity. The Elizabethan ear was no doubt different from our own, as people were not spoken to or entertained in the same way. A modern voice has to engage us in a different way in order to make us truly listen in a society that seems to rely solely on the belief that image is truth, that it is more important to show than to tell.

Sometimes, we say that a speech in Shakespeare, or even an entire production, is not well-spoken, not up to standard. What do we mean by that? Evidently, there are a certain number of "guidelines" that any actor now has to know when working on a classical text. Yet, even when these are known, actors still have to make choices when they speak. A sound is not a sound without somebody to lend an ear to it: rhetoric is nothing without an audience.

There are a certain number of factors that affect the receiver's ear. These can be cultural factors such as the transition between different acting styles or the level of training that our contemporary ear has had. There are also personal and emotional factors. Often we feel the performance was not well-spoken because, somehow, it did not live up to our expectations of how we think it should have been performed. Is it that many of us have a self-conscious model, perhaps our own first experience of Shakespeare, that meant something to us and became our reference point for the future (some treasured performance kept under glass)? Nothing from then on can quite compare with that experience.

Most of the time, however, it is more complex than nostalgia. Take, for example, the thorny area of accent. I remind myself constantly that audibility is not embedded in Received Pronunciation or Standard American. The familiarity that those in power have with speech and the articulate confidence gained from coming from the right quarters can lead us all to hear certain types of voices as outshining others. But, to my mind, the role of theater is at least to question these assumptions so that we do not perpetuate those givens but work towards a broader tolerance.

In Canada on a production of *Twelfth Night*, I was working with an actor who was from Newfoundland. His own natural rhythms in speaking seemed completely at home with Shakespeare's. Is this because his root voice has direct links back to the voice of Shakespeare's time? It does seem that compared to British dialects, which are predominantly about pitch, many North American dialects have a wonderful respect and vibrancy in their use of vowels. Shakespeare's language seems to me very vowel-aware. How useful it is for an actor to isolate the vowels in the spoken words to hear the music they produce, the rich patterns, their direct connection to feelings. North Americans more easily respond to this and allow it to feed their speaking. I can only assume it is closer to how the Elizabethans spoke.

In *Othello* the very names of the characters have a direct connection to one vowel in particular. All the male names, except the Duke, end in the sound OH: Othello, Cassio, Iago, Brabantio, etc. Furthermore, the sound OH ripples through the play both consciously and unconsciously. "Oh" occurs repeatedly and, more interestingly, is contained within other words: "so," "soul," and "know." These words resonate throughout the play, reinforcing another level of meaning. The repetition of the same sounds affects us beyond what we can quite say.

Vowels come from deep within us, from our very core. We speak vowels before we speak consonants. They seem to reveal the feelings that require the consonants to give the shape to what we perceive as making sense.

Working with actors who are bilingual (or ones for whom English is not the native language) is fascinating because of the way it allows the actor to have an awareness of the cadence in Shakespeare. There seems to be an objective perception to the musical patterns in the text, and the use of alliteration and assonance are often more easily heard not just as literary devices, but also as means by which meaning is formed and revealed to an audience.

Every speech pattern (i.e., accent, rhythm) is capable of audibility. Each has its own music, each can become an accent when juxtaposed against another. The point at which a speech pattern becomes audible is in the dynamic of the physical making of those sounds. The speaker must have the desire to get through to a listener and must be confident that every speech pattern has a right to be heard.

SPEAKING SHAKESPEARE

So, the way to speak Shakespeare is not intrinsically tied to a particular sound; rather, it is how a speaker energetically connects to that language. Central to this is how we relate to the form of Shakespeare. Shakespeare employs verse, prose, and rhetorical devices to communicate meaning. For example, in *Romeo and Juliet*, the use of contrasts helps us to quantify Juliet's feelings: "And learn me how to lose a winning match," "Whiter than new snow upon a raven's back." These extreme opposites, "lose" and "winning," "new snow" and "raven's back," are her means to express and make sense of her feelings.

On a more personal note, I am often reminded how much, as an individual, I owe to Shakespeare's spoken word. The rather quiet and inarticulate schoolboy I once was found in the speaking and the acting of those words a means to quench his thirst for expression.

NOTES:

(1) Peter Brook, *The Empty Space* (Harmondsworth: Penguin, 1972)

(2) Ted Hughes, *Winter Pollen* (London: Faber and Faber, 1995)

(3) Michael Redgrave, *The Actor's Ways and Means*
    (London: Heinemann, 1951)

In the Age of Shakespeare

Thomas Garvey

One of the earliest published pictures of Shakespeare's birthplace, from an original watercolor by Phoebe Dighton (1834)

The works of William Shakespeare have won the love of millions since he first set pen to paper some four hundred years ago, but at first blush, his plays can seem difficult to understand, even willfully obscure. There are so many strange words: not fancy, exactly, but often only half-familiar. And the very fabric of the language seems to spring from a world of forgotten assumptions, a vast network of beliefs and superstitions that have long been dispelled from the modern mind.

In fact, when "Gulielmus filius Johannes Shakespeare" (Latin for "William, son of John Shakespeare") was baptized in Stratford-upon-Avon in 1564, English itself was only just settling into its current form; no dictionary had yet been written, and Shakespeare coined hundreds of words himself. Astronomy and medicine were entangled with astrology and the occult arts; democracy was waiting to be reborn; and even educated people believed in witches and fairies, and that the sun revolved around the Earth. Yet somehow Shakespeare still speaks to us today, in a voice as fresh and direct as the day his lines were first spoken, and to better understand both their artistic depth and enduring power, we must first understand something of his age.

REVOLUTION AND RELIGION

Shakespeare was born into a nation on the verge of global power, yet torn by religious strife. Henry VIII, the much-married father of Elizabeth I, had

From *The Book of Martyrs* (1563), this woodcut shows the Archbishop of Canterbury being burned at the stake in March 1556

Map of London ca. 1625

defied the Pope by proclaiming a new national church, with himself as its head. After Henry's death, however, his daughter Mary reinstituted Catholicism via a murderous nationwide campaign, going so far as to burn the Archbishop of Canterbury at the stake. But after a mere five years, the childless Mary also died, and when her half-sister Elizabeth was crowned, she declared the Church of England again triumphant.

In the wake of so many religious reversals, it is impossible to know which form of faith lay closest to the English heart, and at first, Elizabeth was content with mere outward deference to the Anglican Church. Once the Pope hinted her assassination would not be a mortal sin, however, the suppression of Catholicism grew more savage, and many Catholics— including some known in Stratford—were hunted down and executed, which meant being hanged, disemboweled, and carved into quarters. Many scholars suspect that Shakespeare himself was raised a Catholic (his father's testament of faith was found hidden in his childhood home). We can speculate about the impact this religious tumult may have had on his plays. Indeed, while explicit Catholic themes, such as the description of Purgatory in *Hamlet*, are rare, the larger themes of disguise and double allegiance are prominent across the canon. Prince Hal offers false friendship to Falstaff in the histories, the heroines of the comedies are forced to disguise themselves as men, and the action of the tragedies is driven by double-dealing villains. "I am not what I am," Iago tells us (and himself) in *Othello*, summing up in a single stroke what may have been Shakespeare's formative social and spiritual experience.

If religious conflict rippled beneath the body politic like some ominous undertow, on its surface the tide of English power was clearly on the rise. The defeat of the Spanish Armada in 1588 had established Britain as a global power; by 1595 Sir Walter Raleigh had founded the colony of Virginia (named for the Virgin Queen), and discovered a new crop, tobacco, which would inspire a burgeoning international trade. After decades of strife and the threat of invasion, England enjoyed a welcome stability. As the national coffers grew, so did London; over the course of Elizabeth's reign, the city would nearly double in size to a population of some 200,000.

Hornbook from Shakespeare's lifetime

A 1639 engraving of a scene from a royal state visit of Marie de Medici depicts London's packed, closely crowded half-timbered houses.

FROM COUNTRY TO COURT

The urban boom brought a new dimension to British life—the mentality of the metropolis. By contrast, in Stratford-on-Avon, the rhythms of the rural world still held sway. Educated in the local grammar school, Shakespeare was taught to read and write by a schoolmaster called an "abecedarian", and as he grew older, he was introduced to logic, rhetoric, and Latin. Like most schoolboys of his time, he was familiar with Roman mythology and may have learned a little Greek, perhaps by translating passages of the New Testament. Thus while he never attended a university, Shakespeare could confidently refer in his plays to myths and legends that today we associate with the highly educated.

Beyond the classroom, however, he was immersed in the life of the countryside, and his writing all but revels in its flora and fauna, from the wounded deer of *As You Like It* to the herbs and flowers which Ophelia scatters in *Hamlet*. Pagan rituals abounded in the rural villages of Shakespeare's day, where residents danced around maypoles in spring, performed "mummers' plays" in winter, and recited rhymes year-round to ward off witches and fairies.

The custom most pertinent to Shakespeare's art was the medieval "mystery play," in which moral allegories were enacted in country homes and village squares by troupes of traveling actors. These strolling players—usually four men and two boys who played the women's roles—often lightened the moralizing with bawdy interludes in a mix of high and low feeling, which would become a defining feature of Shakespeare's art. Occasionally even a professional troupe, such as Lord Strange's Men, or the Queen's Men, would arrive in town, perhaps coming straight to Shakespeare's door (his father was the town's bailiff) for permission to perform.

Rarely, however, did such troupes stray far from their base in London, the nation's rapidly expanding capital and cultural center. The city itself had existed since the time of the Romans (who built the original London Bridge), but it was not until the Renaissance that its population spilled beyond its ancient walls and began to grow along (and across) the Thames, by whose banks the Tudors had built their glorious palaces. It was these two contradictory worlds—a modern metropolis cheek-by-jowl with a medieval court—that provided the two very different audiences who applauded Shakespeare's plays.

Londoners both high and low craved distraction. Elizabeth's court constantly celebrated her reign with dazzling pageants and performances that required a local pool of professional actors and musicians. Beyond the graceful landscape of the royal parks, however, the general populace was packed into little more than a square mile of cramped and crooked streets where theatrical entertainment was frowned upon as compromising public morals.

Just outside the jurisdiction of the city fathers, however, across the twenty arches of London Bridge on the south bank of the Thames, lay the wilder district of "Southwark." A grim reminder of royal power lay at the end of the bridge—the decapitated heads of traitors stared down from pikes at passersby. Once beyond their baleful gaze, people found the amusements they desired, and their growing numbers meant a market suddenly existed for daily entertainment. Bear-baiting and cockfighting flourished, along with taverns, brothels, and even the new institution of the theater.

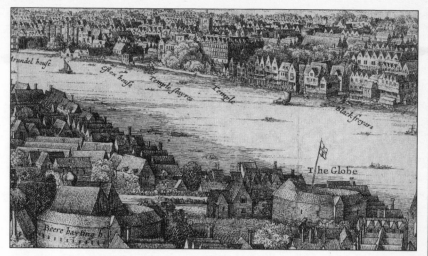

Southwark, as depicted in Hollar's long view of London (1647). Blackfriars is on the top right and the labels of Bear-baiting and the Globe were inadvertently reversed.

THE ADVENT OF "THE THEATRE"

The first building in England designed for the performance of plays—called, straightforwardly enough, "The Theatre"—was built in London when Shakespeare was still a boy. It was owned by James Burbage, father of Richard Burbage, who would become Shakespeare's lead actor in the acting company the Lord Chamberlain's Men. "The Theatre," consciously or unconsciously, resembled the yards in which traveling players had long plied their trade—it was an open-air polygon, with three tiers of galleries surrounding a canopied stage in a flat central yard, which was ideal for the athletic competitions the building also hosted. The innovative arena must have found an appreciative audience, for it was soon joined by the Curtain, and then the Rose, which was the first theater to rise in Southwark among the brothels, bars, and bear-baiting pits.

Even as these new venues were being built, a revolution in the drama itself was taking place. Just as Renaissance artists turned to classical models for inspiration, so English writers looked to Roman verse as a prototype for the new national drama. "Blank verse," or iambic pentameter (that is, a poetic line with five alternating stressed and unstressed syllables), was an adaptation of Latin forms, and first appeared in England in a translation of Virgil's *Aeneid*. Blank verse was first spoken on stage in 1561, in the now-forgotten *Gorboduc*, but it was not until the brilliant Christopher Marlowe (born the same year as Shakespeare) transformed it into the "mighty line" of such plays as *Tamburlaine* (1587) that the power and flexibility of the form made it the baseline of English drama.

Marlowe—who, unlike Shakespeare, had attended college—led the "university wits," a clique of hard-living free thinkers who in between all manner of exploits managed to define a new form of theater. The dates of Shakespeare's arrival in London are unknown—we have no record of him in Stratford after 1585—but by the early 1590s he had already absorbed the essence of Marlowe's invention, and begun producing astonishing innovations of his own.

While the "university wits" had worked with myth and fantasy, however, Shakespeare turned to a grand new theme, English history—penning the three-part saga of *Henry VI* in or around 1590. The trilogy was such a success that Shakespeare became the envy of his circle—one unhappy competitor, Robert Greene, even complained in 1592 of "an upstart crow...beautified with our feathers...[who is] in his own conceit the only Shake-scene in a country."

Such jibes perhaps only confirmed Shakespeare's estimation of himself, for he began to apply his mastery of blank verse in all directions, succeeding at tragedy (*Titus Andronicus*), farce (*The Comedy of Errors*), and romantic comedy (*The Two Gentlemen of Verona*). He drew his plots from everywhere: existing poems, romances, folk tales, even other plays. In fact a number of Shakespeare's dramas (*Hamlet* included) may be revisions of earlier texts owned by his troupe. Since copyright laws did not exist, acting companies usually kept their texts close to their chests, only allowing publication when a play was no longer popular, or, conversely, when a play was *so* popular (as with *Romeo and Juliet*) that unauthorized versions had already been printed.

Demand for new plays and performance venues steadily increased. Soon, new theaters (the Hope and the Swan) joined the Rose in Southwark, followed shortly by the legendary Globe, which opened in 1600. (After some trouble with their lease, Shakespeare's acting troupe, the Lord

penďeſt on to meane a ſtap . Baſe minďeď men all thꝛee
of you,if by my miſerie you be not warnď:foꝛ vnto none
of you (like mee) ſought thoſe burres to cleaue : thoſe
Puppets(I meane)that ſpake from our mouths, thoſe
Anticks garniſht in our colours. Is it not ſtrange,that
I,to whom they all haue beene beholding: is it not like
that you,to whome they all haue beene beholding, ſhall
(were yee in that caſe as I am now) bee both at once of
them foꝛſaken ? Yes truſt them not : foꝛ there is an vp-
ſtart Crow, beautifieď with our feathers, that with his
Tygers hart wrapt in a Players hyde, ſuppoſes he is as
well able to bombaſt out a blanke verſe as the beſt of
you : anď beeing an abſolute Iohannes fac totum,is in
his owne conceit the onely Shake-ſcene in a countrey.
O that I might intreat your rare wits to be imploieď in
moꝛe pꝛofitable courſes : ꝙ let thoſe Apes imitate your
paſt excellence, anď neuer moꝛe acquaint them with
your admireď inuentions . I knowe the beſt huſbanď of

Greene's insult, lines 9–14

Chamberlain's Men, had disassembled "The Theatre" and transported its timbers across the Thames, using them as the structure for the Globe.) Shakespeare was a shareholder in this new venture, with its motto "All the world's a stage," and continued to write and perform for it as well. Full-length plays were now being presented every afternoon but Sunday, and the public appetite for new material seemed endless.

The only curb on the public's hunger for theater was its fear of the plague—for popular belief held the disease was easily spread in crowds. Even worse, the infection was completely beyond the powers of Elizabethan medicine, which held that health derived from four "humors" or internal fluids identified as bile, phlegm, blood, and choler. Such articles of faith, however, were utterly ineffective against a genuine health crisis, and in times of plague, the authorities' panicked response was to shut down any venue where large crowds might congregate. The theaters would be closed for lengthy periods in 1593, 1597, and 1603, during which times Shakespeare was forced to play at court, tour the provinces, or, as many scholars believe, write what would become his famous cycle of sonnets.

THE NEXT STAGE

Between these catastrophic closings, the theater thrived as the great medium of its day; it functioned as film, television, and radio combined as well as a venue for music and dance (all performances, even tragedies, ended with a dance). Moreover, the theater was the place to see and be seen; for a penny

Famous scale model of the Globe completed by Dr. John Cranford Adams in 1954. Collectively, 25,000 pieces were used in constructing the replica. Dr. Adams used walnut to imitate the timber of the Globe, plaster was placed with a spoon and medicine dropper, and 6,500 tiny "bricks" measured by pencil eraser strips were individually placed on the model.

you could stand through a performance in the yard, a penny more bought you a seat in the galleries, while yet another purchased you a cushion. The wealthy, the poor, the royal, and the common all gathered at the Globe, and Shakespeare designed his plays—with their action, humor, and highly refined poetry—not only to satisfy their divergent tastes but also to respond to their differing points of view. In the crucible of Elizabethan theater, the various classes could briefly see themselves as others saw them, and drama could genuinely show "the age and body of the time his form and pressure," to quote Hamlet himself.

In order to accommodate his expanding art, the simplicity of the Elizabethan stage had developed a startling flexibility. The canopied platform of the Globe had a trap in its floor for sudden disappearances, while an alcove at the rear, between the pillars supporting its roof, allowed for "discoveries" and interior space. Above, a balcony made possible the love scene in *Romeo and Juliet*; while still higher, the thatched roof could double as a tower or rampart. And though the stage was largely free of scenery, the costumes were sumptuous—a theater troupe's clothing was its greatest asset. Patrons were used to real drums banging in battle scenes and real cannons firing overhead (in fact, a misfire would one day set the Globe aflame).

With the death of Elizabeth, and the accession of James I to the throne in 1603, Shakespeare only saw his power and influence grow. James, who considered himself an intellectual and something of a scholar, took over the patronage of the Lord Chamberlain's Men, renaming them the King's Men; the troupe even marched in his celebratory entrance to London. At this pinnacle of both artistic power and prestige, Shakespeare composed *Othello*, *King Lear*, and *Macbeth* in quick succession, and soon the King's Men acquired a new, indoor theater in London, which allowed the integration of more music and spectacle into his work. At this wildly popular venue, Shakespeare developed a new form of drama that scholars have dubbed "the romance," which combined elements of comedy and tragedy in a magnificent vision that would culminate in the playwright's last masterpiece, *The Tempest*. Not long after this final innovation, Shakespeare retired to Stratford a wealthy and prominent gentleman.

BEYOND THE ELIZABETHAN UNIVERSE

This is how Shakespeare fit into his age. But how did he transcend it? The answer lies in the plays themselves. For even as we see in the surface of his drama the belief system of England in the sixteenth century, Shakespeare himself is always questioning his own culture, holding its ideas up to the light and shaking them, sometimes hard. In the case of the Elizabethan faith in astrology, Shakespeare had his villain Edmund sneer, "We make guilty of our disasters the sun, the moon, and stars; as if we were villains on necessity." When pondering the medieval code of chivalry, Falstaff decides, "The better part of valor is discretion." The divine right of kings is questioned in *Richard II*, and the inferior status of women—a belief that survived even the crowning of Elizabeth—appears ridiculous before the brilliant examples of Portia (*The Merchant of Venice*), and Rosalind (*As You Like It*). Perhaps it is through this constant shifting of perspective, this relentless sense of exploration, that the playwright somehow outlived the limits of his own period, and became, in the words of his rival Ben Jonson, "not just for an age, but for all time."

track 38

Conclusion of the Sourcebooks Shakespeare **The Tempest**
Sir Derek Jacobi

About the Online Teaching Resources

The Sourcebooks Shakespeare is committed to supporting students and educators in the study of Shakespeare. A web site with additional articles and essays, extended audio, a forum for discussions, as well as other resources can be found (starting in August 2006) at www.sourcebooksshakespeare.com. To illustrate how the Sourcebooks Shakespeare may be used in your class, Jeremy Ehrlich, the head of education at the Folger Shakespeare Library, contributed an essay called "Working with Audio in the Classroom." The following is an excerpt.

One possible way of approaching basic audio work in the classroom is shown in the handout [on the site]. It is meant to give some guidance for the first-time user of audio in the classroom. I would urge you to adapt this to the particular circumstances and interests of your own students.

To use it, divide the students into four groups. Assign each group one of the four technical elements of audio – volume, pitch, pace, and pause – to follow as you play them an audio clip or clips. In the first section, have them record what they hear: the range they encounter in the clip and the places where their element changes. In the second section, have them suggest words for the tone of the passage based in part on their answers to the first. Sections three and four deal with tools of the actor. Modern acting theory finds the actor's objective is his single most important acting choice; an actor may then choose from a variety of tactics in order to achieve that objective. Thus, if a character's objective on stage is to get sympathy from his scene partner, he may start out by complaining, then shift to another tactic (asking for sympathy directly? throwing a tantrum?) if the first tactic fails. Asking your students to try to explain what they think a character is trying to get, and how she is trying to do it, is a way for them to follow this process through closely. Finally, the handout asks students to think about the meaning (theme) of the passage, concluding with a traditional and important tool of text analysis.

As you can see, this activity is more interesting and, probably, easier for students when it's used with multiple versions of the same piece of text. While defining an actor's motivation is difficult in a vacuum, doing so in relation to another performance may be easier: one Othello may be more concerned with gaining respect, while another Othello may be more concerned with obtaining love, for instance. This activity may be done outside of a group setting, although for students doing this work for the first time I suggest group work so they will be able to share answers on some potentially thought-provoking questions…

For the complete essay, please visit www.sourcebooksshakespeare.com.

Acknowledgments

The series editors wish to give heartfelt thanks to the advisory editors of the series, David Bevington and Peter Holland, for their ongoing support, timely advice, and keen brilliance.

We are incredibly grateful to the community of Shakespeare scholars for their generosity in sharing their talents, collections, and even their address books. We would not have been able to put together such an august list of contributors without their help. Our sincere thanks go to our text editor, Richard Preiss, for his brilliant work, and to Curt Tofteland, Tom Garvey, Doug Lanier, and Andrew Wade for their marvelous essays.

Our research was aided immensely by the wonderful staff at Shakespeare archives and libraries around the world: Susan Brock, Helen Hargest, and the staff at The Shakespeare Birthplace Trust; Jeremy Ehrlich, Bettina Smith, and everyone at the Folger Shakespeare Library; and Gene Rinkel, Bruce Swann, and Tim Cole from the Rare Books and Special Collections Library at the University of Illinois. These individuals were instrumental in helping us gather audio: Justyn Baker, Traci Cothran, Janet Benson, and Barbara Brown. The following are the talented photographers who shared their work with us: Donald Cooper, George Joseph, Michal Daniel, Richard Termine, and Carol Rosegg. We appreciate all your help. Extra appreciation goes to Doug Lanier for all his guidance and the use of his personal Shakespeare collection.

From the world of drama, the following shared their passion with us and helped us develop the series into a true partnership between the artistic and academic communities. We are indebted to: Liza Lorenz, Lauren Beyea, and the team from the Shakespeare Theatre Company, Amy Richard and the team from the Oregon Shakespeare Festival, and Nancy Becker of The Shakespeare Society.

With respect to the audio, we extend our heartfelt thanks to our narrating team: our director, John Tydeman, our esteemed narrator, Sir Derek Jacobi, and the staff of Motivation Studios. John has been a wonderful, generous resource to us and we look forward to future collaborations. We owe a debt of gratitude to Nicolas Soames for introducing us and for being unfailingly helpful. Thanks also to the "Speaking Shakespeare" team: Andrew

Wade for that wonderful recording, and Joe Plummer for his excellent work on the audio analysis.

Our personal thanks for their kindness and unstinting support go to our friends and our extended families.

Finally, thanks to everyone at Sourcebooks who contributed their talents in realizing The Sourcebooks Shakespeare. Special mention to Eileen Foley and Elizabeth Lhost, assistants extraordinaire for the Sourcebooks Shakespeare.

So, thanks to all at once and to each one (Macbeth, 5.7.104)

Audio Credits

In all cases, we have attempted to provide archival audio in its original form. While we have tried to achieve the best possible quality on the archival audio, some audio quality is the result of source limitations. Archival audio research by Marie Macaisa. Narration script by Joe Plummer and Marie Macaisa. Audio editing by Motivation Sound Studios, Marie Macaisa, and Todd Stocke. Narration recording and audio engineering by Motivation Sound Studios, London, UK. Mastering by Paul Estby.

Narrated by Sir Derek Jacobi
Directed by John Tydeman
Produced by Marie Macaisa

The following are under license from Naxos of America www.naxosusa.com ℗ HNH International Ltd. All rights reserved.
Tracks 4, 7, 13, 15, 19, 22, 26, 30, 34

The following are under license from The CBC Stratford Festival. ℗ 2004. All rights reserved.
Tracks 3, 10, 16, 21, 25, 28, 33

The following are selections from The Complete Arkangel Shakespeare ℗ 2003, with permission of BBC Audiobooks America. All rights reserved. Copyright exists on all recordings issued by BBC Audiobooks America. Any unauthorized broadcasting, public performance, copying or rerecording of such recordings in any manner whatsoever, will constitute an infringement of such copyright.
Tracks 6, 12, 18

The following are under license from IPC Media ℗1962. All rights reserved.
Tracks 9, 24, 29, 32

Audio from *Shakespeare Behind Bars* is under license from Philomath Films ℗ 2006. All rights reserved.
Track 36

Photo Credits

Every effort has been made to correctly attribute all the materials reproduced in this book. If any errors have been made, we will be happy to correct them in future editions. Photos are credited on the pages in which they appear.

Costume renderings by Deborah M. Dryden from the Oregon Shakespeare Festival's 2007 production directed by Libby Appel are courtesy of the Oregon Shakespeare Festival.

Image of "The Magic Grottoes", 1870 rendering by Currier & Ives, is courtesy of the Library of Congress.

Photos from *Forbidden Planet* (1956) directed by Fred M. Wilcox are courtesy of Douglas Lanier.

Photos from the Joseph Papp Public Theater's 1995 production directed by George C. Wolfe are © 1995 Michal Daniel.

Photos from the 2000 Shakespeare's Globe production directed by Lenka Udovicki are © 2000 Donald Cooper.

Photos from the Royal Shakespeare Company's 1957 production directed by Peter Brook are courtesy of Angus McBean © Royal Shakespeare Company; from its 1978 production directed by Clifford Williams are © 1978 Donald Cooper; from its 1982 production directed by Ron Daniels are © 1982 Donald Cooper; from its 1993 production directed by Sam Mendes are © 1993 Donald Cooper; from its 1995 production directed by David Thacker are © 1995 Donald Cooper; from its 1998 production directed by Adrian Noble are © 1998 Donald Cooper; from its 2000 production directed by James Macdonald are © 2000 Donald Cooper.

Photos from the Delacorte Theater's 1962 production directed by Gerald Freedman are © 1962 George Joseph.

Photos from Mitzi E. Newhouse's 1974 production directed by Edward Berkeley are © 1974 George Joseph.

Photos from the New York Shakespeare Festival's 1981 production directed by Lee Breuer are © 1981 George Joseph.

Photos from the Ninagawa Company's 1992 production directed by Yukio Ninagawa are © 1992 Donald Cooper.

Photos from the Shakespeare Theatre Company's 1997 production directed by Garland Wright are © 1997 Carol Rosegg; from its 2005 production directed by Kate Whoriskey are © 2005 Richard Termine.

Photos from the West Yorkshire Playhouse's 1999 production directed by Jude Kelly are © 1999 Donald Cooper.

Photos from the documentary *Shakespeare Behind Bars* (2005) by Philomath Films are courtesy of Philomath Films © 2005 Hank Rogerson.

Sketch of *The Tempest* in 1845 by Kenny Meadows permission of the Shakespeare Birthplace Trust.

William Shakespeare's signature (on the title page) courtesy of Mary Evans Picture Library. Other images from the Mary Evans Picture Library used in the text are credited on the pages in which they appear.

Images from "In the Age of Shakespeare" courtesy of The Folger Shakespeare Library.

About the Contributors

TEXT EDITOR
Richard Preiss received his Ph.D. from Stanford University and is now Assistant Professor in the Department of English at the University of Utah, where he teaches Shakespeare and Renaissance literature. His published articles include *Natural Authorship* (Renaissance Drama, 2006), *Robert Armin Do the Police in Different Voices* (from *Performance to Print in Shakespeare's England,* ed. Peter Holland and Stephen Orgel, 2006), and *Mucedorus: A Play Finally Anonymous* (*Shakespeare Yearbook,* 2007). He is currently completing a book-length study of early modern stage clowning and its role in the emergence of dramatic authorship.

SERIES EDITORS
Marie Macaisa has a bachelor degree in computer science from the Massachusetts Institute of Technology and a master's degree in artificial intelligence from the University of Pennsylvania. She worked for many years on the research and development of innovative applications of computer technology before becoming the series editor of *The Sourcebooks Shakespeare* in 2003. Marie contributed the *Cast Speaks* essays in previous volumes and is the producer of the accompanying audio CDs.

Dominique Raccah is the founder, president, and publisher of Sourcebooks. Born in Paris, France, she has a bachelor's degree in psychology and a master's in quantitative psychology from the University of Illinois. She also serves as series editor of *Poetry Speaks* and *Poetry Speaks to Children.*

ADVISORY BOARD
David Bevington is the Phyllis Fay Horton Distinguished Service Professor in the Humanities at the University of Chicago. A renowned text scholar, he has edited several Shakespeare editions including the *Bantam Shakespeare* in individual paperback volumes, *The Complete Works of Shakespeare* (Longman, 2003), and *Troilus and Cressida* (Arden, 1998). He teaches courses in Shakespeare, renaissance drama, and medieval drama.

Peter Holland is the McMeel Family Chair in Shakespeare Studies at the University of Notre Dame. One of the central figures in performance-oriented Shakespeare criticism, he has also edited many Shakespeare plays, including *A Midsummer Night's Dream* for the Oxford Shakespeare series. He is also general editor of Shakespeare Survey and co-general editor (with Stanley Wells) of Oxford Shakespeare Topics. Currently he is completing a book, *Shakespeare on Film,* and editing *Coriolanus* for the Arden 3rd series.

ESSAYISTS

Thomas Garvey has been acting, directing, or writing about Shakespeare for over two decades. A graduate of the Massachusetts Institute of Technology, he studied acting and directing with the MIT Shakespeare Ensemble, where he played Hamlet, Jacques, Iago, and other roles, and directed *All's Well That Ends Well* and *Twelfth Night.* He has since directed and designed several other Shakespearean productions, as well as works by Chekhov, Ibsen, Sophocles, Beckett, Moliere, and Shaw. Mr. Garvey has written on theatre for the *Boston Globe* and other publications.

Douglas Lanier is an associate professor of English at the University of New Hampshire. He has written many essays on Shakespeare in popular culture, including "Shakescorp Noir" in *Shakespeare Quarterly* 53.2 (Summer 2002) and "Shakespeare on the Record" in *The Blackwell Companion to Shakespeare in Performance* (edited by Barbara Hodgdon and William Worthen, Blackwell, 2005). His book *Shakespeare and Modern Popular Culture* (Oxford University Press) was published in 2002. He is currently working on a book-length study of cultural stratification in early modern British theater.

Curt L. Tofteland has 29 years of professional theatre experience as an equity actor, director, producer, playwright, and college professor. Curt is the Founder and Artistic Director of the critically acclaimed Shakespeare Behind Bars program at the Luther Luckett Correctional Complex in LaGrange, Kentucky. Curt is an adjunct theatre professor at Bellarmine University, University of Louisville, Indiana University Southeast, and Jefferson

Community College. Awards include the Al Smith Fellowship in playwriting from the Kentucky Arts Council, the Mildred A. Dougherty Award for communication from the Greater Louisville English Council, and a Distinguished Theatre Alumni Award from the University of Minnesota, where he received his M.F.A. in Acting.

Andrew Wade was head of voice for the Royal Shakespeare Company from 1990 to 2003 and voice assistant director from 1987 to 1990. During this time he worked on 170 productions and with more than 80 directors. Along with Cicely Berry, Andrew recorded *Working Shakespeare* and the DVD series on *Voice and Shakespeare,* and he was the verse consultant for the movie *Shakespeare In Love.* In 2000, he won a Bronze Award from the New York International Radio Festival for the series *Lifespan,* which he co-directed and devised. He works widely teaching, lecturing, and coaching throughout the world.

AUDIO CONTRIBUTORS

Sir Derek Jacobi (Series Narrator) is one of Britain's foremost actors of stage and screen. One of his earliest Shakespearean roles was Cassio to Sir Laurence Olivier's Othello in Stuart Burge's 1965 movie production. More recent roles include Hamlet in the acclaimed BBC Television Shakespeare production in 1980, the Chorus in Kenneth Branagh's 1989 film of *Henry V,* and Claudius in Branagh's 1996 movie *Hamlet.* He has been accorded numerous honors in his distinguished career, including a Tony award for Best Actor in *Much Ado About Nothing* and a BAFTA (British Academy of Film and Television) for his landmark portrayal of Emperor Claudius in the blockbuster television series *I, Claudius.* He was made a Knight of the British Empire in 1994 for his services to the theatre.

Joe Plummer (Audio Analyst) is the Director of Education for the Williamstown Theatre Festival and Assistant Professor of Shakespearean Performance with Roger Rees at Fordham University's Lincoln Center Campus. He has taught several Master classes on Shakespeare and performance at Williams College, the National Shakespeare Company and Brandeis University, and also teaches privately. Joe is currently the Artist-In-Residence and Director of Educational Outreach for The Shakespeare Society in New York City and is the founder and Producing Artistic Director of poortom productions, the only all-male Shakespeare Company in the U.S. He has performed extensively in New York and in regional theaters.

John Tydeman (Series Director) was the Head of Drama for BBC Radio for many years and is the director of countless productions, with 15 Shakespeare plays to his credit. Among his numerous awards are the Prix Italia, Prix Europa, UK Broadcasting Guild Best Radio Programme (*When The Wind Blows* by Raymond Briggs), and the Sony Personal Award for services to radio. He has worked with most of Britain's leading actors and dramatists and has directed for the theatre, television, and commercial recordings. He holds an M.A. from Cambridge University.